ON TURNER'S TRAIL

Turner on a Sierra Club hiking trail in 1904 with his daughter Dorothy. (From the author's collection)

Wilbur R. Jacobs

ON TURNER'S TRAIL
100 Years of Writing Western History

UNIVERSITY PRESS OF KANSAS

© 1994 by the University Press of Kansas

Published by the University Press of Kansas (Lawrence, Kansas 66049), which was organized by the Kansas Board of Regents and is operated and funded by Emporia State University, Fort Hays State University, Kansas State University, Pittsburg State University, the University of Kansas, and Wichita State University

Library of Congress Cataloging-in-Publication Data

Jacobs, Wilbur R.
    On Turner's trail : 100 years of writing western history / Wilbur R. Jacobs.
       p.   cm.
    Includes bibliographical references (p.) and index.
    ISBN 0-7006-0616-5 (hardcover : alk. paper)
    1. West (U.S.)—Historiography.   2. Turner, Frederick Jackson, 1861–1932—Influence.   I. Title.
    F591.J33   1994
    978′.0072—dc20   93-38244

British Library Cataloguing in Publication Data is available.

Printed in the United States of America

10 9 8 7 6 5 4 3 2 1

The paper used in this publication meets the minimum requirements of the American National Standard for Permanence of Paper for Printed Library Materials Z39.48-1984.

For my Ph.D.s, of whom I am very proud: John R. Alley,
Robert D. Brunkow, George Frakes, Albert L. Hurtado,
Steven W. Ireton, David Kamens, Yasuhide Kawashima,
Calvin Luther Martin, Christopher L. Miller, Duane Mosser,
Michael Mullin, Georgiana Nammack, Sean O'Neill,
Robert Righter, James Alan Rogers, Gregory L. Schaaf,
David A. Sloan, Curtis Solberg, Rick W. Sturdevant,
Robert A. Trennert, and Chad Wozniak

CONTENTS

Part V.   New Trails and New Challenges by
              the New Westerners

ILLUSTRATIONS

PREFACE

Every book has its own trajectory that may take one to unintended trails and reveal new points of view. These perspectives on Turner's trails began a number of years ago with my father's interest in "extension" history courses at the "Southern Branch of the University of California" (UCLA) taught by history professor Louis Knott Koontz, who became a dinner guest at our home in Altadena. Koontz, a professional in his field, astonished me with his ready associations with other historians, among whom was Lawrence H. Gipson, the colonialist, who also was our guest. I can recall one dinner table conversation about the young George Washington in the wild lands of the colonial West, with Gipson and Koontz talking about Indian hunting practices. My father, who was concerned about wildlife preservation, spoke about the philosopher Arthur Schopenhauer's interest in animals. My mother, leader of a group of antivivisectionists in Southern California, then brought out some grisly pictures of animals being brutalized in laboratories. Both Gipson and Koontz were shocked. Gipson maintained (mistakenly as I later determined) that such things did not happen in England. Eventually the conversation returned to what Koontz called the Old West.

I soon learned that Koontz knew the famous Frederick Jackson Turner (and later verified their relationship through letters in the Huntington Library's collection of the frontier historian's papers). Koontz persistently called upon Turner to speak before a new historical group, the Pacific Coast Branch of the American Historical Association, and he did give at least one talk. Koontz, a Johns Hopkins man as Turner had been, was a Turnerian enthusiast whose own doctoral dissertation dealt with the Virginia frontier in the era of the French and Indian War. Koontz steered me to Indian frontier history and to the study of two major historians of that era, Francis Parkman and Turner. More important, when I was still an undergraduate at UCLA he took me to the Huntington Library where I learned for the first time that Turner had done research there and had left his papers in the library's vaults. As Koontz said with a smile, "Now you have been to the holy of holies."

There was still another Turner connection: My father was a member of the Pasadena Unitarian (Neighborhood) Church in the late 1920s and early 1930s, where Turner, Robert Millikan the scientist, and other leaders of old Pasadena congregated to hear the fabulous sermons of Theodore Soares relating to philosophy, science, world affairs, and the culture of the nation. Although my father was only a passing acquaintance of Turner's, the important thing was that I heard about it.

I began to follow Turner's path as a hobby and as a vocation. Returning to graduate school after some four years of World War II military service, I resumed Turnerian research. Why not write about him by canvassing his former students? For an article on Turner as teacher I sent out questionnaires (see Appendix B) to a host of enthusiastic historians who remembered their former teacher well. Herbert Bolton, Merle Curti, Avery Craven, Homer C. Hockett, and Edgar Eugene Robinson were among the respondents. Bolton, who sent a long handwritten reply, became a friendly acquaintance at the Bancroft Library even though he could never remember my name or that I had written several times to thank him for his memories of Turner. My colleague, Philip W. Powell, who saw Bolton frequently reported to me that Bolton had said, "There's a Wilbert James in Santa Barbara who will not thank me for a long letter I wrote to him on Turner!" I eventually caught up with Bolton in Berkeley. I thanked him once more, and he in turn gave me a viewing of a new University of California extension film he had made proving that one of his students had found an original Sir Francis Drake "Plate" on the shores of the San Francisco Bay. I can still see his eyes sparkle as he spoke of Turner and the Drake plate; he had unbounded enthusiasm for both.

I followed up by contacting other former students of Turner for personal interviews; they were generous in sharing their recollections. A clumsy type of tape recorder was coming into vogue in the early 1950s, but unfortunately I did not use it. I talked many hours with Edgar E. Robinson during my first two years of teaching at Stanford. At the University of California, Santa Barbara, to my delight I found a quiet Quaker gentleman named Homer C. Hockett occupying a sunny cottage on West Valerio Street. How many pleasant afternoons I spent with him. He told me a great deal about writing history and about his affection for Turner. Later, when I had a temporary post as academic assistant to President Clark Kerr at Berkeley, I had the joy of getting to know John Hicks better. At the Faculty Club round table we had noonhour talks about Turner and history: Hicks was a Wisconsin Turnerian through and through.

There are other historians mentioned whose words I recalled from conversations and interviews and jotted down in a series of notebooks. In the 1960s and 1970s I spent may hours with Ray A. Billington at the Huntington Library and at social events at his home and at mine. Allan Nevins was also my friend and counselor as I worked on books about Turner and on Native American history. Nevins teased me about my tolerant view, referring to "Will Jacobs's Epworth League Indians who could do no wrong." From my conversations with Nevins, I am reasonably sure that Nevins himself was the knowledgeable individual who suggested that a Pulitzer Prize committee examine Turner's book on sectionalism, which did indeed win that prize in 1933.

At Harvard in the late 1950s where I spent summers and a year's sabbatical leave, I had the pleasure of knowing Frederick Merk and his charming wife Lois. Although I did not mention a dispute he had had with Ray A. Billington, we talked about Turner (Merk showed me several letters he had received from Turner), western history, and historic wars and conflicts. As a one-time pacifist, I shared an interest in the latter with my mentor-teacher at Johns Hopkins University, Charles A. Barker, who with Merle Curti was a cofounder of the History of Peace Society. It did not take me long to appreciate Curti's wide knowledge about Turner, his former teacher. Otey M. Scruggs, Rodman Paul, and Father Paul Prucha shared their memories of Frederick Merk with me. So, in a sense, many individuals cited in the notes are longtime friends, some of them no longer here to see the book in publication. I am grateful to all of them. In an effort to be objective, I have tried to keep my recollections separate from my records of conversations and interviews, but I may not always have succeeded. Readers can judge for themselves after reading chapter 14, in which I recount personal memories of an old friend and rival.

As I began my research and writing on Turner, first by studying his papers in the Huntington collection and then by making a nationwide search for his letters in other repositories, I found my work stymied by the historian Fulmer Mood, who controlled the Huntington collection. I had actually plunged into the Turner papers and had an article in press, but the director of research at the library, the kindly Robert Glass Cleland who had given me permission to use the papers, suddenly called a halt. Even though my article was in galleys I was nevertheless obliged to remove any reference to the Turner Papers at the Huntington.

There is more to this tangled story in the final chapters of this book. As I moved through Turner's books, notes, and correspondence, I became increasingly critical of him and his work. As a result, my lectures and essays about him reflected this view, a consequence largely stemming from my parallel investigations in ethno- and environmental history. In a missive to the AHA newsletter, in a presidential address at the Pacific Coast Branch of the American Historical Association, and finally in the book *Dispossessing the American Indians*, I found myself on the attack. How could I write approvingly on the frontier-sectional theory of American history and at the same time ignore the pile of evidence indicating that Turner saw our history through a strangely refracted lens?

This book explains my seemingly entangled perspectives. Allan Nevins once told me that one deserves to be treated with favor in the first biography, but after that anything goes. Ray Billington has given us a laudatory biography, but my interpretation extends beyond his admiring view. The trajectory of my book carved its own trail in a direction that I had not intended to go.

Part One introduces the youthful Turner who wrote an essay that rocked the historical profession of his day. How did he do it, and what kind of education did he have? Behind the watershed of the 1893 essay was a story of growing up in a marvelously productive atmosphere of stimulating teachers who taught him how to teach and how to probe the knowledgeable world of Yankee scholarship with its Germanic origins.

Part Two explores the emerging Turner and his attempts to channel a flooding river of data. Why not keep it within the boundaries of a theory of frontier-sectionalism? To find out how completely successful Turner was I followed his path and the paths of his disciples to discover that both American colonial history and agricultural history were completely within the compass of Turnerian thought and methodology.

Part Three examines an era about which Turner did not write, the twentieth century. Yet his papers and notes include a series of amazing proposals involving the creation of international political parties, a world government, and suggestions to cope with the "threats" of overpopulation and a scarcity of resources. Here Turner is at his best. Unfortunately these views never reached print because of his commitment to expanding his frontier-sectionalism studies of nineteenth-century American history.

Part Four takes up the unique story of the tremendous impact Turner had as a teacher-scholar in a package of thought I call the "realwestern" history, and the evolving professorial "war" in high circles of academia for the possession of Turner's "realwestern" history is examined. Frederick Merk, chosen by Turner, carried the flag, but it was taken from him by the talented and enterprising Ray Billington. For the first time we have data available that reveals the fascinating struggle for power and possession among the heirs of the Turnerian legacy.

Part Five plunges into a new controversy, the story of the new western history rebels who seek to erase Turner and Billington from the landscape of what is now called the history of the West. Richard White's 1991 textbook, *"It's Your Misfortune and None of My Own," A History of the American West,* challenges the place of Billington's text, the book on the western frontier that Merk had so long resented. Patricia Limerick had predicted the view that appears in White's textbook, the now accepted alternative to Billington's *Westward Expansion.* And Limerick is supported by Don

Worster, the eloquent scholar of America's dustbowl and rivers of empire. But the argument in William Cronon's *Nature's Metropolis* is a dissent not only from Turner but also from some of the main arguments about the West's being a place instead of part of a Turnerian frontier. Cronon is ambivalent on Turner and uses him as a foil in a dramatic narrative on Chicago's growth and decline as a "gateway" city. Yet Turner, despite his shortcomings, has become a link binding the old western historians and the new.

The Epilogue focuses on the more positive aspects of the Turnerian legacy and the meaningful accomplishments of the man and his major disciples, Merk and Billington. The new westerners have a formidable range of rocky mountain tops to blast if they hope to level the peaks of achievement attained by the old master.

I am indebted to Turner himself, to his descendants, and to the Huntington Library for the opportunity to write about him and to use his papers. Turner himself would not mind, since he wanted scholars to consult his collection; I fear, however, that he would not always agree with what I have said. I am especially appreciative of the assistance I have had at the Huntington Library from Peter Blodgett, curator of western history manuscripts (who read an early draft of my book); Martin Ridge, senior research associate; John Steadman, senior research associate; Susan Green, editor of the library's *Quarterly;* Paul Zall and Andrew Rolle, research scholars; and Robert Ritchie, director of research. William Moffett, librarian, has given me new faith in the academic freedom of libraries and insight into the uses and abuses in consulting collections. I also have benefited from talks about historiography with Robert Skotheim, president. Other Huntington Library staff members, Robert Schlosser, Alan Jutzi, Jill Cogen, Virginia Renner, Linda Williams, Cathy Martin, Barbara Quinn, Rebecca Saad, Janet Hawkins, and Lee Zall, have shared their knowledge to help me in what seemed to be neverending investigations. Former members of the library's staff, Mary Isabel Fry, Norma Cuthbert, Constance Lodge, and John Pomfret, have also helped me along the way. Carol Pearson made an excellent index for the book.

I am particularly grateful to Allan Bogue and David Wrobel for their suggestions concerning early drafts of the chapters in Part

Five and to Susan Green for her valuable suggestions after reading
an early draft of chapter 16. My students, some of them now
professors themselves, have read and commented on a number of
other chapters. They are Timothy O'Donnell, Peter Neushall, Ken
Smith, Michael Mullin, Duane Mosser, Coy F. Cross, and Sean
O'Neill. O'Donnell, as a research assistant, did yeoman work in
gathering data on the "realwestern" history. My typists, Alice
Kladnick and Judith Parker, patiently worked on drafts of chapters, some of which found their way into fugitive publications. My
young son William, assisted by his younger sister Emily, made a
xerox copy of the entire manuscript. Three unknown readers of
the original copy for the University Press of Kansas have given me
invaluable assistance as has Cynthia Miller, editor-in-chief and
Megan Schoeck, production manager. Staff members at the State
Historical Society of Wisconsin have assisted me in locating letters
written by Ray A. Billington and other scholars in the Merle Curti
Papers and the William Hesseltine Papers. W. Eugene Hollon has
permitted me to examine his correspondence with Ray A. Billington and has made his papers available at the University of
Toledo Library. Paul Wallace Gates in interviews has remembered
his experiences and his friendship with Frederick Merk, his mentor at Harvard University; and Richard Leopold has recalled his
long associations with Frederick Merk and Ray A. Billington in
several letters. Ray A. Billington himself (the subject of one of my
chapters) often talked with me about his attitudes toward Frederick Merk, Frederick Jackson Turner's legacies, and his identification with Turner and the Huntington Library collection of Turner's
papers. Earl Pomeroy, Allan Bogue, and Howard Lamar have
given me the benefit of their recollections and associations with
leading historians of western history.

I am grateful to the University of California, Santa Barbara, the
faculty committee on research, and the Huntington Library for
financial support. My longtime friends Alexander DeConde and
Allan Bogue have given the benefit of their wise counsel. Peter
Loewenburg of UCLA and Andrew Rolle, both skilled practitioners in psychoanalysis, aided me in drawing conclusions about
the behavior of academics who develop parsimonious attitudes in
their taking possession of sources of information.

Since the 1950s I have been writing about Frederick Jackson

Turner. My publications on Turner have appeared in Spain, France, Australia, the former Yugoslavia, the former Soviet Union, and in several encyclopedias including the two latest editions of *The Encyclopedia Britannica*. As I worked through the large Turner collection at the Huntington Library I put my findings on Turner's unpublished essays and his correspondence into the first two volumes of my trilogy, *Frederick Jackson Turner's Legacy*, in the *Historical World of Frederick Jackson Turner*. I appraised his significance in conservation and in Indian policies in my *Dispossessing the American Indians*. Additionally, I have written more than a dozen essays on and relating to Turner in such publications as *American Heritage*, the American Historical Association *Newsletter, Pacific Historical Review, American West, Journal of American History, Agricultural History,* and *Pacific Northwest Quarterly*. A number of my Turner pieces are listed in *Frederick Jackson Turner, A Reference Guide*, edited by Vernon Matteson and William E. Marion (Boston, 1985). I mention these publications because my present book is in many respects distilled from my previous work, but it is at the same time a distinct and new interpretation of Turner. For instance, I would like to rewrite an essay on Turner that I published in *Western Historical Quarterly* some years ago, but I agree with myself to the extent that a recent essay in *Pacific Northwest Quarterly* seemed so appropriate that it has been incorporated into this book, *On Turner's Trail*.

Wilbur R. Jacobs
Huntington Library

PART ONE

THE TRAILHEAD

We must now obtain a new theory of Society.

    ——Frederick Jackson Turner's Commonplace Book (1883)

The gentlest, justest, most scholarly man I ever knew.

    ——Turner on his teacher, William F. Allen (1889)

I have sufficient respect for the learning and the personality of Prof. Allen to feel a decided modesty in urging any claims of mine to succeed him. . . . The knowledge that this was his wish . . . is chiefly what permitted me to allow my name to be used.

    ——Turner to Woodrow Wilson (1890)

Of America as a social organism growing and changing in reaction with its environment, we hear very little. . . . Our history is one of social and institutional modification.

    ——"Some Sociological Aspects of American History" (1895)

CHAPTER ONE

TURNER'S ESSAY OF 1893
The Frontier as a Molding Force

A celebrated event in the world of historical scholarship took place in Chicago on July 12, 1893, when thirty-one-year-old Frederick Jackson Turner, a professor from the University of Wisconsin, delivered an address, "The Significance of the Frontier in American History," at a meeting of the American Historical Association. His address was surely a personal as well as a professional expression of history.

Turner was the product of the upper midwestern town of Portage, Wisconsin, and had an urban middle-class background. Learning Republican party politics at his journalist-editor father's dinner table, Turner was exposed to the real world of rural democracy at work. At the same time, he saw the wide variety of northern European immigrants who flooded Wisconsin and rivaled the original Yankee settlers in farming, lumbering, and small businesses. In high school he won prizes for orations dealing with such topics as the power of the press. Graduating from the University of Wisconsin in 1884, the year the American Historical Association came into existence, he established himself as an exceptional orator by winning the Burrow Prize. Having been exposed to a stellar combination of teachers, first at the University of Wisconsin and then at Johns Hopkins University where he received his doctorate, Turner returned to the university at Madison to begin his career, teaching both rhetoric and history. Here, in 1889, soon after his marriage to Caroline Mae Sherwood of Chicago, Turner's role as a full-fledged historian began. Following the death of his mentor and friend, William F. Allen, Turner accepted the acting chairmanship of the history department, and, soon with the aid of Richard T. Ely, his former economics teacher from Johns Hopkins whom he persuaded to come to Madison, Turner set up an interdisciplinary program of study for students.

The people who were to hear Turner in 1893 already knew him as a brilliant orator-lecturer and a budding interdisciplinary historian with knowledge of medieval and ancient history as well as the history of his own country. Because of his Johns Hopkins' affiliations, Turner was already familiar to the prominent scholars who arranged the program as a speaker who could deliver a worthwhile address. It was a magnificent opportunity to gain exposure and to make a name for himself. The fact that Turner had won prizes for oratory seems to have given him special prominence.[1]

Thus, when Turner traveled to Chicago, he contracted to speak at one of the congresses at the World's Columbian Exposition, known today as the Chicago World's Fair of 1893.[2] Turner spoke at an evening session in the handsome new Art Institute building fronting Lake Michigan. He was the last speaker of five, and the listeners had had to endure a heavy body of historical discourse, a challenge for even the most enthusiastic of audiences. One of those speakers, Turner's friend and camping companion Reuben Gold Thwaites, lectured on a relatively uninteresting topic, "Early Lead Mining in Illinois and Wisconsin."[3] Despite the lateness, a number of concerned and loyal members of the audiences remained to hear Turner speak. There can be no doubt that Turner belonged to an elite group of "Hopkins men" who were to occupy prominent places of leadership among historians of America, a set including Charles Homer Haskins, J. Franklin Jameson, and Woodrow Wilson. We are not sure about the membership of the audience, but we do know that Turner's doctoral mentor at Hopkins, Herbert Baxter (H. B.) Adams, was on hand.[4] And we can be sure that Turner's own graduate students were there to hear him. One of them had already surfaced as a possible participant in the program at the cost of Turner's name being deleted. Fortunately, the chairman of the program committee had decided to accept Turner's address, even though Turner had asked that his student's proposal be "put in the place of my own paper."[5]

Turner and his wife, Caroline Mae Turner, ca. 1893, when he read his noted essay at the Chicago World's Fair. (From the author's collection)

One can, with some imagination, see the youthful Turner on the podium. Blond, handsome, of small to medium height, he had an athletic build and a firm step and was unusually trim because of summer woodland hikes. He spoke in a pleasant, agreeable manner and was, in a sense, a model academic about to set forth a challenging theory of American history.[6] It is no exaggeration to say that after Turner presented his theoretical arguments, the telling of American history was never quite the same. Turner's address, although lengthy, was far from humdrum. One reason that it at once received favorable attention was that the eminent historian H. B. Adams devoted a large portion of his report to Turner's paper. Although Adams's glowing remarks may be traced partly to enthusiasm for his former student, Adams nevertheless did pick out effective generalizations that became almost classic statements of Turner's frontier theory. For instance, Adams noted Turner's impressive words: "Up to our own day . . . American history has been in large degree the history of colonization of the great west. This ever-retreating frontier of unoccupied land is the key to our development."[7] When Turner stated that the frontier was the key to American historical development, he implied that his interpretation would replace other theories about our national origins. He needed all his eloquence as a historian-orator to persuade others that his was the accurate view of what had happened to the American people.

Turner's view, for instance, would replace the "germ theory" of American history. Yet the question arises, How do we reconcile Turner's use of the germ theory and his self-proclaimed reaction to it? The answer in part is that Turner never completely disregarded the importance of the European heritage. The concept of the germ theory, adopted by Turner in his doctoral dissertation, presented the thesis that "germs" of American institutions evolved in the forests of Europe among the ancient Teutonic tribes. Moreover, H. B. Adams, an ardent proponent of the theory, had written on the subject and had told his seminar of advanced students that "American [germ] institutional history had been well done [and] that we had better turn next to European institutions." Turner, as a specialist in American history, seems to have been angered by this assertion. He declared in one of his letters that his "frontier was pretty much a *reaction* from . . . my indignation."[8] Turner was willing to give lip service to his teacher's pet theory in his doctoral dissertation and in his frontier essay, cleverly incorporating Adams's idea into his own thesis ("germs of [social] processes repeated at each successive frontier"), probably to mitigate any opposition from his teacher. Turner, however, eventually abandoned the idea and the word "germ" and instead wrote about the European heritage.[9]

Turner's skills in presenting his frontier theory were based upon at least a decade of theorizing. This experience enabled him to generalize on an original theme and to make his arguments convincing. For instance, members of his audience in 1893 were probably aware of the fact that he had already published two thought-provoking addresses, "The Significance of History" and "Problems in American History."[10] In these two pieces Turner set the stage for his frontier theory by arguing that one must "know the elements of the present by understanding what came into the present from the past." Further, he broke the ice on his evolutionary approach to American social history by arguing that "society is an organism, ever growing. History is the self-consciousness of this organism."[11] And finally he asserted that the West was the "point of view" for the study of "our history":

> What the Mediterranean Sea was to the Greeks, breaking the bond of custom, offering new experiences, calling out new institutions and activities, that ever retreating Great West has been to the eastern United States, and to the nations of Europe more remotely.[12]

When Turner formed an eloquent phrase he sometimes repeated it in essay after essay, and his comparison of the American frontier to the Mediterranean Sea was no exception. Word for word, it appeared in the conclusion of the address in 1893. He also duplicated phrases about "the process of evolution" that had appeared in earlier writings.

Time and again Turner impressed his audience with the idea that the westward-moving frontier could be seen as a kind of mirror of America's history that permitted one to gaze backward from the present to the origins of the frontier experience. Turner maintained that by understanding these phenomena one could see how the frontier opened for new opportunities. It functioned as a gate to freedom, as a means of escape from old bondages. In his view American society was best understood as a kind of biological organism evolving from frontier beginnings. Turner in his various writings stressed that the frontier created unique opportunities, different from other settings. At the same time he implied that the frontier offered freedom to pursue familiar dreams in these new settings.

His chain of reasoning was based on the assumption that Europeans began to shed their cultural baggage, or traditional lifestyles (to use a modern word), almost from the moment they set foot on the raw, fresh land. In time, as settlers, they became less and less dependent upon the Old World. Sheer necessity made them more self-sufficient in their frontier homeland. This lessening of dependence and their gradual adjustment to another environment occurred over a period of some three hundred years. Families and their descendants traveled inland over routes and trails from the Atlantic Coast to cross frontiers of the Appalachians and then passed on to successive Wests in the Mississippi Valley, the Rocky Mountains, the Sierra Nevada, and the Pacific Coast.

During a period of hundreds of years of westward migration, Turner argued, a social process of "Americanization" made its impact upon frontier peoples. As this process grew, it spread and left its imprint on the entire nation. And it was a dual process: The Americanization of immigrants was accompanied by frontier expansion. The frontier became a unifying force. "It was democratic and non sectional if not national . . . rooted strongly in material prosperity. It was typical of the modern United States." The frontier, then, was a modifying force in the sectional rivalry between North and South. Turner ascertained that the "nationalizing tendency" of the frontier "transformed the democracy of Jefferson into the national republicanism of Monroe and the democracy of Andrew Jackson."[13]

On the western frontiers changing institutions, different ways of life, attitudes, intellectual traits, and methods of self-government evolved as pioneers discarded older habits brought from their eastern homelands. Just as England had been the original mother of the early British colonies, so was the eastern seaboard the mother of western settlements on the frontier. As eastern social and governmental functions were cast off, frontier circumstances demanded the need for self-sufficiency. These evolutionary changes occurred in hundreds of pioneer communities where settlers were forced to cope with "primitive" (a favorite word of Turner's) living conditions in a wilderness environment. Indian attacks often forced the settlers to band together to defend themselves.

When pioneers on each frontier solved the Indian "question," set up a political organization, and allocated the public domain, their procedures served as a guide for settlers on the next frontier. There was a continual penetration of multiple frontiers in different locations. Soon wilderness hamlets swelled into towns and cities, and unique composite populations occupied vast frontier lands and tiers of new western states. Here germs of social institutions developed in evolutionary processes so that after a passage of time frontier communities differed from their prototypes in the East.

Composite blends of pioneer culture gradually evolved, Turner maintained, because of the availability of free land, or virtually free land, which gave individuals the chance to improve their lot in life. It was on the frontier, with its mix of eastern and western peoples, that the wilderness environment made its full impact. Turner, echoing the French-American colonial writer Hector St. John de Crevecoeur, declared that a "new man" emerged as a historic process of Americanization took place in the wilderness land called America. The frontiering experience, at least as Turner perceived it, created Americans who were quite different from their European counterparts.

One can imagine Turner's audience following his discourse as he unfolded his argument in an attempt to persuade them to accept his theory. Let us examine some significant excerpts from his address of 1893:

> The existence of an area of free land, its continuous recession, and the advance of American settlement westward, explain American development. . . .
>
> Thus American development has exhibited not merely advance along a single line, but a return to primitive conditions on a continually advancing frontier line, and a new development of that area. . . .
>
> The wilderness masters the colonist. It finds him in European dress, industries, tools, modes of travel, and thought. It takes him from the railroad car and puts him in the birch canoe. It strips off the garments of civilization and arrays him in the hunting shirt and moccasin.

Turner went on to describe the United States as "a huge page in the history of society." Standing at the eastern Cumberland Gap one could see a long, winding procession of Indians, fur traders, and cattle raisers, followed by farmers. At the South Pass in the Rocky Mountains a century later, a similar line passes through, this time with ranchers and miners preceding a procession of farmers.

Within this tableau of history one could recognize, he asserted, that an emerging "frontier individualism has from the beginning promoted democracy." Conditions of frontier life promoted intellectual traits of "profound importance. . . . That coarseness of strength combined with the acuteness and inquisitiveness; that practical, inventive turn of mind, quick to find expedients; that masterful grasp of material things . . . that restless, nervous energy; that dominant individualism . . . which comes with freedom—these are the traits of the frontier. . . . America has been another name for opportunity. . . . the stubborn American environment is there with its imperious summons to accept its conditions."[14]

One can draw a number of conclusions after reading Turner's statements setting forth his frontier theory for reinterpreting American history. First, and most obvious, his call for a complete revision of the views on historical causation was bound to challenge other historians and thereby cause controversy. He tells us, for instance, that free land and its recession "explain American development" without acknowledging the consequence of such subjects as the growth of cities or the importance of the large immigrant populations that poured into these cities. Charles A. Beard, a Turner critic, argued that he overlooked the cities and exaggerated the importance of free land as a "factor" in America's history. Beard also quarreled with Turner's use of the term Americanization. "About the only test I can apply [to that word]," Beard wrote, "is that of plain loyalty in a crisis."[15]

One can identify other flaws in Turner's work. He states, for example, that "the wilderness masters the colonist" and that "frontier individualism has from the beginning promoted democracy." Yet this activity took place as society reverted to "primitive" modes of living. Just exactly how sophisticated methods of self-governance emerged from "primitive" societies, preoccupied in scratching a living out of land where sod had to be broken for the first time, Turner does not explain. Such questions were ignored as Turner described the various frontier people who conquered the West.

There is wearisome repetition in much of Turner's work. The

address of 1893, published as the opening chapter in his book of essays, *The Frontier in American History* (1920), contains the main arguments for his thesis but repeats phrases and ideas from his earlier publications. The subsequent essays supplement his arguments, especially his "Social Forces in American History," delivered as a presidential address before members of the American Historical Association. But all the essays echo themes already stated in 1893. Turner himself acknowledged that there was considerable duplication in his writings.[16]

One theme repeated in practically all of Turner's work, especially in his 1893 essay, is that of environmental determinism. We can therefore conclude that Turner's statement that "the stubborn American environment is there with all its imperious conditions" reveals an interpretation that environmental conditions were a first cause for the formation of a unique frontier society. The course of this argument flows into an explanation of American politics: great frontier leaders such as Thomas Jefferson, Andrew Jackson, and Abraham Lincoln (who signed the Homestead Act) led America's democratic political development. According to Turner, this environmental concept also explains a social view of American communities as having evolved from primitive frontier hamlets into modern cities. And Turner's environmentalism helps to explain the evolution of American communities such as Trempealeau County in Wisconsin.[17]

Turner adopted an environmental-evolutionary view of society that social Darwinists of the nineteenth and early twentieth centuries accepted. He also attributed America's prosperous history to the treasure of free land, a kind of safety valve to guard against discontent. But the treasure hunt for free land came to a virtual halt when the frontier reached the western edge of the continent in 1890 as the census of that year shows.

Another conclusion we can draw from Turner's frontier theory is that it set forth a popular, patriotic self-image that generations of Americans (particularly middle-class white Americans) have liked. When Turner described our traits of individualism, inventiveness, and our exuberance for freedom that grew from the "conditions of frontier life," he rang a historical freedom bell that has not stopped pealing.

Whatever may be said about Turner's theory of frontier development, we must acknowledge that he remains one of America's major historians. He is remembered as a gifted theorist in his understanding of and accounting for the varied origins of American civilization. In his frontier theory, later blended into a frontier-sectional concept, Turner gave us a realistic model that shows a theoretical basis for auxiliary levels of causation. His frontier-sectional theory is perhaps the best explanatory model for America's development that we have from any historian. Moreover, he stimulated hundreds of other historians to explore beyond his own ideas. The very fact that he did not foreclose debate has made his writings almost as popular today as when they first appeared in print. Throughout his life, in the world of historians Turner was a man with a mission—to rectify gross distortions of old historians of an old frontier, a body of flawed writing. That he was successful there can be little doubt. The vigorous debate over his interpretations today, found in leading newspapers such as the *Los Angeles Times* and the *New York Times* together with news magazines, historical journals, and monographs, shows that Turnerian thought is alive in the 1990s.[18] Turner's thought prospers partly because his ideas provoke debate. Many of his central points (such as the safety-valve theory) are attacked for lack of credibility, but they nevertheless endure as valuable jumping-off points in theorizing about our past.

Thus we have an essay by a younger historian whose work became a watershed in American history. Precocious as he was, Turner managed to thrust himself into the limelight so that his 1893 essay also became a watershed in his own career. In looking back on the young Turner's intellectual growth, by examining the plethora of extraordinary sources that he immersed himself in, we can say that Turner was on a rapid intellectual ascent in his thirties. During these years when he was formulating the ideas for his frontier essay, he invaded the mainstreams of current thinking— in history, geography, economics, and sociology and in European historical methodology and thought. His commonplace books and his pilot essays show the diversity of his reading in literature, politics, history. He found particular stimulus in Walter Bagehot, Henry George, Charles Darwin, Achille Loria, Francis Parkman, Francis Walker, Woodrow Wilson, Hermann Von Holst, Percy

Bysshe Shelley, and Theodore Roosevelt, among other writers.[19] To an amazing degree he distilled the thought of the best of these writers in putting together his frontier-sectional thesis. Equally important, he based his theorizing upon thousands of historical references and statistics relating to a westward-moving population. The result was a kind of intellectual explosion. For Turner the 1893 essay was a high point of literary exuberance.

According to some critics, Turner seems, for a time, to have run his course. In published and unpublished essays, we find him cannibalizing the frontier theory, stating and restating his ideas. As Richard Hofstadter has argued, Turner, having exhausted the frontier idea, felt the need to formulate another central historical concept. He had already mentioned several times in early essays the notion that an important sectional rivalry had emerged in the wake of the frontier advance.[20] Sectionalism then became the thrust of his argument in *Rise of the New West*.

An able Turnerian convert, Michael Steiner, argues that the idea of sectionalism is so compelling a concept that it should be recognized on a par with Turner's frontier theory because the two ideas are in a sense one. Moreover, Turner's explanations of sectionalism provide the historical root for our newer concepts of regionalism in American history.[21] The frontier story remains incomplete without accounting for the accompanying sections that arose in its terminal moraine. Turner rightly saw the frontier, as Steiner maintains, as a self-destroying phenomenon.[22] After the passing of the frontier in the 1890s, pioneers settled in new homelands, which in turn gradually became separate regions or sections.

Ray A. Billington, in his writings and in his luncheon orations on Turner at the Huntington Library, tended to downplay the sectional interpretation as a viable theme. He was so convincing that most historians agreed with him. For Billington, the sectionalism thesis lacked the tremendous suggestiveness, what Hofstadter called the "important truth." If we examine Turner's notes and research materials another "important truth" becomes evident. The veracity of the sectional theme is compromised by evidence that Turner, its originator, appears to have become intellectually stagnated. Reading his sources and research notes reveals that he neglected to keep up with new developments in the social sciences and related fields. Although he had had an early interest in German writers, the mature Turner appears to have been unaware of the sociological scholarship in the era of Max Weber. He seems to have completely bypassed American writers such as William James and John Dewey in philosophy, Thorstein Veblen in economics, John Muir in conservation, and Franz Boas in anthropology together with the earlier impact of Lewis H. Morgan. The political scientists of his day, Charles E. Merriam and J. Allen Smith, and even more important, Charles A. Beard, intentionally or unintentionally escaped his notice. Perhaps his innate conservatism caused him to ignore Fabian socialism in England or the growth of American socialism. And there is no mention in his notes of Karl Marx except for his horror over the Bolshevik Revolution. Hofstadter argues that the extent to which Turner fell behind could be seen in comparing him with Charles A. Beard during the years 1908–1920.[23]

Turner had demonstrated genuine characteristics of greatness as a young man. But he seems to have had a period of arrested intellectual development in addition to a writing block. When one examines his thousands of three-by-five notecards (thirteen file drawers with notes, references, and references to other references) we can see that he was overwhelmed by his data. He was confronted with an unusable factual apparatus, although he continued to add to it with the vision of incorporating parts of it into a frontier-sectional theory to fit twentieth-century international problems.[24]

Turner's voluminous notes and rewritings of his frontier and sectionalism themes reveal that more and more he merged the two concepts into one. In his 1893 essay Turner on three occasions linked sectionalism with the advancing frontier. In his youth Turner tended to emphasize the frontier; in his mature years he stressed sectionalism. In practically all his writings he saw his two theories as interconnected.[25] I therefore refer to Turner's central interpretation of history as the frontier-sectional theory.

He had, he believed, emancipated American history from the germ theory, tracing the origins of our institutions to the German tribes. He opposed, if we make a joking reference, the "Turnerver-ein" school of the past. In its place was the new Turnerian asser-tion that democracy came "stark and strong and full of life out of the American forest." As we shall see, early critics greeted this kind of rhetoric with disdain, calling it a trumpet of rural provin-cialism. But Turner and his frontier-sectional concepts survived all attacks. His theory had an inherent strength and vitality of its own. In the safety-valve idea, for instance, Turner gave us a third theory linking both the frontier and the section. If all else about Turner is forgotten, this remaining idea has national and interna-tional implications for all the years to come.

CHAPTER TWO

TURNER'S APPRENTICESHIP
The Waspish Trail

Turner's ardent enthusiasm for the frontier can be traced in part to his early life. His entire youth was spent in the frontier town of Portage, Wisconsin, where, he tells us in his autobiographical letters, he saw the frontier firsthand. He was born there on November 14, 1861, and attended the town's high school where he was awarded a prize for his graduation oration, "The Power of the Press." He worked part-time as a typesetter in his father's newspaper office and observed his father's role as a political leader in a pioneer community.

Turner attended the University of Wisconsin in Madison where he studied history and completed his B.A. and M.A. degrees while supporting himself as a lecturer-tutor in rhetoric and oratory. After receiving his Ph.D. at Johns Hopkins University, he embarked upon a distinguished career as a professor of history at the University of Wisconsin. After much soul-searching he later left for Harvard University, but while in Cambridge his letters tell us that he yearned for the West. When he retired in 1924, he returned to Madison but then moved to Pasadena, California, in 1926. At the Huntington Library, he joined his friend Max Farrand in building an Anglo-American historical and literary research center. Turner died on March 14, 1932, after a brief illness, leaving two books on frontier-sectional themes to be published posthumously.

We know that Turner may have considered writing an autobiography because he was meticulous in assembling data about his

16

Turner at the age of eighteen, in 1879, upon entering "the preparatory department of the University of Wisconsin." (Courtesy, State Historical Society of Wisconsin)

family and autobiographical fragments in pocket notebooks, and on several occasions he wrote lengthy letters to admirers and former students detailing highlights of his life. Of course, Turner also thought that his biography would eventually be written and that the many little notes would be of tremendous help in tracing the main currents of his life.

More than anything else, as we read through his voluminous correspondence and unpublished speeches (some about himself and the reasons he wrote what he wrote), we encounter Turner's self-consciousness about his Yankee heritage, which proved to be a force in shaping his life and work. Undoubtedly he was tempted to write about himself at great length because of a justified pride in his accomplishments. He gave much thought to his reputation and to the fame he might have with future generations. His letters indicate he was aware of his influence on younger scholars.

A good example of the enormous shadow Turner cast upon his own generation can be seen in the career of John Hicks as revealed in his autobiography.[1] Unfortunately, Hicks, a popular historian of the era 1930–1960, reached intellectual maturity at the zenith of Turner's influence, and indeed to live in Turner's shadow was to live in an intellectual atmosphere that tended to stifle originality. Like Turner, Hicks traced his ancestors to colonial times and then to the Midwest. Also like Turner, Hicks attended the University of Wisconsin and later became a professor there, carrying on the tradition established by Turner and continued by Fredric L. Paxson of teaching frontier history.

Hicks writes, "I was flattered, rather than offended," when now and then comments were made about the Turner-Paxson-Hicks overemphasis on western history.[2] As an advanced student and then as a teacher, Hicks felt the almost overpowering presence of Turner. When his first important book, *The Populist Revolt*,[3] was published, Hicks made a thorough attempt to convince his readers that the farmers' discontent arose from the closing of the frontier, a Turnerian perspective later demolished by revisionist scholarship.[4] "When I wrote *The Populist Revolt*," Hicks regretfully concluded, "I was still uncritical, as were most American historians, of Turner's theories, and found greater significance in the passing of the frontier than I would now think reasonable."[5]

Hence it was not until middle life, after his move to the University of California in Berkeley, that Hicks's teaching career, modeled around a popular social history course, finally broke away from the powerful Turnerian tradition that had shaped his early professional life. The break seems to have come during 1933–1935, after Turner's death, when Hicks felt free to write a critical review of Turner's book, *The Significance of Sections*. The story of Hicks is significant because it shows the strength of the Turnerian tradition, how it might well hold back creative thinking and perhaps endanger a productive career in historical scholarship. Hicks eventually escaped Turner's shadow after the beginning of intelligent criticisms of Turner in the 1930s; he had also moved away from Madison, where such criticism of the master was slow to take form.

Turner's own career was similar to Hicks's. The main difference, of course, was that the adult Turner was surrounded by an intellectual atmosphere of his own creation, a body of doctrine he and his followers had created, which in time became a ruling theory of history. It was surprising even to Turner that his ideas were so well known that advanced students were often familiar enough with them to predict his lectures. At Harvard, after 1910, he was frustrated by pupils who thought his lectures such "old stuff" that "I seemed to be plagiarizing myself when I developed the phase of a theme. . . . I was criticized for seeming to follow too closely the work of some of my students."[6] Surely there are few creative thinkers who have had the opportunity to witness the imprinting of their own ideas on the intellectual fabric of their time. Turner moreover was continually reminded of his essay of 1893, "my frontier," as he affectionately called it in his letters. Even so, the pride in this essay concealed his frustration over his inability to duplicate what he had accomplished in his youth. There is little question that the essay haunted him in his later years.

The incubation of Turner's thinking about the nature of the frontier began, as he often said in telling the story of his youth, with his colorful childhood in Portage, a pioneer community on the portage of the Fox and Wisconsin rivers where in terms proposed by Erik Erikson, Turner enjoyed a boyhood of trust and security. He perceived his ancestors as having been a part of the Yankee march to the West, gradually winding their way with the frontier migrations from New England and New York to various midwestern settlements and finally to Portage. Their migrations, their hopes and aspirations in making homes in frontier areas and civilizing the wilderness were part of the social experience many other families shared in attempting to better their lot. Turner loved to reminisce in letters to former students about the Turners and the Hanfords, the paternal and maternal branches of his family who pioneered the midwestern frontier. Although he never claimed a connection with the old patrician families of New England, he nonetheless seems to have admired them and their descendants, especially the Brahmin Yankee gentlemen whom he encountered as a Harvard faculty member.[7] He was conscious enough of his New England origins to complain sometimes about his reticence: "I have enough ancestral Puritanism in me not to be able to express my deeper feelings,"[8] he told Mrs. Alice Forbes Hooper, his closest friend during his tenure at Harvard. Turner felt pride in his Puritan background because these people had been conquerors of the wilderness hinterlands. Eulogizing New England in his letters and essays, Turner sometimes went overboard in extolling his frontier theme of progress when he talked about how much America owed to the Puritan pioneers. "New England," he wrote, "may appreciate and be proud of the part she herself has had in helping to build up a society in what was once a splendid wilderness."[9] Turner had lived long enough in the Midwest, however, to know that too much of such talk might be offensive. There were Americans who were "sensitive about being civilized by New England."[10] As he told Mrs. Hooper, the special importance of New England families was their role in building ideals that made possible "marvelous growth." He wrote to her that it was "seldom realized by the families of those who have been active in the making of America, and who have profited from its marvelous growth, that the children have a duty to preserve its history and ideals." Later generations should pass on the "hope and determination to make a better world" by their "optimistic faith" in our progress.[11]

Turner was willing to concede that although families like Mrs. Hooper's could claim glory in the pioneer past by building eastern railroads and establishing profitable western trunk lines, his own ancestors were more common folk, the actual settlers, the farmers who had broken virgin soil and fought the Indians. The most central of these figures was one Humphrey Turner, a tanner from Essex, England, who arrived in Plymouth, Massachusetts, in 1628.[12] In giving an account of his own life and work for the Harvard History Club, Turner proudly spoke of his family as one that "runs back to the beginning of the Puritan migrations to New England." As they "pioneered westward to Michigan and Wisconsin" in successive generations, they "became a part of the influence that shaped my thinking toward a less sectional view and a more dominant American view."[13]

The wider "American view" that Turner believed he had adopted was thus partly the result of having ancestors who were the "pioneer stock." One of these on his mother's side, a Connecticut clergyman, the Reverend Thomas Hanford, gained some notoriety

Turner's mother, Mary Hanford Turner, the village schoolteacher, and his father, Andrew Jackson Turner. (From the author's collection)

because his speech, affected by bad teeth, was sometimes misunderstood by his congregation. As Turner said, Cotton Mather had remarked that Hanford made "much smoke" from "a little fire." Turner also joked that Cotton Mather would criticize the Puritan-like Hanfords who went west "beyond the hedge" of settlement "into the frontier wilderness."[14]

Turner's father, who was a newspaper editor, local historian, and politician, met his mother, "the village school-ma'am," in the quaint village of Friendship in Adams County, Wisconsin, which Turner termed "a transplanted Yankee town." Mary Hanford was so pretty that "Jack" (who was born in 1832 and named after Andrew Jackson) declared when first meeting her, "I'm going to marry that red-headed girl."[15] Actually, Turner's gentle schoolteacher mother, who loved to give him history books—especially those on classical Greece and Rome, had "rich brown rather than red hair."[16] A photograph of her as a young woman shows an attractive, intelligent round face crowned by a full head of dark hair parted in the middle and pulled back from her ears to allow for hanging earrings. Her self-confident and steady gaze seems to follow the movements of the observer. There is no question that she had a quiet influence on her older son Fred as well as on her younger son and daughter. Turner often recalled that "my mother's ancestors were preachers. Is it strange that I preached of the frontier?"[17]

In picturesque Portage, an area where Marquette and other explorers had traveled, Andrew Jackson Turner established himself as editor and publisher for the *Wisconsin State Register*; he also became a leader in Republican politics, lecturing to the immigrant European settlers in editorials in between his terms as chair of the local board of supervisors. Turner reminisced about his father's influence upon him, a man of "strong gentle presence . . . who helped his fellows and stood for good things." "What I was conscious of was that father had come of pioneer folk, that he loved the forest, into which he used to take me fishing."[18] Certainly Turner's passion for fishing and for woodland vacations can be traced to his boyhood outings with his father, but Jack Turner influenced his son in other ways, too. His letters to his son stress the Puritan ethic of hard work and the wise use of money and time. He told his son of his pioneer home where "every stone, stump, and tree has its history," and he urged him to "be punctual to Sunday School."[19]

The father also gave his son a thousand chances to see politics in action by allowing young Fred, or "Fritz" as he was affectionately called, to set type in the family-owned newspaper office. What especially impressed Fred was his father's editorializing on Yankee virtues for the benefit of the mixed community of Swiss, German, Scandinavian, Irish, and Scottish workers and farmers who settled in the Portage area. "Father," Turner once wrote with pride, "shepherded these new people in the county-board meeting; lectured them on politics and farming in his editorials, and was followed by them wonderfully."[20]

Portage for young Fred was a fascinating world of immigrants carving new homes in the wilderness. There were Yankees from all parts of New England as well as from New York, and they had no option but to blend their lives in the cultural milieu increasingly dominated by northern European settlers. "When I went to Europe," Turner remembered, "it was familiar. I had seen it in Portage. When I went to Harvard I found that I had met the Puritan in the flesh long years before."[21] There were also Indians and a few lonely blacks, who were not part of the blending. Turner particularly remembered the social flux that occurred among the northern Europeans and the Yankees, the conflicts of the boisterous Irish raftsmen, and the stone throwing of some Pomeranian children. He often described Portage as a representative melting pot of pioneer cultures to admiring readers of autobiographical letters to show that he himself was a product of the frontier.

The census count of Portage when Turner was ten years old was nearly 4,000. As the town boomed and improvements came, Turner recalled, old French graves were exhumed for the grading of roads. The sight of the old cemetery when he was about six years old caused him to speculate about "those mouldering relics" for years.[22] This expanding port city was passing through what Turner later termed "the frontier process." In one of his letters to Carl Becker, Turner described the enormous impact of his boyhood upon his writing.

> I have poled down the Wisconsin in a dug-out with Indian guides from "Grandfather Bull Falls," through virgin forest of balsam firs, seeing deers in the river,—antlered beauties who watched us come down with curious eyes and broke for the tall timber,—hearing the squaws in their village on the high bank talk their low treble to the bass of our Indian polesman,—feeling that I belonged to it all. I have seen a lynched man hanging to a tree as I came home from school in Portage, have played around old Fort Winnebago at its outskirts, have seen the red-shirted Irish raftsmen *take* the town when they tied up and came ashore, having plodded up the "pinery road" that ran by our house to the pine woods of Northern Wisconsin, have seen Indians come in on their ponies to buy paint and ornaments, and sell their furs; have stumbled on their camp on the Baraboo, where dried pumpkins were hung up, and cooking muskrats were in the kettle, and an Indian family bathing in the river—the frontier in that sense, you see, was real to me, and when I studied history I did not keep my personal experiences in a watertight compartment away from my studies. Early I got hold of Droysen's dictum that history is the self-consciousness of humanity, and

conceived of the past as the explanation of *much* of the present—not *all* of it, however, thank God.[23]

What can be made of this outpouring of boyhood recollections? It so resembles the descriptions that Turner wrote his friends Alice Forbes Hooper and Constance L. Skinner that it could not have been completely spontaneous. For instance, in a letter a few years earlier to Mrs. Hooper about his youth, Turner wrote that

> the Wisconsin River rafts came down and tied up at Portage, where the red-shirted profane, hard-drinking and virile Irishmen came ashore and took possession. Talk about he-men, and red blood! They had it one hundred percent plus. Then there was that inviting "pinery" road that ran past our house to the pine forest in upper Wisconsin. . . . I remember . . . a narrow aisle cut like a gash through the wonderful white pine forest . . . hearing a duet-like conversation between the boatmen and their squaws . . . the gutteral of the buck and the sweet, clear, laughing treble of the squaw . . . the antlered deer who stood at a bend among the balsam firs.[24]

What romance and excitement: tough Irishmen, a pinery road, and the world of nature—white pines, antlered deer, and Indians, a "buck" and his "squaw" (then, as now, Indians considered these terms insulting). Even as late in his life as 1921, when Turner wrote this letter, the Indians were still part of the wildlife, not part of the pioneer community. When Turner wrote to Constance Skinner about a year later, he offered a similar hometown profile:

> There were still Indian Winnebago tepees where I hunted and fished, and the Indians came into stores to buy paints and trinkets and sell furs. Their Indian ponies and dogs were familiar street scenes. The town was a mixture of raftsmen from the "pineries" . . . Pomeranian immigrants (we stoned each other) . . . Scotch . . . Welsh . . . Germans . . . Yankees from Vermont and Maine and Conn . . . "New York-Yankees" . . . southerns . . . a few negroes; many Norwegians and Swiss, some Englishmen, and one or two Italians."[25]

Somehow the various settlers adjusted to each other. Turner's father helped through his leadership in harmonizing "rival tongues" and by shepherding such a "composite flock." Turner himself "set up" the local news and could follow every step of the frontier's blending of differences: the social transformation or the Americanization of the settlers. As he told Constance Skinner, "We all 'got on together' in this forming society."

This concept of the melting pot, a basic evolutionist theme in Turner's historical writing, was not original with him, despite the tone of his autobiographical writings. At least two writers whom Turner had studied at length during his formative years, Francis Parkman and Theodore Roosevelt, had already described the ethnic blend of Northern European peoples in the Allegheney woodlands. Roosevelt's *Winning of the West* in a deluxe edition was treasured throughout Turner's life. Parkman's brief note complimenting him on his Wisconsin fur-trade thesis was another valued possession.[26] The extent of Roosevelt's influence on Turner should not be underestimated: Turner was captivated by Roosevelt's idea that a frontier "hunter type" emerged from this woodland cultural melting pot.[27] The concept of a frontier type became a central theme in Turner's writing.

Roosevelt and Parkman wrote descriptive accounts of these blending ethnic frontier communities, but Turner made the melting-pot concept a determining factor in history. Here in Darwinist context was the determinist argument for the frontier as the originator of American national characteristics. Turner's home of Portage, equally populated by European immigrants and native Yankees, was for him a microcosm of social history bringing about transformation through Americanization. Turner had seen in his boyhood a rough but friendly blending of people in a rustic setting where pioneers became progenitors of our basic institutions and democratic ideas. In evolving his thesis, Turner went far beyond Roosevelt and Parkman in applying the melting-pot concept.[28]

Turner's background, as the son of a public figure, was different from that of other Wisconsin pioneers. The Norwegian Thorstein Veblen, for example, a contemporary who lived north of Portage in Manitowoc County, experienced a boyhood of exhausting farm labor and cultural isolation as a "Norske" youth. Ridiculed as a "Norwegian Indian" and cheated by Yankee land speculators and "businessmen" magistrates, Veblen adopted a cynical view of leisure-class Americans. Veblen defended Indian rights during the Sioux uprisings of the time,[29] and Turner, who lacked sympathy for the Indians in their dealings with whites and who presented an idealistic view of white society, eventually came to share some of Veblen's pessimism.

It was John Muir who saw sufficient waste and greed in white frontier trade to make him a conservationalist for life. Growing up in the Portage area about fifteen years before Turner, Muir in his autobiography recounted the greedy exploitation of the soil and the "gory business" of slaughtering thousands of birds and small animals by collecting their heads in bloody bags during "head hunt" jamborees. The farmers believed this annual extermination of wildlife would benefit them.[30]

Muir was involved in the debate Scottish pioneers had begun over the dispossession of the Wisconsin Indians. He wrote that his father and his neighbor, another Scotsman, often discussed the morality of taking Indian land. His father had argued that God never intended for the Indian hunting society, unskilled in agriculture, to hold vast fertile land that could be tilled profitably by whites. The neighbor just as tenaciously held that the immigrants were themselves wasteful and that a truly "scientific" farmer could grow five times as much on the same Wisconsin land, hence the land might profitably be left to the Indians. Muir decided that his father never won the argument but that nevertheless the Indians had lost out completely.[31]

During Turner's youth, the Indians and the wildlife disappeared as the pioneers advanced through the Portage area, and the magnificent pine forests of Wisconsin shrank. Turner remembered the romance of "Pinery road" and the cuts through the forests made by lumbermen and Irish raftsmen, but he never appreciated the dimensions of the ecological disaster to Wisconsin's white pine. How could this exploitation so visible around the Portage area have escaped Turner's notice? Indeed, he believed that awareness of conservation as an issue emerged only after free land had disappeared around 1890,[32] illustrating the extent to which the frontier theory dominated his view of history. When Turner's good friend, Charles Van Hise, wrote a book on conservation in 1910, Turner made a number of notations about the size of America's "original forests," but he passed over references to the ravaging of Wisconsin's white pine.[33] If timbermen stole with impunity, they also acted with boldness and energy; Turner admired these latter aspects of the frontier character because of his boyhood experiences, and this value pervaded his professional writing.

The "West" that had captivated Turner in his formative years was actually the Midwest, the large woodland area his ancestors had helped to clear as they followed fur traders into the fertile river valleys that had been the home of Indian tribes. And when Fred Turner left Portage to study at nearby Madison, his travels were largely restricted to a Portage-Madison circuit as he visited his parents or his younger sister. He seems to have separated himself from his younger brother Will, who, living in the shadow of a gifted older brother, worked as a railroad brakeman and hardware dealer after minimum schooling in Portage.[34]

Fred Turner polished his high school education by taking a Greek class, a special college preparatory unit of the University of Wisconsin. Aware of the emphasis on classical studies at Madison, Andrew Jackson Turner saw the need to prepare his older son for college entrance requirements.[35] Young Turner was also drawn to oratory, a particular qualification for politicians of the time. When Turner was growing up, there were countless speakers who rivaled the politicians as they lectured through the small towns. Such distinguished figures as Ralph Waldo Emerson used the lecture platform to set forth themes of literary historical interpretation. Turner's newspaper scrapbook is filled with quotations from the writings and speeches of Emerson, Charles Dickens, Thomas Carlyle, and Robert G. Ingersoll, "the great agnostic" who saw in Darwin's *Origin of the Species* scientific evidence for his view. Certainly Ingersoll, an eloquent speaker, lawyer, and debater, was a model of excellence in oratory for Turner. These matters were often of interest to Turner's family as well as to the newspaper office where conversation about political rivalries among parties and candidates was constant.

Fred Turner's own ability as an orator won him a graduation

The Wisconsin State Register *in Portage, Wisconsin, where Turner worked as a typesetter.* (Courtesy, Henry E. Huntington Library and Art Gallery)

prize for his argument in June 1878 that the power of the press contributed to the making of history, particularly the history of the United States.[36] Praised for its originality, style, and manner of delivery by a "self-possessed and very ernest" young man, the speech was published in his father's newspaper and preserved with other clippings in Fred's scrapbook. He was one of a half-dozen student speakers, but Turner gained the advantage through his ability to stir his audience. The speech was more than an ordinary high school graduation speech. Turner had not yet been overwhelmed by Ingersoll's humanistic rationalism, and so he unhesitatingly rounded out his eloquent passages with biblical overtones. As a family friend wrote Fred's parents, "very few men of his age could produce" such a piece.[37] At the same time, Turner did argue his case within the context of an evolution of ideas through the centuries. By surveying highlights of biblical, classical, and modern European and American history, the young orator demonstrated how the wisdom of great writers and the events

Andrew Jackson Turner on the spacious front porch of his home in Portage, one of the town's most attractive and gracious houses. (Courtesy, Henry E. Huntington Library and Art Gallery)

of history are preserved in print. Through the "baptism of ink" centuries are rolled away as "the past becomes the Present." Further, the press as an instrument of progress was "of unspeakable good in the diffusion of education upon which the whole social and political fabric depends." The youthful Turner argued that the press was "a wonderful influence in shaping the morals and customs of a people." As the great orators kept alive the accumulated wisdom of mankind, letterpress printing, "one of the greatest inventions," made possible an even greater transfer of knowledge from generation to generation. The printing of books allowed great events of past ages to be "re-enacted" and thus permitted "the genius" of figures like Homer, Aristotle, Shakespeare, and Bacon to stand side by side on the library shelves. Turner had recently seen such a library, presumably at the State Historical Society in Madison, which his father frequently visited.

The appeal of Turner's youthful speech lay in his ability to call forth imagery to represent the events of the past, a technique he later used in his famous 1893 essay on the frontier. Fred told his high school audience that "Washington appears," "Napoleon startles the world by his genius," "Civil War rages in our Union and Lincoln steps forward to save the land from a martyr's death." He said, "The curtain falls on events transpired," linking the past with "the existing." The press had actually "joined the Past and Present and made them one." Books preserved the words of "Kings of Thought," and newspapers carried "the torch of freedom" to the masses of people.

This speech held the theory of progress for Fred Turner as a Portage High School orator. Certainly he believed what he said, for he said much the same thing for the rest of his life; for example, he never stopped theorizing about how common people better themselves through stages of progress. He believed that linking the past with the present through the study of history would make this social process more visible and more understandable, and he found support for this concept in the writings of historians such as Johann G. Droysen.[38] Some change did occur in his thought, however. He never again conceived of American progress as "the New Jerusalem [rising] in its divine beauty."[39] He turned away from interpretations deriving from traditional Christianity and toward the Darwinism taught at the state university.

Turner had been doing his homework well in Portage before he left for Madison. He conceived the ideas for his high school graduation address while writing a column in his father's newspaper, "Pen and Scissors,"[40] filled with quotations from Samuel Johnson, Ralph Waldo Emerson, Charles Dickens, Walter Scott, and William Shakespeare. Some of the references may have been lifted from a book of quotations, although Bartlett seems not to have been his major source. At least part of his theory of progress via the press came from Isaiah Thomas's popular *History of Printing in America*,[41] which presented books and newspapers as a cultural index of society's progress toward a better life.

One might think that when Turner entered the University of Wisconsin in fall 1878 he might have forgotten about his "Press" theory of progress, but such was not his way. Once he developed a theory, he would apply it in every conceivable way to explain historical events and epochs. His college commonplace books reveal an astonishing series of revisions he made on his high school oration; these three volumes show that Turner over the next five years never completely strayed from the basic ideas of that speech. He restated and revised them repeatedly in an oration he called "Imaginativeness of the Present." Since in his first two years he largely concentrated on drill in the classics and on English composition and mathematics, it was not until his junior year that he could revise his oration for classes in rhetoric and oratory.[42]

Of course, Turner's involvement with the press and with history was related to his experience at home, which he once confided had shaped his life as a "practical experience."[43] In fact Turner left college after graduation to work for a brief period as a journalist for Chicago and Milwaukee newspapers, and his close friend, the journalist-editor-historian Reuben Gold Thwaites, almost persuaded him to follow journalism as a career. Not surprisingly, Turner wrote to himself in his 1881 notebook, "develop ideas of the Press and the effect which it had on starting the great undercurrent by making knowledge cheap. . . . Growth at present as shown by the press. . . . Read up on Evolution. . . . the glorious influence of the Press. . . . Americans erected a republic based on the great progressive possibilities of a free people. . . . The past dreamed. The present acts."

More and more these drafts eulogize "Evolution" as that which "the present believes" to explain man's social development.[44] The press, Turner argued in page after page, recorded the ways in which men progressed toward a better way of life. The expansion of his high school oration held young Turner in a sort of intellectual captivity until 1883 when he finally discarded the press and concentrated exclusively on Darwinian themes. His prize-winning oration, "The Poet of the Future," delivered at the end of his junior year, contended that there were no poets to express the spirit of an age in which "the locomotive is a type of our grand civilization." As the "reign of aristocracy" passed, "that of humanity begins. Democracy is waiting for its poet." Where were those bards who would "sing" of Darwin, Spencer, Lincoln, and Watt?[45]

In the commonplace book of June 1883, Turner jubilantly expounded on a singular "new theory of society."[46] Although part of "The Poet of the Future" is repeated here, Turner stressed the idea that "Evolution . . . is now the intellect," that Comte, Darwin, and Spencer were the thinkers who could teach us lessons, that the "social problem" of the lower classes was now making itself known, even to the poor. "Our age is a turning point. We have a new system of nature. We must now obtain a new theory of society." In still another oration, his commencement address of 1884, "Architecture through Oppression,"[47] Turner further developed a distinct Darwinian theme, arguing that Old World temples were built by the toil of the common people, but "now the world begins to see that true progress, true enlightenment, means the progress, the enlightenment of all . . . when the greatest happiness of the greatest number shall have something of a reality" as a result of "this wave of democratic utilitarianism."

As these orations and drafts make clear, Turner in his college years was an ardent admirer of Charles Darwin and Herbert Spencer. His speculations on poets, architecture, and the press were laced with evolutionist determinism as he traced the historic origins of Anglo-Saxon and American democracy. Jeremy Bentham's utilitarianism, the practical outlook on social problems, also permeated his thinking. Underneath the practicality is the social obligation of the person telling the story, the patriotic aim of the historian to probe the nature of the past so that citizens could chart their future. Finally, there is the more elusive fact that the historian approaches the past wishing to impose "independent thought" on historical phenomena and to educe theory about the past.

In one of his handwritten autobiographical fragments during his Harvard teaching years, Turner extolled the "mind that drew light and heat from the resources of scholarship . . . passing on the impulse to independent and incisive thinking." Turner argued that "such incitement to thought is more important than the precise form of thought." It was this type of historical motivation that Turner admired in others, "even if I do not find myself able at all times to agree with the thinker."[48]

Thus Turner viewed his own work as "independent and incisive thinking," a trenchant burrowing into the past that could be done only by creating patterns of thought to explain the facts. In his early years, the Darwinian theme lay at the theoretical center of the interpretations he set forth in discussing the press, poets, or architecture. Turner found in his writing and rewriting that such variations on one theme could be presented neatly in the form of an oration. Thus Turner's entire background of reading, with references to almost every great author he had ever read, is telescoped with rhetorical flourishes in these remarkable orations. Turner's later essays, particularly his famous "Significance of the Frontier in American History," were enormously successful because each was a model oration.[49]

CHAPTER THREE

THE MAKING OF A HISTORIAN
Yankee Perspectives

Turner's commonplace books confirm that he was an avid reader. Although he dropped out of college for a brief period after his sophomore year, his records of his reading tell us that in 1880 he read over thirty volumes, including novels by Dickens, Swift, and Cooper and works by Milton, Macaulay, and Irving. His reading lists for the immediate years thereafter concentrate on Carlyle, Horace "in original Latin,"[1] Lucretius, Tacitus, Emerson, Parkman, Shelley, Dante, Herbert Spencer, and Darwin. His commentary, expressed largely in quotations for inclusion in orations, reveals that Turner was fascinated with literature protesting conformity to authority and defining man within a universe governed by Darwinian law.

The state university in Madison was like an advanced high school and operated under the constant supervision of a board of regents who told the president, John Bascom, what textbooks to use, how to discipline students, how to allocate funds, how to run the library, and whom to appoint to the faculty. Bascom, however, was an energetic administrator who fought this interference. Exasperated on one occasion, he asserted, "No president can draw the free breath of manhood in the University of Wisconsin as it is now organized."[2] Bascom, who had a flowing beard and the penetrating eyes of a religious prophet, successfully fought the regents with Calvinist resolution. And, as a member of the faculty, he taught constitutional law, philosophy, psychology, and ethics.[3] Bascom survived the regents' attempts to force him out of office

34

Francis Parkman, ca. 1855, shortly after the publication of the Conspiracy of Pontiac *in 1851. Parkman was an early model for Turner.* (Courtesy, Massachusetts Historical Society)

and began a courageous administrative initiative that would eventually transform the university into a research center. Yet the university of Turner's day was still primarily a teaching institution where overworked faculty attempted to introduce professional standards in scholarship. Their efforts were supplemented by many visiting lecturers expounding social change. Bascom, a progressive on such topics as the regulation of interstate commerce, shared his faculty's acceptance of Darwinian ideas in analyzing contemporary subjects. In 1878, the year Turner entered the college, barely twenty years had passed since Darwin had put forth his ideas, and they had become the current doctrine to be followed in the social sciences and the humanities as well as in the sciences. Turner, who was befriended by some of the faculty, readily absorbed this teaching as part of his intellectual development.

Prof. Rasmus B. Anderson, who taught history, was a Scandinavian studies enthusiast and liked to talk about ancient Norse culture and the Viking voyages. He also tried to win over any student who appeared to be of Norwegian descent; staring at the student through his gold-rimmed spectacles, he would say, "Young man, you ought to be in my class studying the language of your ancestors."[4] It is unclear whether Anderson urged Norse studies on Turner, but the two men did talk about the ancient Norsemen and how a "genius" like Carlyle, with a few terse comments in *Heroes*, could project, as Anderson stated it to Turner, "as good, if not a better idea of those subjects, than another man could in a lifetime of study in volumes of writing."[5]

Carlyle himself, Anderson told Turner, "had some elements of littleness about him. . . . We like him better for that. For my part, I do not like a perfect man. To tell me a man has no faults disgusts me." Turner in reply asked, "Why should we be so impatient with perfectionists." "Because," Anderson said, "human nature is very imperfect and we cannot sympathize with which we have nothing in common—like the perfect man." Anderson concluded, according to Turner's record of their conversation in his commonplace book, "I don't like angels."[6] If Turner learned anything from Anderson, it was probably that historians are human beings too and thus share their shortcomings.

Another teacher Turner admired was his talented instructor in rhetoric and oratory, Prof. David Bower Frankenburger.[7] He not only advised and tutored Turner but also trained some of Turner's future students. A venerable professor of quiet personal charm, an amateur poet, and a subtle critic of those students who ornamented their presentations with inappropriate epithets and literary flourishes, Frankenburger was a skilled professional. He used his seminar-sized groups to expose each participant to a variety of criteria for excellence: choice of words and examples, structure of argument, tone of voice, and stance. Frankenburger was an expert in stylistic techniques dealing with philosophical or historical generalizations. Behind the wall of criticism that all students experienced in their pilot orations (for Frankenburger was never at a loss for congenial faultfinding), was the reward of a smile, a kind remark, and often some real humor and fun. The students competed eagerly for Frankenburger's favor and appreciated him. There is the anecdote of the football player who in his oration emphatically declared: "There was a shadow of a doubt!" Frankenburger's eyes twinkled: "You know, young man, you must learn that you do not know that there is such a thing as no shadow of a doubt!"[8]

Turner, under Frankenburger's training, won two oratory prizes in his junior and senior years, and after his experiment as a journalist following graduation, he returned to assist his mentor as a tutor in rhetoric and oratory for three years. Much later, when Turner spoke at his teacher's funeral at the local Unitarian church, he talked not only about Frankenburger as the ideal colleague and teacher but also, one suspects, of his own personal aspirations as a teacher:

> What Frankenburger's life meant to his associates, what it meant to the great body of students who through nearly thirty years came into affectionate touch with his instruction and his uplifting sympathy. . . . He was a teacher. But he taught his students more than formal expression. Those of us who in our plastic years came under his influence will never forget that rare questioning smile; that invitation to the best and the highest. . . . He had the glad expectancy, the appealing sympathy . . . that drew forth the bud and blossom of our best endeavor.
>
> No other member of the faculty was so absolutely bound up in the University of Wisconsin. His life was one of unselfish devotion to his students. Others might teach classes, he taught the individual. . . . No student ever brought his imperfect work to him without going away heartened by encouragement, aided by helpful suggestions, and above all inspired to do something better. . . . His face was aglow with expectancy . . . new truth, new beauty, new good.[9]

Turner preserved this funeral oration carefully in an envelope, which suggests that he wanted future biographers to know what

William F. Allen, Turner's teacher and lifelong friend at the University of Wisconsin. Allen, who had studied at universities in Berlin and Göttingen, passed on to his students a belief in "scientific inquiry," which came to shape Turner's writings. (Courtesy, Henry E. Huntington Library and Art Gallery)

kind of man his teacher had been. The original handwritten oration shows much revision and indicates that Frankenburger was the sort of teacher Turner trained himself to become: a person intent on touching the lives of individual pupils.

Frankenburger also exposed Turner to the type of oratory that

(left, courtesy, Henry E. Huntington Library and Art Gallery) *David P. Frankenberger, Turner's instructor in rhetoric and oratory at the University of Wisconsin;* (right, from the author's collection) *Richard T. Ely, Turner's teacher at Johns Hopkins University and later a colleague at the University of Wisconsin.*

can serve as the basis for the literary essay. An admirer of Emerson, Frankenburger may well have been responsible for Turner's reading every essay that Emerson ever wrote. As Turner's career gradually shifted from oratory to history, Emerson became Turner's teacher almost as if his physical presence had been in the classroom; consciously or unconsciously, Turner came under his shadow, the preacher, orator, lecturer, and essayist whose prose was distilled from his journals.

Turner was a disciple of Emerson in method as well as in intellect. In method, Turner gradually mastered the technique of writing essays that had the vitality of the spoken word. In intellect, Turner adopted some of Emerson's ideas on evolution, nature, and the individual. Turner's orations were punctuated with phrases about human dignity, self-reliance, and "life in harmony with nature" although he was slow to appreciate the relevance of this last dictum to conservation. Emerson's Unitarianism provided still another influence and was reinforced by the beliefs of David Frankenburger and of Turner's mentor in the teaching and writing of history, William F. Allen. Turner's commonplace books contain phrases such as the "broader ideas of religion," "the democratic, ethical spirit of Christ," and "the anthropomorphic God."[10] Turner's stress on individualism and on the term "self-reliance"[11] can be traced to Emerson's gentle mysticism, which did not directly confront traditional Christianity. Turner also adopted the Unitarian resistance to the virulent fundamentalism so vigilantly opposed to Darwinian ideas at that time.[12]

According to Turner's reminiscences, neither Frankenburger nor Anderson was as influential a teacher as William Francis Allen. Turner filled his letters with accolades to Allen though other Wisconsin faculty faded from his memory; Rasmus Anderson was scarcely mentioned and David Frankenburger was ignored, despite Turner's obvious indebtedness to him. The omissions could be explained in part because Turner never considered himself a professional in the field of oratory and rhetoric, but in truth the specialty had lost its prestige in the curriculum even before Frankenburger died. Turner's correspondence and autobiographical notes show a hunger for recognition, and he had no incentive to acknowledge his dependence upon this outmoded field even though he used oratorical techniques extensively to argue historical points.

William Francis Allen was shrewd enough to perceive his protégé's position as he confronted two diverging professional paths within college teaching. "You have to make a decision," Allen told Turner. "It is either oratory or history. It cannot be both."

Allen was convincing and persuasive, demonstrating the use of the scientific method in his historiography. He gave Turner professional advice, arranged fellowships, and sent him to Johns Hopkins for doctoral work where he could write a doctoral dissertation on a subject that he had already investigated in writing his M.A. thesis. When Allen died in 1889, Turner took his first post as an assistant professor, filling the vacancy on the staff of the Wisconsin history department. A memorial volume was published the next year, and

Frankenburger wrote an affectionate tribute to Allen, describing the making of a Yankee schoolteacher who rose to become a leading intellectual force in the fledgling midwestern university.[13] Turner prepared an extensive bibliography of his master's writings.

Allen, a prolific writer of the 1880s, published manuals on Greek and Latin, *A Short History of the Roman People,* an edition of slave songs in the United States, commentaries on higher education, and some 900 essays and reviews on such diverse topics as history, politics, literature, ethnology, Asiatic studies, the classics, and the medieval church. With his slim, finely chiseled, sensitive face framed by dark sideburns and hair brushed close over his high forehead, Allen projected a somewhat feminine image in his portrait. Turner called him "the gentlest, justest, most scholarly man I ever knew."[14] Born in Massachusetts, educated at Harvard with supplementary study at two German universities, Allen enjoyed a varied career. He was a member of the Sanitary Commission during the Civil War and taught at Antioch College before accepting the chair of ancient languages and history at Wisconsin.

The gentle and thoughtful expression in Allen's portraits concealed the strict discipline that governed his life in teaching and writing. His teaching methods were grounded in an iron rigidity cast in the mold of the "topic system," a method of examining evolutional shifts in a Darwinian scheme of historical development. He was a hard taskmaster, requiring masses of source and reference work from his students in their mastery of a topic. As Turner recalled, it was a test of survival, but the experience was never forgotten. Indeed, Allen's topic method became Turner's method, a controlled approach to American history, providing guidelines for teaching, lectures, investigation, and writing itself. Far-ranging in surface considerations, deep in cutting through to the historical facts, and interdisciplinary in probing for the right direction of interpretation, Allen's method brought the neophyte and his subject, the historical "topic," together at once.[15]

In the course of explaining how he absorbed Allen's techniques, Turner in one of his letters detailed the experience the student confronted in the master's "territorial and dynastic history," which "covered the world." Aiming toward an understanding of the origin of "institutions" in Roman, medieval, and English "constitutional" development, each undergraduate prepared a lecture. This procedure provided each student a chance to appear before the class and gave the overworked Allen a respite from an apparently exhausting teaching schedule, In preparing the lecture, each student was subjected to layers of data and information. "First," Turner reports, came "the dry bones of geography & tables of kings. Second the political institutions, by retracing the same field, using lectures on the basic mimeographed documents—(Latin & Anglo-Saxon), which he put in our hands, laws. . . . Then finally the world of ideas, culture."[16]

After exposure to this data and interpretation, only the fittest survived, "for," as Turner tells us, "it worked very well for those who lived to the end." Survival of such disciplined study was for Turner especially rewarding because it was done under the supervision of a master guide. Throughout the ordeal Allen was constantly there encouraging and urging greater depth in research and critical evaluation of data.[17] Here indeed was a unique introduction for the undergraduate to the problems of evaluation of sources and the search for evidence. Allen "made me realize," Turner wrote, "what scholarship meant; what loyalty to truth demanded. I never had, in Hopkins or elsewhere, his equal as a scholar and simple sincere *acute* mind."[18]

Turner and his fellow students, gallantly attacking topics such as "Charlemagne" or, in American history, "Puritanism" or "The Town Meeting," could always confer with Allen when the topic seemed overwhelming. In Turner's correspondence with Allen, we see that the master teacher seldom failed as an adviser. Allen seems to have known a little bit about almost everything. His letters cover an enormous range of topics in history and literature, but he always returned to the unifying idea of holding onto the threads of "scientific inquiry" so that history could be kept in "scientific channels" by "applying laws."[19] His approach to studying the church and medieval rulers gave insight into how medieval "institutions in their formative period" evolved.

The astonishing influence that Herbert Spencer, Darwin, and other writers of evolutionary themes exercised on Allen's conception of history is clear from Allen's classroom lecture notes and from the notes that Turner took as an undergraduate listening to these lectures. If Allen insisted upon any concept, a "fundamental" for him was that "society is an organism." There were many such societal "organisms"; to understand any one of these, for instance the New England town meeting, one had to study "how it is affected by surrounding organisms." Of particular significance were society's institutions that developed and modified their behavior "upon certain *lands* with changes at certain times." Historical surveys were necessary to take "account of these changes and their causes" in light of "geography and chronology."[20]

Shifting from topic to topic, from the ancient German *comitatus* to the New England town meeting, Allen encouraged students to study the "organism vertically" for its "inheritance," "horizontally for the interaction of conditions," "physically" for environment, and "sympathetically" for its "peculiar conditions." Here was Allen's "laboratory method," which Turner adopted and used for the rest of his life. It was an approach to history designed to pinpoint modifications in social change. As Turner wrote in detailing the topic method, his goal in mastering any topic was "to know all about it," to master the "essential facts." The amassing of facts required the compilation of dates. As a student Turner made dreary lists of dates, not unlike Hayden's *Dictionary of Dates* (one suspects he borrowed much of his data).[21] About the time Turner began graduate work in the late 1880s, he also began compiling his data on three-by-five cards. His scheme was to compile the entire history of the United States on these cards, thousands of them, filed chronologically under topics. Allen had been an effective teacher of method.

Allen had other refinements in theory, which the impressionable Turner also wrote down in his American history notebooks. There were glimmerings of the frontier theory in these early notes stressing the importance of land, geography, and the growth of society as it adjusted to its environment. Turner asks in these early notes, "What were the conditions leading to this new chapter in history—the discovery and occupation of a new continent? The law of continuity," he assures us, "demands that we investigate the cause of this discovery." One of his conclusions is a prelude to much of his later writings: "The history of the people who occupied the savage territory that is now the U.S.—the story of this occupation and the ideas which here arose . . . is part of the old story of the Aryan race—the latest chapter."[22] In his mid-twenties, Turner had already envisioned his major concern in his conceptualization of American history, the occupation of a wilderness by the Aryan race, the most recent chapter in an old story of conquest. The history of the American people, he argued later with supporting documentary evidence, was largely the story of society's expansion into frontier territory. The organism of American society, for Turner, consisted of the melding of Aryan people on the frontier where the traits of self-sufficiency, independence, and democracy were developed in the savage American wilderness. This theme was echoed repeatedly in his most influential essays, particularly in "The Significance of the Frontier in American History" and in his thoughtful and persuasive piece, "The Development of American Society."

Allen's personal lecture notes permit a further insight into Turner's development; in them one finds the precise sources of Allen's theme of social Darwinism. Attempting to answer the formidable question, "What is civilization?" Allen assured his students that they should read three of his most trusted sources, Henry Thomas Buckle, Lewis Henry Morgan, and Herbert Spencer. To understand the growth of civilization, Buckle urged his readers to think in terms of "society and progress, the degree in which society has come in possession of its several interests": religion, science, literature, art, wealth, liberty, order, and government. From Morgan's *Ancient Society* and other works, Allen found anthropological evidence that under the natural law of progress, man gradually emerged through stages of development to attain the threshold of civilization. And from Spencer, Allen set forth the borrowed idea that the social organism, though differing from the animal organism, was subject to similar "laws" in the struggle for existence, an inevitable part of social evolution.[23] Allen's lectures followed the theory of social Darwinism to the disturbing extent that any topic his students might choose to investigate required analysis according to the predetermined format of Darwinist "law." Thus within this framework, Turner chose his topics, including the subject of his M.A. thesis and later his doctoral dissertation.

Turner's notebooks give the impression that most of his reading centered on evolutionary themes. Much of this reading was part of his attempt to master the available data on the topic in historical and literary works. Emerson's evolutionism is pervasive in his notes, supplemented by poets such as Shelley, whose passionate statements against cruelty and oppression moved Turner to express a vision of "the ultimate renovation of man & the world" and a "beginning of modern life." Among the ancient writers, he found Lucretius' *De rerum natura,* the fifth book of which sets forth an incipient theme of evolutionism stressing the significance of sociological growth as a result of environmental experiences. Even Benjamin Franklin contributed to Turner's education with a powerful insight into the frontiersman's attitudes in early American history: "The boundless woods . . . are sure to afford freedom and subsistence to any man who can bait a hook or pull a trigger."[24]

Turner slowly culled much of the data from a wide range of sources for inclusion in his college orations. At the same time, the theoretical foundations of certain orations became the guidelines for further reading and historical investigation. Turner explained in one of his letters to Carl Becker how Allen's assignment of a topic (in this case a "thesis") led to his first foray into the fur-trade records at the State Historical Society, then under the direction of Lyman C. Draper, one of the foremost authorities on midwestern frontier history at that time.

> Allen assigned me, in one of his classes, a thesis on the subject "Common lands in Wisconsin.". . . I soon saw that it wasn't a subject which would get me far, and while I was looking over the material, Dr. Draper happened in the library . . . and looking over my shoulder said that I might be interested in some old French fur traders' letters from those villages. Of course I was glad to see them, and he let me loose on a box of papers, waterstained, tied in deer skin thongs, written in execrable French which, however, did me no harm, for I was guiltless of any knowledge whatever of French. . . . I found I could, with a dictionery, get on. . . . So I learned Kanuk French, and fur trade history. . . . Thus while a junior, I did the thesis, which in substance, I later turned in for a doctoral dissertation. It was my own idea—by accident.[25]

Allen's assignment resulted in Turner's research publication demonstrating that the town of Portage evolved from an Indian trader's campsite in 1793 into a community with an ethnic blend of

European and Yankee settlers. In "The History of the 'Grignon Tract' on the Portage of the Fox and Wisconsin Rivers," published in the Portage *State Register* for June 23, 1883, Turner exhibited skill in using documentary sources such as the *Annals of Congress* and manuscript deeds. Here also could be seen the social evolution of an individual town that in a period of two generations had been occupied by Indians, French traders, and then the American pioneers.

The Grignon tract paper was not the same essay as Turner's thesis on the Indian trading post later composed for his graduate degrees. But both pieces dealt with early Wisconsin fur trading, and it was logical that Turner might confuse his first two research projects with somewhat similar subject matter. Further, both essays were organized to set forth factual data around a theory of Aryan progress. Although the details and points of emphasis differed, the lesson was the same. Turner relied upon a familiar cycle of interpretation, the progress of the Aryan race in occupying a savage continent. Whether examining the growth of a town around a key land tract or the penetration of Indian trading posts in the hinterlands of Wisconsin, he told the same story. Both were part of what Turner later called "the frontier process," and the "institution" of the trading post was central to an understanding of his 1888 master's thesis, *The Character and Influence of the Fur Trade in Wisconsin*. It is no accident that the Darwinist theme could satisfy his mentor for both an M.A. and a doctoral dissertation. Allen was a close friend of Herbert Baxter Adams and often recommended Adams's writings on the evolution of institutions in New England towns to his classes. Even Turner's piece on the Grignon tract appears to have been stimulated by Allen's correspondence with Adams about the need for studies of midwestern towns and the evolution of parallel institutions.

When Turner arrived in Baltimore in 1888 to spend a hectic year working on his doctorate at Johns Hopkins, he was readily disposed to themes of Anglo-Saxonism. His correspondence indicates he was immersed in the German "scientific methodology." Allen's shadow still followed him, for both Allen and Adams, his more recent mentor, were the disciples of Leopold Von Ranke. At that time Turner claims that he rebelled against Adams's declaration to the advanced-seminar students that the group, "having dealt with American local institutions, had exhausted the opportunities for new contributions in the field of U.S. history and would turn to European history for its next work."[26] But it is clear from Turner's correspondence with Adams that the two men still agreed on Darwinist concepts. Indeed, Adams developed an affection for his new protégé from Wisconsin. To some extent, Turner exaggerated Adams's negative influence on his intellectual development when he remarked that Adams's declaration became "a challenge to me to work out my own ideas."[27] Adams welcomed Turner's fur-trade dissertation and was pleased by Turner's idea that the trading post was a potent enough "institution" to be traced to Phoenician times.

Adams seems to have confirmed for Turner the Darwinist evolutionary theme that made Turner a successor to Adams as historical spokesman for the Protestant, Anglo-Saxon culture then shaping the American nation into its early maturity. He had accepted and applied Allen's and Adams's faith in progressive development toward a "higher" culture. Turner was also exposed to Adams's germ theory, which traced the development of political institutions from their medieval and Teutonic origins. Turner used this idea in his doctoral dissertation and never completely abandoned it in his later writings that stressed the significance of European cultural heritage and an evolutionary environmentalist theory of American social development.

Adams taught and wrote about a unique application of the germ theory, "the continuity of human history." He greatly admired Edward A. Freeman, the English constitutional historian who argued that "the continuity of history was a life principle of . . . philosophy." When the distinguished Freeman visited Johns Hopkins in 1883, Adams was proud to report that the English scholar "found this principle bearing fruit in the Johns Hopkins University." Indeed, "with Bacon's folio edition of the laws of Maryland before him, [Freeman] pointed out to Maryland young men . . . the continuity of Old English institutions in their native state." Freeman also had found to his pleasure that the law of continuity was even "germinating" in the public schools of Baltimore.[28]

The continuity principle seems to have had sufficient Darwinian

Turner's littered desk at Johns Hopkins University, ca. 1889. Among the wall portraits, William F. Allen's photograph is the centerpiece. (Courtesy, Henry E. Huntington Library and Art Gallery)

connotations for Adams to have considered it a virtual "law" of history. The phrase "the law of continuity" appears in Turner's notes even when he studied in Wisconsin, so widespread was the general acceptance of this principle. Adams took on a moralistic tone in expounding this law when he wrote that Puritan institutions carried over from "the mother country" were "historical monuments deserving not only watchful guardianship, but scientific attention." Whether he wrote about the Germanic origin of New England towns or about Norman constables and Saxon tithing men in New England, he noted that "these institutions for the strict and wholesome governments of neighborhoods were transmitted to us by another society."[29] Adams would countenance no qualifications about the matter; the reproduction of such institutions was like the growth of plants, "the process was so quiet, so unobtrusive . . . so gradual, so like the vegetable in springtime—so *natural*, that it seems to have escaped the notice of many historians."[30] This Darwinian process of reasoning to support the law of continuity or the germ theory is disturbing because of the pseudoscientific manner in which it presents Germanic institutions as sacrosanct in bringing a "wholesome government."

The extent to which this Darwinist approach influenced some of Adams's students is illustrated in the 1884 book by Charles Howard Shinn, *Mining Camps: A Study of American Frontier Government*, which is filled with comparisons of "folk-moots" in Old England to meetings in the mining camps of the Sierra Nevada.[31] Shinn was typical of those students indoctrinated with the Freeman-Adams continuity law. And James Phelan, the historian and politician who had studied history when Adams had, asserted in the middle of his narrative history of Tennessee that the "new school of historical investigation [Herbert Adams and the essayists writing articles about New England townships] already formulated as a general law the absolute continuity of political institutions. There are changes and modifications, readaptations and revivals, but rarely new inventions."[32]

Turner's rebellion against Adams's germ theory gradually turned him from the determinist position of Adams and Freeman toward a new determinist concept emphasizing the frontier environment as key in the evolution of American society. The shift is visible in

Turner's early publications. He became more militant against the notion of Teutonic origins while still taking some care not to offend his mentor by outright contradictions. Turner's dissertation had presented the trading post as an institution evolving continuously from ancient times through Teutonic society and finally into the present. The later version for publication shows heavy revisions stressing how migrations of peoples filtered through the trading posts. This institution was especially significant because of its "elevating influence" bringing "the disintegrating and transforming influence of a higher civilization." Through trade, Turner concluded, "a continuously higher life flowed into the old channels, knitting the United States together into a complex organism."[33]

In the essay of 1891, "The Significance of History," Turner, still under the watchful eye of Adams, echoed Adams's germ theory and law of continuity: "Says Dr. H. B. Adams, American local history should be studied as a contribution to national history. This country will yet be viewed and reviewed as an organism of historical growth, developing from minute germs, from the very protoplasm of state-life." Then in his own terms Turner asserted, "History has a unity and a continuity; the present needs the past to explain it; and local history must be read as a part of world history."[34]

For Adams, Turner's maturation as an exuberant disciple gave tremendous satisfaction, as their correspondence affirms. Turner's provocative 1892 essay, "Problems in American History," so impressed Adams that he arranged for his protégé's presentation of another "such paper" at the 1893 American Historical Association.[35] The 1892 essay stressed the study of "our political institutions" and the various "processes" sectionalizing America. Turner summarized by saying that "in this progress from savage conditions [are] topics for the evolutionists." The "colonization of the Great West," the "ever retreating frontier of free land," were processes that should be linked in continuity. "American history needs a connected and unified account of the progress of civilization across the continent. . . . Let the student survey this organism, the American commonwealth."[36]

Turner at this point was still conforming to the Darwinist interpretation that dictated how to analyze any historical data on Anglo-

American history. His syllabi, carefully organized for extension lectures, listed topics: "The Colonization of North America from Earliest Times to 1763" and "A Half Century of American Politics, 1789–1840." After 1891, another evolutionary theme appeared, the colonization of the West, as his "Problems" essay illustrated.[37] The "mother colonies" settled the West in much the same fashion that the "mother country planted" her settlements on the North American coast. Turner states in his 1893 syllabus that his students will learn how America was shaped by "European contributions, through the influence of the native races and of physiography; and . . . will trace, in this era of planting, many of the germs of the United States today."[38]

But by 1893 when Turner composed his frontier essay, he had moved away from Adams's position that American institutions were reproduced without change like growing plants. Instead Turner stressed that the coastal colonies were contributing to a new culture for the interior wilderness. Yet if Turner was turning away from a rigid application of the law of continuity, he still accepted an organismic view of history. In his critique of Hermann Von Holst's writings, Turner made one of his strongest defenses of this perspective:

> In my opinion, more harm may be done by an improper perspective or by omissions, than by defects in regard to accuracy of statement. If I aim to describe an elephant and give only an account of his feet, alleging at the same time that this constitutes the elephant, the microscopic accuracy and keenness of criticism of these organs will not atone for the failure to speak of the rest of the animal. Nor will it do to speak even of the feet or trunk as seen simply in a state of rest. Unless I describe them in *action* and in *growth,* I have failed to describe the animal.[39]

The contributing factors in Turner's maturation as a historian include two concepts. First, society is an organism with action and movement, and second, America's Anglo-Saxon and Aryan institutions must be traced in their evolution. The frontier was the arena that gave the American frontiersmen their peculiar character, which grew from their struggle to adapt themselves to the refractory natural conditions, the attack of Indians, and the ongoing fight for survival. Add to this theme Turner's training as an orator, and the power of "The Significance of the Frontier in American History" becomes understandable.

In that essay, Turner broke with Adams for the first time in print by rejecting the influence of Germanic institutions upon American history. Although he admitted that "our early history is the study of European germs developing in an American environment," he asserted that "too exclusive attention has been paid by institutions . . . to Germanic origins, too little to American factors."[40] Turner then moved to his second premise: "The frontier is the line of most rapid and effective Americanization." Hereafter he developed the melting-pot theme: "The wilderness masters the colonist" but in time the colonist "transforms the wilderness." "The frontier promoted the formation of a composite nationality for the American people. . . . In the crucible of the frontier the immigrants were Americanized, liberated and fused into a mixed race. . . . The process has gone on from early days to our own."[41] Turner, having established the moving frontier as a determinist factor in molding American nationality, developed the survival doctrine in a "contest for power" developed between rival religious sects. This survival experience brought forth a tough new breed of people with "coarseness and strength combined with acuteness and acquisitiveness" and with "that masterful grasp of material things," people who had "that buoyancy and exuberance which comes from freedom." That toughness resulted from battling "the stubborn environment" that ultimately provided "opportunity, a gate of escape from the bondage of past."[42]

At this point Turner was evidently blending concepts of growth and heredity into his theory of social evolution and progress. The frontier, the progressive agent of American history, was dynamic in its transformation of the American nationality because "an intellectual stream from New England sources fertilized the West."[43] Although "Pennsylvania had been the seed-plot of frontier emigration," Turner stressed the profound New England Yankee role in forming the western type. In this 1893 essay, Turner made his most convincing argument that the type more than the individual is the proper concern of Americanists. Turner had written an early draft of an essay on the hunter type about 1890, based largely upon his examination of Theodore Roosevelt's first volume, *The Winning of the West,* and had eulogized backwoods virtues ("They loved to hear the crack of their long rifles, and the blows of the ax in the forest"), but the romanticism, even sentimentalism, of this piece contrasts with Turner's bold rhetorical assessment of the new breed that, according to his 1893 essay led the nation to its conquest of the wilderness.[44]

More than portraying a type of aggressive frontiersman, Turner presented a "prototype": the Yankee colonial confronting the frontier. At the "edge of the Indian country," he wrote, the early Massachusetts frontier was a prototype of what was to come. Such a frontier "calls out militant qualities and reveals the imprint of the wilderness upon psychology and morals as well as upon institutions and people."[45] Such men as Thomas Jefferson, Andrew Jackson, and Abraham Lincoln were political leaders of successive advances into the frontier. They were not so much individuals as national figures whose folk virtues were distillations of the American frontier character. And finally, under political leadership from the West, the frontier was at last conquered by progressive traders, miners, cattle raisers, and farmers, giving Americans a free and prosperous country.

Turner portrayed the mixing of nationalities on the frontier as an agent of progress and as a process of adaptation for the social organism. On this point Turner parted company with Adams and the law of continuity because Turner was asserting that ancestral institutions could, in fact, *had* to transform themselves. The woodland-frontier melting pot, to Turner, was "compelled to adapt," a phrase he used earlier in his "Problems" essay of 1892.

As William Coleman pointed out, Turner's Darwinism had become a "Lemarckism with Spencerian fittings."[46] L. B. LeMarck, in his *Philosophie zoologique,* had stated that the environment triggers events that cause psychic changes, such as need or desire, an idea that was later challenged by environmental Darwinists.[47] Turner, however, did not know the technical aspects of this debate, and simply drawing his ideas from such writers as the historical evolutionists Walter Bagehot (*Physics and Politics*), Richard Ely, and his own former teachers, he proposed an environmentalist determinism in which the environment brings about practically inevitable transformations.[48]

In his later writings Turner vacillated between determinism and the more moderate "possibilism."[49] Although Turner's work presents genuine contradictions, he consistently promulgated a historical doctrine of progress based upon Darwinian environmentalism, with the frontier's melting pot operating as the determining agent of American history. When the frontier was gone, the nation was still in the process of "changing as it adjusts to its environment."[50]

Turner was not rigorous at the theoretical level; although somewhat aware of the current debates over evolution, he was not a careful student of the sciences and he misunderstood the doctrine of "multiple working hypotheses," a subject about which he often wrote and lectured.[51] The important point is that Turner proposed a lopsided Darwinist concept of progress that had the effect of distorting the conceptual framework used by American historians for half a century.

"How does civilization march?"[52] This question, raised by Turner's most perceptive student, was answered by Turner's pointing to the miraculous frontier, which, through its evolutionary process of "perennial rebirth," produced the new society, a white race of mixed Europeans. Our early history was "the study of European germs developing in an American environment,"[53] a process repeated on each frontier. Indeed, Turner had seen the frontier type, the frontier ideals, in Portage as he grew up. And in Madison, where he espoused the vigorous Unitarianism of his teachers and friends, he set forth ideals of progress in his college orations that created the impression that all civilization was growing toward nineteenth-century liberalism.

In giving us a saga of noble Yankee progress across a continent, Turner virtually ignored Indians, blacks, Mexican-Americans, and Asians. Although it did not directly appear in his published writings, his private correspondence reveals that as a writer he thought in terms of concepts that were markedly racist, even by standards of his own time.[54] His personal letters contain disturbing anti-Semitic statements and a certain rural boorishness, especially apparent in the letters he wrote as a young man.[55] A number of newspaper articles he wrote on immigration show his hostility toward the immigrants who were flooding America during his middle years.[56] Turner does not take a racist stand against non-whites and southern Europeans in his better-known essays, but his lesser-known writings and personal correspondence show that the tone and emphasis of his published work were conditioned by an Anglo-Saxon bias.

In eulogizing the frontier type, Turner, like other prophets of progress, underestimated or ignored the destructive power of the pioneers and the irrationality that fueled their actions against Indian tribes. As Richard White has pointed out, Turner tended to confuse nature and culture when he wrote about frontiersmen accepting canoes and moccasins from the wilderness frontier. Deer and birch trees were from nature's forest; moccasins and canoes were created by culture and not by wilderness.[57]

This misconception of Turner's, confusing culture with nature, was undoubtedly not intentional, but it permitted Turner to give support to the violence and prolonged wars against native people in his writings about frontier advance in the seventeenth, eighteenth, and nineteenth centuries. For many who have not studied American Indian history, the incredibly brutal wars to rid the frontier of Native American people are hard to accept. And along with them, the nineteenth-century frontier expansion was accompanied by an astonishing "war against the animals" that makes one think that we are fortunate to have any wildlife left. In another book (in progress), I document the astonishing slaughter of millions upon millions of birds and mammals (by private and commercial hunters, by furmen, frontiersmen, midwestern farmers, Mormons, California miners) that were, along with the Indians, literally blasted out of the landscape.

Thus Turner, in detailing a story of progress, gave himself no vantage point from which to evaluate the polarization of classes in the cities, the violence of mobs against minorities, the bitter slave rebellions, the filibusterings, the lynchings, the wars between capital and labor, or the widespread lawlessness and fraud. His view of war, until his reexaminations during his last years, glorified expansion.

Indeed Turner was continuing in much the same vein as his

nineteenth-century predecessors, but he applied his approach to the American frontier. To a conservative reading public, he was accounting for the growth of a vigorous, liberty-loving democracy that had reached what Richard Hofstadter called "an orgy of material development marked by the emergence of a vulgar plutocracy and crass machine politics."[58] This Turner ignored. Committed to progress, he could not come to grips with the consequent land exploitation, the stultifying evil of slavery, political corruption, or the pre–Civil War breakdown of political institutions that had endured since the Revolutionary era. Confronted with the conflict between national ideals of freedom, democracy, and unity versus the reality of destructive economic rivalries, the decimation of Native Indian populations, the ravaging of land, and unnecessary war, Turner ignored the challenge and let the positive side of the story prevail. Turner's frontier theory, especially in his earlier writings, is as significant for what it leaves out as for what it says.

The theory of progress has become an unacceptable element for other historical scholars who have tried to incorporate it into their writings. Although the theory has rational foundations, "It is untenable as a scientific explanation of historical movement."[59] The moral tone of his writings is particularly disturbing because he sets forth an ethical hypothesis to give sanctity to what he writes. The continuing popularity of the theory of progress that he wrote about is attested to by the fact that it became firmly established at all levels of public policy. It also was uncritically presented in influential textbooks and monographs. Fortunately, within recent decades, questions have been raised about public policy supporting unlimited growth and land exploitation by the Sierra Club and other conservationist groups. At the same time, minority groups have challenged, often with success, WASP presumptions. Indeed the belief that historical progress is somehow rooted in natural law has been obliterated by the example of Nazi Germany and Hitler's Final Solution.[60] The relationship between the doctrine of Nordic superiority and that of Euro-American accomplishments on the frontier becomes apparent when we consider such events as the massacre of Indians at Wounded Knee or the internment of Japanese-Americans during World War II. Yet we must not resort to censuring Turner on the issue of Anglo-Saxonism by singling him out as a lone figure of his time. His influence was important, but it should be measured against the impact of many other writers.[61] As Reginald Horsman argues in *Race and Manifest Destiny, Origins of American Racial Anglo-Saxonism*, the concept of a westward-moving empire in the Mississippi Valley occupied by Anglos was widespread. Here in the great valley, "perhaps human intelligence [was] to reach its loftiest manifestations" with "Anglo-Normans" the "bearers of religion, science, and liberty." There were writers who put forth this romantic, racial, nationalistic theme fifty years before Turner presented his ideas in the essay of 1893.[62]

Still, Turner's impact in these matters should not be understated. He was particularly effective because he couched his ideas in the format of a ruling theory that appeared to encompass other interpretations of history. How did he do it? The answer lies in an examination of Turner's shifting but outwardly credible methodology, the subject we shall examine next.

CLEARING THE TRAILS IN FRONTIER HISTORY

The race question. It is plain that if the English constitution were put in French hands it would operate differently. Race affects politics.

—Turner's critique of Von Holst's *History* (1889–1890)

The truth is that I found it necessary to hammer pretty hard and pretty steadily on the frontier idea to "get it in." . . . I hope to add a companion piece (the Section) . . . to attempt a coordination of these old and new viewpoints.

—Turner to Arthur M. Schlesinger (1922)

I, as you perhaps recall, valued [Thomas] Chamberlin's paper on the Multiple Hypotheses, which I have aimed to apply to history as he to geology.

—Turner to Merle Curti (1928)

CHAPTER FOUR

DEVELOPING A RULING THEORY

One of the most intriguing aspects of Turner's methodology is a leitmotiv that seemed always to be present in his inner mind. Anyone who has had the pleasure of reliving the ups and downs of Turner's literary life by reading through his papers at the Huntington Library is impressed by Turner's open-mindedness and by his assertion to his students or anyone else who would listen that he looked at history through the prism of "multiple hypotheses." A special refraction of this viewpoint is continually seen in Turner's writings: his "scientific" thrust. How did he prove his impartial, scientific approach to historical research? By citing the example of a scientist whom he had known at the University of Wisconsin, the geologist and one-time president of the university, Thomas C. Chamberlin.

Especially significant is the result that Turner's leading students such as Homer C. Hockett and Merle Curti came to echo the words of their master's claim that he relied upon the concept of multiple hypotheses.[1] If Turner was trying to dupe his followers, he was successful, so successful that even Ray Allen Billington, his major biographer, believed him. Detailed analysis demonstrates that there is an element of pretense on Turner's part, either consciously or unconsciously. Indeed we shall never know if Turner used Chamberlin's ideas without understanding them or if he appropriated them to justify his own ruling theory of the frontier and section in American history. Let us look at this curious, even mysterious part of Turner's writings, for here we may find the very soul of his work.

The founding fathers of the State Historical Society of Wisconsin; (left) Lyman C. Draper, secretary, 1854–1886; (right) Reuben Gold Thwaites, secretary and president, 1887–1912. (From the author's collection)

The question of the extent to which Turner actually adopted Chamberlin's methods is important, not only because Turner believed Chamberlin's methodology to be as consequential for the serious study of history as it was for geology but also because Turner's own approach to historical research has exercised so great an influence on modern historical writing.[2] Since Turner hoped that the procedures that he himself developed would help to make historical scholarship a more impersonal field of endeavor and perhaps bring historical scholarship closer to (even within the magic circle of) the sciences, it is relevant to examine the extent to which his own work satisfied the demands he made upon scientific scholarship and the extent to which it satisfied the criteria set forth by Chamberlin.

In 1882, the year that Chamberlin left Beloit College to become

Turner in his office at the State Historical Society of Wisconsin in the state capitol. (Photograph attributed to Reuben Gold Thwaites, ca. 1892; reproduced courtesy, State Historical Society of Wisconsin)

president of the University of Wisconsin, Turner was an undergraduate there. After earning his doctorate at Johns Hopkins, Turner returned to Wisconsin as an assistant professor in 1890.[3] One year earlier, Chamberlin had read a paper at a meeting of the Society of Western Naturalists entitled "The Method of Multiple Working Hypotheses," to which was appended the provocative subtitle, "With this method the dangers of parental affection for a favorite theory can be circumvented." Revising the piece for the *Journal of Geology* some years later,[4] Chamberlin wrote that it had "been freely altered and abbreviated so as to limit it to aspects related to geological study."[5] This latter version has been reprinted a number of times, and in its approach to geological research, it is still valid today. Marland P. Billings of Harvard in his volume, *Structural Geology,* cites Chamberlin's essay and notes that above all, the field geologist must use the method of "working multiple hypotheses" to deduce the geological structure. While the field work progresses, he should conceive as many interpretations as are consistent with the known facts. He should then formulate tests for those interpretations, checking them by data already obtained, or checking them in the future by new data. Many of these interpretations will be abandoned, new ones will develop, and those finally accepted may bear little resemblance to hypotheses considered early in field work.[6]

In 1888, Turner and Chamberlin had collaborated in writing an essay on Wisconsin for the ninth edition of *The Encyclopedia Britannica*.[7] Five years later, at the meeting of the American Historical Association held at the World's Fair in Chicago, Turner presented his epoch-making paper, "The Significance of the Frontier in American History"; in 1910 he left Wisconsin for Harvard, where he continued to tell his students about his indebtedness to Chamberlin. The geologist, in the meantime, had left Wisconsin for the University of Chicago to assume the chair of its newly established department of geology.[8]

A comparison of the original and the revised versions of Chamberlin's paper on multiple working hypotheses reveals that he remained consistent about methodology. The practicing theorist, Chamberlin insists, was constantly exposed to the temptation to formulate premature conclusions on the basis of facts revealed by investigations. "The mind," he notes, "lingers with pleasure upon the facts that fall happily into the embrace of the theory, and feels a natural coldness toward those that assume a refractory attitude."[9] But even when the investigator attempts to maintain an impartial attitude, the problem of "unwarranted vacillation" exists—the danger that, in considering the various working hypotheses, the investigator, unwilling to take a stand, will sway from one line of policy to another.[10] This tendency to vacillation and procrastination springs from the difficulties inherent in the search for knowledge—"the imperfections of evidence," the vast unknown in science and in life itself that make the investigator wary of judging too quickly.[11]

Despite the limitations implicit in the method of multiple working hypotheses, Chamberlin held that its use was obligatory in the scientific world; and, indeed, it might even be applied to "the varied affairs of life," where almost unlimited opportunities for its application—especially in teaching—might be found.[12] According to Chamberlin, scholars needed to learn to recognize the proper time for decision making—to withhold judgment until sufficient evidence has accumulated to justify conclusions.[13]

Chamberlin always referred to "multiple working hypotheses." By stressing the word "working"—which Turner seems never to have used in this context—Chamberlin placed particular emphasis on the tentative nature of the hypothesis; the scientist, he insists, must maintain complete detachment from pet theories that may all too easily become ruling theories. "The working hypothesis," Chamberlin argues, "differs from the ruling theory in that it is used as a means of determining facts rather than as a proposition to be established."[14] The function of the working hypothesis was to suggest lines of inquiry: "The facts are sought for the purpose of ultimate induction and demonstration." Under the ruling theory, by contrast, the facts are sought in order to support the theory.[15]

Chamberlin repeatedly warns against the tendency of the working hypothesis to slip quietly into the role of the ruling theory. A hypothesis by its very nature may quickly become a "beloved intellectual child" and finally "a controlling idea." The ideal investigator, Chamberlin notes, should be "the parent of a family of hypotheses"; among these offspring are "intellectual children (by birth or adoption)." Some may die before reaching healthy maturity, but all must survive "the results of final investigation." "The effort," Chamberlin concludes, "is to bring up into view every rational explanation of new phenomena, and to develop every tenable hypothesis respecting their cause and history."[16] Chamberlin's method, as his disciple Bailey Willis observes, "calls upon the student to lay aside a natural preference for the theory which seems plausible and to consider as sincerely that which holds out small promise of development."[17] The investigator must avoid being entrapped by the ruling theory at all costs.

It was not simply Chamberlin's scientific approach that fascinated Turner; methodology alone did not make him a lifelong disciple of the geologist. In fact, he was very much interested in the influence of geological and geographical factors on the history of a country, and Chamberlin's work provided him with a rich source of relevant geological information. Therefore it is not surprising that Turner's offprint of Willis's article dealing with Chamberlin's theories concerning the effect of atmospheric carbonic acid on glaciers is heavily underlined and replete with marginalia.[18] This interest in a field not normally associated with American history repeatedly emerges in Turner's work. For example, in a lecture delivered at the California Institute of Technology, "The Sectionalism of Politics," Turner pointed out that

in the election of 1856, the counties that voted in favor of Fremont almost exactly coincided with this second glacial ice sheet . . . the land of the basin of the Great Lakes and the prairies rejected by the Southern settler and occupied by Greater New England.[19]

Turner's geological interests were also evident in the works of his students—such as Orin G. Libby's doctoral dissertation, "The Geographical Distribution of the Vote of the Thirteen States on the Federal Constitution 1787–8,"[20] which proved to be a milestone in the geological-geographical approach to American history and which developed out of Turner's lectures on the constitutional and political history of the United States.[21] The technique of map analysis used in this study later proved helpful to Turner in his sectional studies.

Many of the concepts historians have associated with Turner—the fall line, the Appalachian barrier, the geological-geographical syndrome—were based upon the study of the topographical maps published by the United States Geological Survey. Turner found these maps especially helpful; he used them for charting election results and population movements and for studying the correlations between types of soil and areas of white illiteracy.[22] He even had an annotated set of topographical maps placed in the library at Harvard, and students in his History 17 course were required to consult them.[23] The lectures of the geologist Charles Richard Van Hise, his Madison colleague and friend, provided Turner with another useful source of geological inspiration. He took copious notes on subjects that interested him; one of these was Van Hise's lecture on the Gulf Plains, which described not only the rocks and soil of the area, the deposits made by the Mississippi and its tributaries, and the crops and natural resources of the region but also its history.[24] Van Hise touched on the theme of America's vanishing mineral and lumber resources—a topic that became almost an obsession with Turner after his retirement, when he was gathering material for a book on problems resulting from overpopulation, war, and the depletion of food supplies.[25]

Of course geology was only one of the disciplines that could contribute to the study of history, according to Turner. When Turner was told that he behaved like a sociologist, he answered that he did not care what he was called,

> so long as I was left to try to ascertain the truth, and the relation of the facts to cause and effect in my own way. . . . I have been dubbed by the Sociologists an economic determinist (which I am not!), by the geographers as a geographer. . . . And I as you perhaps recall, valued Chamberlin's paper on the Multiple Hypothesis, which I have aimed to apply to history as he to geology.
>
> Perhaps at the bottom the belief that all the social sciences were one, and related to physical science has influenced my work.[26]

The difficulties facing the would-be scientific scholar in his attempts to achieve "historical fairmindedness" were readily apparent to Turner: "unconscious interpretation, selection, emphasis, . . . conscious, but unsuccessful interpretation, selection and emphasis. 'We're all poor critters!'" he once wrote, "especially F.J.T."[27] The modesty of this statement was perfectly sincere, but it was meant to emphasize the rather obvious fact that truth is hard to apprehend. In fact, Turner firmly believed that he was applying Chamberlin's scientific approach to history. "One must adopt," he noted, "the geologist's use of the multiple hypothesis to explain complex areas; and must not attempt to give a decisive reason for the political complexion of a given county at a given election."[28] That Turner emphasized the scientific nature of his work was understandable, for he was indeed more objective, more farsighted, more open-minded than those scholars who had dealt with American history before him.

Yet at the same time Turner cannot be accepted at face value when he insists that he is applying Chamberlin's scientific methodology to history. There is the distinct impression that Turner confused Chamberlin's multiple working hypotheses with multiple causation. Chamberlin felt that one value of the theory of multiple working hypotheses was that it could lead to the discovery that some phenomena are the result of a number of causes (but this did not have to be so), whereas the ruling theory and even a single working hypothesis could lead to a monocausational interpretation. When examining Turner's writings, one notes that though Turner called upon the social sciences in his interpretations of American history and made use of the comparative method in arriving at conclusions, his work as a whole was nevertheless shaped by the two theories for which he is usually remembered—the frontier theory and the theory of sections. Turner used these theories to construct a framework within which the seemingly pointless minutiae of history take on form and become usable ingredients for the historian's analytical alchemy. American history, as Turner viewed it, consisted of a long process of change, an extended adjustment to conditions on the American continent. The various societies created across the country as the settlers moved west, lured by the promise of plentiful free land, passed through the several stages separating a backward society from a highly developed one; and as they did so, they developed sectional interests and sectional characteristics. But the pattern that helped Turner pick his way through the past vitiated his claim that he was following the theory of multiple working hypotheses. Original as it was, Turner's work reveals rather too clearly his affinities with those unscientific investigators whom Chamberlin scorned—those scholars who practiced the "ruling theory" approach.

But in all fairness to Turner, to judge the value of his work by the degree to which he followed, or failed to follow, Chamberlin's method is to bind him unnecessarily in a straitjacket—albeit in one of his own making. Indeed Turner can be admired for a number of different reasons—for his ingenuity and freshness of mind, for his willingness to erase the boundaries separating disciplines, for the wealth of ideas scattered through his writings (ideas taken up and expanded by more recent historians), for the clarity with which he makes us aware of the complexity of his subject matter, for his unerring instinct for the important, for his skill in emphasizing the larger trends—not, however, for the scientific character and completeness of his work. On the contrary, as Avery Craven points out in his essay "Frederick Jackson Turner, Historian,"[29] Turner must be excused certain unscientific traits of mind since these are associated with the intellectual characteristics we value in him:

> There was something of the poet and much of the philosopher about Turner. He had the ability to see deep into the meaning of things and the power to catch the universals. This did not weaken his capacity for scientific research nor lessen his interest in details, but it did cause him to emphasize trends and flavors, to attempt to deal with intangibles, to sweep over minor things in the effort to get at the larger truths. This method has its dangers if history is to be viewed as a pure science and not as a mixture of science and art.[30]

Moreover, Turner himself recognized the special, at best semi-scientific, nature of history, which requires that each new generation write *"the history of the past anew with reference to the conditions uppermost in its own time."*[31] An "ultimate" history—a really scientific history—he therefore knew could never be written. Even if the nature of history had not precluded a strictly scientific approach, Turner's enthusiasm for his subject matter and his patriotic pride in his country would have made him the wrong man to attempt the job. "This progress of society from pioneer life on a seashore, to the colonization of successive sections, and to the final occupation of a continental empire," he wrote, "is one of the most wonderful chapters in human history."[32] Since Turner's feelings lent a somewhat rosy hue to his discussion of the frontier and its inhabitants, it is hardly surprising that his frontier-sectional theory became widely known and widely accepted. Here was the new national history, the theoretical basis for understanding the American character; the special qualities of American democracy could be explained by the frontier experience and by the evolution of sections.

Early in his career Turner concluded that if he were to use the vast resources of those disciplines outside history, he would have to identify guidelines to cope with the jungle of data confronting him.[33] While he was in the process of establishing a kind of order, he developed his theories of the frontier and the section, yet at the same time he quickly recognized the importance of other theories and hypotheses. An enthusiastic reader of Darwin and Spencer,[34] Turner placed considerable emphasis on the doctrine of evolution in the drafts of his student orations[35] as well as in his later essays, especially when he stressed that American society went through "successive stages of social evolution."[36] He thought of society as an "organism," and history was actually the self-consciousness of that organism.[37] Turner at times also emphasized the economic theory of history; in his teaching he gave so much importance to economics that he felt obliged to tell one class that "this is not a course on that subject, economic history."[38] Still another idea that Turner set forth in writing and in teaching is now called the culture-concept, or theory, the idea that old and new emigrants brought their particular ethnic heritage into developing areas. In his last book, *The United States, 1830–1850: The Nation and Its Sections*, Turner developed this concept in discussing the growth of regional cultures.[39] These ideas and others, then, were incorporated into Turner's theory of sections, which is in a sense a means of objecting to theories, for it posits the complexity of historical causation. It was through his theory of sections that Turner explored the interrelationships of social, geographical, political, evolutionary, cultural, and economic forces in the development of American society.

Thus it was natural for Turner to encourage his students and associates to investigate a wide range of historical interpretations although he did not develop them as his own hypotheses. Turner's letters abound with friendly suggestions for investigation as, for instance, in his encouragement of Arthur M. Schlesinger in 1922 to give further attention to "the phenomena of great city development and the results and problems in many fields thereto."[40]

Turner certainly was not responsible for a narrow view of American history, as a few of his followers have insisted.[41] Yet it is true that he devoted his life to gathering the material with which to support his own interpretation of the American past. His belief that he had applied Chamberlin's method to historical research was quite sincere; but in fact he confused the interdisciplinary, comparative method of investigation with the methodology of multiple working hypotheses. Furthermore, he seems also to have confused the idea of multiple causation in history with both the comparative method and Chamberlin's technique. Nevertheless, the approach that he did pioneer has widened enormously the scope of historical investigation; the Chamberlin approach, which he failed to apply, may well be inapplicable to history. Yet Chamberlin's plea for high standards of objectivity from researchers will be echoed by most modern historians, as indeed it was by Turner himself.

Turner's research notes, file drawers of lectures, and various unfinished manuscripts (covering the entire period of his productive life, from the 1880s to the 1930s) support the conclusion that he was primarily a goal-oriented researcher. In the dozens of file drawers and in the large map collection at the Huntington Library there is no single research project or paper or chapter of a projected book that is completely divorced from the sectional-frontier theme. In one of these file drawers there are some seventy unpublished pieces concerned with some aspect of sectionalism, many of them cannibalized from his published work.[42] Indeed, almost everything Turner wrote after 1893 was related to sectionalism—a concern that developed from his frontier theory. He even applied some of his ideas about sectionalism and political parties to problems of international organization and suggested the need for international political parties as a step toward eliminating war.[43] He also began a study of the origin of the city, which he traced in part to economic and social changes on the frontier and in the section.[44] In his later life he placed increasing emphasis upon comparative and statistical methods of study, but his focus remained unchanged.

Turner's lifetime work was built around the dual theme of frontier and section. Certainly this theoretical base provided him with valuable opportunities to study the interplay of historical forces and to reinterpret various phases of history. Nevertheless, Turner's contribution remains but one of many explanations for our national development, a "ruling theory" that has been justifiably contested by a number of other scholars. Turner apparently never regarded his hypotheses with the scientific detachment of a Chamberlin; he never really considered his central ideas as mere hypotheses to be tested and compared with other theories—and possibly rejected. On the contrary, Turner was a loving father to his theories: To them he devoted his life, and for their sake no scholarly effort in gathering data was too great.[45]

How can we explain Turner's extraordinary attitudes toward his frontier-sectional theory? A key may be found in tragedy. Ray Billington in his biography suggests that one of Turner's responses to the death of two of his three children in 1899, when he was thirty-eight, and to Mrs. Turner's uncontrollable weeping was to write a gloomy poem.[46] The agonizing loss of his son and daughter added to the psychic burden that Turner already carried as a man who was essentially what Richard Hofstadter called a "nonwriting writer."[47] It is therefore understandable that Turner, in his early forties, produced a continuous but thin flow of essays, not the output of major books that had been expected of him. Nevertheless, Turner was extremely protective of his essays and argued for their acceptance. The grandson of preachers, Turner developed into a kind of missionary, seeking converts to his historical gospel.

With great persistence, Turner, in low-key classroom lectures, in public speeches, and in essays, promoted what Cushing Strout has called his "first-born intellectual son."[48] The projection of Turner's theory as a "son" also sheds light on Turner's close friendships with the young men who became his devoted student-sons, trained to carry forth his message. They produced a mass of books and articles that Turner, as Strout argues, "could not procreate."[49] Turner also had women disciples and directed the doctoral work of perhaps as many as eight women. He claimed Louise Phelps Kellogg was one of his most important students in a letter to Charles Van Hise, June 19, 1908.[50] Those critics who challenged these academic sons or daughters of the frontier-sectional theory would feel the bite of Turner's anger in hostile book reviews, as Martin Ridge has demonstrated.[51]

Further insight into Turner's emotional attachment to his frontier-sectional theory and into his eagerness to propagandize the concept in essays and lectures, coloring it with the rainbow of multiple hypotheses, is offered by Allan Beckman.[52] Anyone who examines the record Turner left behind must be impressed with his collection of praiseworthy statements about his own work and his folders of drafts, notes, and fugitive sheets with his flowing signature. He not only penned his name on countless sheets and folders, but he also wrote specific comments carefully explaining how various items were linked to the promotion of the frontier-sectional theory. Turner, as this record demonstrates, felt the need for approval. Successful as he was, he still revealed his sense of inferiority. Strout cites Freud in arguing that the kind of inferiority complex Turner exhibited could be found in individuals who had "literary pretensions."[53]

Beckman applies Freud's theory to Turner who as a writer "wrecked by success" became melancholy after having taken over the post of the master who had initiated him into a "life of learning." Beckman's argument is that Turner became chair of the Wisconsin history department after the death of William F. Allen, his mentor and surrogate father. According to Beckman, Turner harbored an unconscious hostility toward Allen that shaded his life, long after Turner had set forth essays on the frontier-sectional theory. Turner, Beckman contends, unconsciously wished to displace Allen as chairman, a desire that produced a legacy of Oedipal guilt. Beckman's thesis is that this "originology" idea explains how Turner's sense of guilt became an emotional factor in producing writer's block.

Perhaps. But we must be aware that blockage is something that has plagued writers and poets through the centuries. Zachory Leader maintains in his volume *Writer's Block* that writers such as Joseph Conrad and Virginia Woolf together with romantic poets such as Samuel Coleridge wrote and agonized about the problem. Some called it "pressure of a great task deferred," "massive . . . inner resistance," "tension reduction," "regression," or "the pleasure principle." Coleridge, we find, like Turner, had a career littered with half-completed undertakings. There were other writers who were "afraid of an ending," although this kind of fear seems not to have been a source of anxiety for Turner. When Leader argues, however, that blockage can give "insight, and with it the

The first page of Turner's unfinished textbook history of the United States. This and other unfinished projects suggest that Turner did indeed have a "writer's block." (Courtesy, Henry E. Huntington Library and Art Gallery) power to write," he points to a paradox. For the blockage itself can link to a "breakthrough" and the two can merge as a healing experience. In a sense, this is what happened to Turner when Albert Bushnell Hart prodded him in 1906 into finishing *The Rise of the New West*.[54] After completing this book, the frustrated Turner found temporary relief in probing sidelines of research in geography, foreign affairs, and immigration history (northern European peoples) and in his studies on sectionalism. In these happy years of research and teaching after the ordeal leading to the publication of *The Rise of the New West*, he wrote fondly to his former students about his scientific methodology of multiple hypotheses.

This theme of multiple causation or multiple hypotheses was repetitious in the sense that Turner used it to explain again and again his wide-ranging interdisciplinary field work carried out in amassing data for his essays. When he wrote in letters to such disciples as Constance Skinner, Carl Becker, and Merle Curti, among many others, we have the suggestion that Turner wanted to be sure that the personal account of his successful rise in the profession would not be overlooked. Even if some of these long missives were lost, enough would still exist for future biographers. Turner, we can be sure, valued fame.

Other aspects of his personality are also revealed in his letters. In my view, Turner is still an enigma because of the tone of these letters. For instance, when I closely examined his correspondence in preparation for *The Historical World of Frederick Jackson Turner*, I detected a distinct mood of the impersonal in his letters. The tone is almost always warm, kindly, thoughtful, and pleasant, but it is equally so to all his correspondents. Even family letters (except those to his fiancée when he was lost in love as a young man) have the same air of detachment. One gradually concludes that letters were not Turner's best medium of communication; very probably conversation was. Possibly this is why he valued personal contacts with advanced students on a day-to-day basis. Yet when one examines the reports of some of his most loyal students, such as Carl Becker, they say much the same thing, that he was friendly, open, thoughtful, and pleasant. Even when he declined to write a letter of recommendation for a poorly qualified student, Turner in a kindly way would state that he could not endorse the student "at this time." Apparently, the master was as skillful in creating and maintaining a loyal following as he was in promoting his theories. Moreover, he maintained a modest posture and was never overbearing with his brood of admiring students.

The creative person, as Peter Lowenberg has written, may be self-depreciating in confronting the line between illusion and reality, but there is sometimes "an ever-present idea" that hovers over all. His narcissistic ego ideal cannot be satisfied with an ordinary career; he must become "much more—a world shaper."[55] One can suggest, therefore, that Turner, the creative person, saw his frontier-sectionalism as the key weapon in an assault on practically all other interpretations of history.

One may not agree with these psychological insights into Turner as a creative writer, but in my judgment they help us to comprehend how his inner conflicts and frustrations were related to his protective attitude toward the frontier-sectionalism theory. The portrait of him as an irresponsible spendthrift, a gifted academic who was underpaid and overworked, and a proponent of the concept of multiple hypotheses falls short; Turner is a complex subject.

CHAPTER FIVE

EXPLAINING COLONIAL AMERICAN HISTORY

Although three of the leading new western historians—Patricia Limerick, Richard White, and Donald Worster—discount Turner's frontier theory as useful in explaining the history and origins of the American West, the theory was apparently well suited for providing an interconnected, intellectual scaffolding for early American history. William Cronon, a fourth member of the group, would probably accept that premise because he has written favorably on the frontier theory and has relied upon it as an intellectual threshold in his analytic study, *Nature's Metropolis, Chicago and the Great West*.[1]

To trace the origins of the Turnerian view and to observe its general acceptance by historians during the decades following 1893, one must turn to an obscure paper read by the University of Washington colonialist, Max Savelle. At a 1948 meeting of the Mississippi Valley Historical Association, Savelle read a paper, "The Imperial School of American Colonial Historians," which discussed the tendency of scholars to assume either an imperialist or a nationalist point of view. The imperialists, among whom were Herbert L. Osgood, George Lewis Beer, Charles M. Andrews, and Lawrence H. Gipson, tended to assume that since the colonies were integral parts of the British Empire, "their history should be studied as history of parts of the Empire." The nationalists, including George Bancroft, John Fiske, and Edward Channing, took an entirely different view of early American history; they looked to the colonial period for the origins of the United States. Savelle then named a third group of early American historians, the "so-called 'frontier school'" of Frederick Jackson Turner, who maintained that transplanted English ideas and institutions were modified and transformed by an ever-westward-moving frontier society.[2] Approximate as Savelle's classification was, its recognition of the existence of a third approach to colonial history indicated that a Turnerian interpretation of early American history was in fact being acknowledged. Indeed the popularity of Turner's frontier approach to colonial history has persisted in varying degrees until today.

The manner in which Turner influenced the historical profession is difficult to describe with any real degree of exactitude. We do know that his concept of the frontier-sectional theory's wider implications was embodied in his published writings, in his classroom and public lectures, and in the careful organization of the accumulating mass of his research materials that he later bequeathed to the Huntington Library.[3] The advanced students who had the greatest exposure to him in everyday contacts and in correspondence after they left his seminars became his most loyal advocates.[4] Some became leading historians who themselves set forth basic themes of the colonial frontier theory; among them were Louise P. Kellogg, James Alton James, Carl L. Becker, Homer C. Hockett, and Orin Grant Libby.[5] Lesser known students, exemplified by the devoted Arthur H. Buffinton, published several articles on such topics as the colonial fur trade in the middle colonies.[6] The charismatic power that Turner exerted over his pupils was described by Carl Becker as "the manner of one who utters moral truths."[7]

A hand-drawn map made by a group of his pupils pinpoints clusters of his former students teaching in leading university centers throughout the United States.[8] In the period between 1907 and 1922 Carl Becker, Arthur M. Schlesinger, and Claude H. Van Tyne had already used basic themes of Turnerian theory to explain the causes of the American Revolution. Other followers included Frederic L. Paxson, Max Farrand, and Ulrich B. Phillips, all of whom incorporated aspects of the frontier-sectional theory in writings on early American history. Even Thomas Jefferson Wertenbaker, who in 1931 joined forces with those critics who questioned the validity of the Turnerian theory, quietly began to include many of the theory's implications in his volumes on colonial history.[9] In 1934 Curtis P. Nettles ventured to say that the frontier theory was an explanation of "a new order rising from native soil" of the colonial past.[10] Paxson, though, writing on the Turnerian theme, tended to shortcut colonial history with a narrative that began after 1763.

During the 1920s and increasingly by the 1930s, historians of early American history published monographs with the words "Westward" or "Frontier" on the title page. For example, Albert T. Volwiler's carefully documented study, *George Croghan and the Westward Movement, 1741–1782*, was published in Cleveland by the Arthur H. Clark Company in 1926 before the company itself moved west to make its headquarters in Glendale, California. Volwiler's book was the first of Arthur H. Clark's "Old Northwest Series" that also included Louis Knott Koontz's 1941 biography, *Robert Dinwiddie, His Career in American Colonial Government and Westward Expansion*. A dedicated teacher at UCLA and a Turner enthusiast, Koontz attracted graduate students who worked on parallel topics. One of these was Kenneth P. Bailey, whose 1939 prize-winning study, *The Ohio Company of Virginia and the Westward Movement, 1748–1792: A Chapter in the History of the Colonial Frontier*, was also printed in the "Old Northwest Series." Koontz's colleague at UCLA, John Carl Parish, developed a friendship with Turner at the Huntington Library in the early 1930s,[11] and as the first editor of *Pacific Historical Review*, he fostered publication of articles on early American frontier history in that journal. Parish's investigation in colonial frontier history were linked with the westward movement as a whole, as he pointed out in a noteworthy essay, "The Persistence of the Westward Movement."[12]

While Koontz and Parish were stimulating the study of colonial frontier history at UCLA, Verner W. Crane at the University of Michigan was writing in the field and encouraging advanced students to carry on similar work. Crane's lively account, *The Southern Frontier, 1670–1732* (Philadelphia, 1929), was followed by a sequel, *John Stuart and the Southern Colonial Frontier, A Study of the Indian Relations, War and Land Problems in the Southern Wilderness, 1745–1775* (Ann Arbor, Mich., 1944), written by John Richard Alden, one of Crane's pupils.

Ideas Turner had set forth were being further developed: Histories taking their inspiration from Turner's work are among the most important works of our own day. Thus Merle Curti's prize-winning *Growth of American Thought* (1943) is appropriately dedicated "to the memory of Frederick Jackson Turner." The title of the first section, "The American Adaptation of the European Heritage," and many of the chapter headings ("Colonial Conditions Modify the Old World Heritage," "The West Challenges Patrician Leadership") show how strongly Turner influenced Curti.[13] John Richard Alden's writings on the emergence of the South contain interpretations that resemble Turner's,[14] and Clarence Ver Steeg finds Turner's frontier theory relevant to his own discussion of the colonial era in *The Formative Years, 1607–1763;* he notes that the social mobility, which Turner recognized as a phenomenon closely connected with frontier life, was especially characteristic of the "Old West," the name used by Turner in 1908 to describe the area between the fall line and the Appalachians.[15] Turner's discussion of social mobility is of continuing interest to contemporary specialists in early American history; his statement that the frontier is "a form of society rather than an area" has a strikingly modern ring.

Daniel J. Boorstin is another modern historian whose writings on early American history have been recognized for their expression of Turnerian themes. Moreover, Boorstin and Turner share a preference for the essay form, perhaps because their complex view of historical causation makes difficult the writing of a conventional narrative history. Indeed, Turner himself confided to his publishers: "My strength, or weakness lies in interpretation, correlation, elucidation of large tendencies to bring out new points of view and in giving a new setting."[16]

Boorstin has not been labeled a Turnerian simply because he writes historical essays stressing "new points of view" and "a new setting." As Cecilia Kenyon in her penetrating review of *The Americans* says of Boorstin, "Although he recognizes the importance of the intellectual and institutional baggage of these early settlers—Puritanism, Anglicanism, the common law, he is at heart a disciple of Turner. His emphasis throughout is on the way in which these ideas and institutions have been modified by the American environment, not on the way in which they shaped that environment."[17] Kenyon, in her analysis of Boorstin's book, is disturbed by this portrayal of a colonial society in which the taming of the frontier, she says, plays so overwhelming a role. She thinks that Boorstin has oversimplified reality by suggesting that most Americans were governed almost completely by the practical facts of life.

This criticism of *The Americans*, although severe, has validity and brings to mind the hostility the late Perry Miller exhibited toward the frontier theory when it was applied to New England's history. One explanation of Miller's response is that he was unwilling to concede that the transforming force of the wilderness brought about significant changes in European culture. Miller seems to have been convinced that European ideas, especially English Puritan ideas, were all-important in determining the social structure and behavior of the colonists, even in shaping the environment of colonial New England. And like Miller, who identified Turner with "the ruling and compulsive power of the frontier" and considered him "the foremost victim—of his fallacy,"[18] Cecilia Kenyon depicted the Turnerian view as an almost slavish devotion to the environmental-frontier theory. Even Page Smith in *The Historian and History* describes Turner as a man who thought "the richest soil produced the most outstanding people, almost as though human beings were a species of turnip."[19]

Turner's evolutionary approach to colonial history has been adopted to explain the enormous changes that occurred during the colonial era—to explain, for example, how thirteen colonies were transformed into an independent nation. Turner and other historians have often borrowed metaphors from nature to explain these changes. For instance, seventeenth-century writers referred to England as "mother," the colonies as "children," and the settling of colonies as "planting." Turner himself said that the colonies "evolved" and "matured," an appropriate metaphorical way to describe change. He also called the original colonies "mothers" of the new colonies in the West. But Turner often used metaphorical language to explain the reality of change and thus was responsible for injecting themes of environmental determinism into early American historiography.[20]

Close examination of early American maps discloses that Turner was also responsible for certain misconceptions about the westward movement, the fall line, and the Appalachian barrier. Clearly the frontier of settlement was not a "line" of land occupation. Maps of the eighteenth century do not show a cutting edge of land settlement moving westward or pausing temporarily at a fall-line boundary between the Piedmont and the coastal plain.[21] The notion of the fall line linking the waterfalls or more specifically the rapids located on some of the coastal rivers flowing across the seaboard into the Atlantic is part of an environmental-determinism theory set forth by Turner and his disciple Ellen C. Semple that is not wholly substantiated in the sources. Turner stressed the idea in his classroom lectures[22] and in his essays, and Semple expanded it in her influential book of 1903, *American History and Its Geographic Conditions*. Modern geologists have indicated that the falls, or rapids, are probably caused by the accentuated slope on the eastern part of the Piedmont. Nor is there evidence to show that certain urban centers or fall-line cities (Baltimore, Maryland; Washington, D.C.; Columbia, South Carolina; and Trenton, New Jersey) originated because of the importance of being located beside these rapids. They became "carrying places" for traders moving into the interior. It is true that such carrying places were marked on early American maps, but generalizations about larger colonial populations following the fall line are of doubtful value.[23]

Another Turnerian misconception about the colonial westward movement is that the Appalachians were an almost impenetrable barrier holding the colonists close to the coast. This theory, expanded by Semple, had been almost universally accepted. But early American maps, especially those of the eighteenth century, reveal that the colonists were not necessarily hemmed in between the Appalachian ranges and the seaboard. In fact, in the colonial era there were many thousands of acres of unoccupied land. Even the modern megapolis of the eastern seaboard encompasses large areas of woodland where in some places the deer population has increased more in the last fifty years than the human population.[24]

A more reasonable explanation than the barrier theory is that if the colonists were confined to the eastern seaboard during most of the eighteenth century, it was partly because of the hostility of the French and Indians. Moreover, the reluctance of the British government to encourage land speculation and settlement west of the proclamation line established in 1763 (revised in 1768) also discouraged westward migration. Turner himself seems to have accepted the idea of the "French barrier" to the colonial westward movement, for he used the phrase as a title for one of his lectures in his undergraduate course on the early American West.

Turner, to be sure, has been criticized for setting forth an oversimplified approach to early American history, but he would argue that the assumption that his views centered entirely on the frontier theory was mistaken. He would protest Perry Miller's assertion that the Turnerian view portrayed a "simple monolithic America." In answer to such complaints Turner would say, as he did on more than one occasion, that he was concerned with "multiple hypotheses"[25] and that his essays on sectionalism practically constituted a theory to do away with theories.

We can examine Turner's published and unpublished essays to obtain a better insight into his thinking. Among his papers is a manuscript essay of 1918, "What Is Colonial History?"[26] refuting his old friend Charles M. Andrews's assertion that the colonies should be studied "from some point outside themselves" so that "for the scholar there is only one point of observation, that of the mother country from which they came and to whom they were legally subject."[27] Turner's answer rejects the narrowness of this viewpoint; two vantage points of observation are necessary, he believed, "both the English home which the colonists left and the American wilderness to which they came."[28] Turner continues in a passage that anticipates some of our modern specialists in early American history: "Was not the more important thing the play of new influences, the grappling with unaccustomed conditions in new surroundings, economic life, the breaking of old customs, the creation of new institutions, the modification of the type?" Writing of the Massachusetts colonist, Turner points out that "whatever old names were attached to his institutions they became essentially different things in their operation, their adjustments, their modification to suit the American conditions. . . . Massachusetts was an American commonwealth at the same time that she was an English colony. She had the American forest at her back door as well as the Atlantic Ocean in front of her. She worked under both influences." Thus the two points of view, the concepts of Massachusetts as "an English colony or an American commonwealth," were, Turner wrote, "mutually interpretive."[29] Turner's own complex view of history quite naturally made him impatient with theories that imposed false limitations on scholarship.

Turner's correspondence and his writings show that he never did abandon the germ theory. To do so would have been to accept an intolerable narrowing of the scope of his investigations. Moreover, he extended the theory by suggesting that the relation between the mother country and the colonies repeated itself as the mother country's colonies themselves became "mothers" of new colonies in the West. Thus, describing a projected paper on the creation of new states in the West during the Revolutionary era, Turner in 1895 wrote J. Franklin Jameson,

> It would be my purpose to bring into a single view the various efforts at state-making in the West in that period, considering the causes, processes, theories, and economic considerations involved in the movement. The paper would cast light upon American political thought in that era. My idea is something like this: the seventeenth century saw the planting of *European* men, ideas, institutions along the Atlantic coast. The close of the eighteenth century saw these coast settlements become, in turn, the mothers of new colonies in this western area of vacant territory. The interaction of American institutions and political ideas, with free land, makes the problem.[30]

In his application of the germ theory to colonial history Turner showed a breadth of perception. His germ theory might seem to ally him with the imperialist school; in fact, however, he was not bound by their assumptions. Turner liked to think of himself as a man not bound by any theory—even a theory of his own developing: "I like to believe," he wrote in 1928 to Merle Curti, "that inherited ideals persist long after the environmental influence has changed; but the environment does change, and society changes— otherwise not history."[31] And so Turner asserted that the historian must turn the theorem around, must look at the past in the light of the present: "The present and its tendencies do cast light upon historically significant events, institutions, ideas, which . . . may have seemed of trivial importance."[32] This germ theory in reverse would be congenial to the nationalists; like them, Turner was interested in examining the origins of the United States from the vantage point of the present. This is not to say that Turner really let go of his frontier-sectionalism theory. It stayed with him even as he argued that he did consider other theories of history.

A point to emphasize is that Turner, in his own mind, seldom drew a sharp line between suggested interpretations. When he wrote about the regulators, he consistently portrayed them as part of a far-flung colonial frontier ranging from the hinterlands of Pennsylvania to Georgia. The revolts of the late eighteenth century in Pennsylvania (the Paxton Riots) and in South Carolina shared certain common denominators with the regulators.[33] Turner also wrote about the rise of towns for retail merchants along the Piedmont frontier in the eighteenth century and pointed to the emergence of inland state capitals, such as Raleigh in 1791.

Turner's talents and inclinations, as he himself recognized, accounted for his fascination with what he called "mass history."[34] "My own work," he wrote Merle Curti, "emphasizes tendencies, institutions, mass movements rather than the exact truth as to details of events, motives of the individual.[35] Thus Turner, in "The Development of American Society," compared United States history to "a human sea—mobile, ever-changing, restless; a sea in which deep currents run, and over the surface of which sweep winds of popular emotion, a sea that has been ever adjusting itself to new shore lines, and new beds. By the side of this westward movement the story of the *individual leaders*, and the narrative of events sink to insignificance. For in America, whatever be the case elsewhere in history, society has shaped its men."[36] And Turner says of himself, "I have been more interested in studying a leader's environment, the society in which he lived, the lesser men whose support he needed and whose opposition modified his policy, than in minutiae of his personal life."[37] Yet even here, where one of Turner's convictions is involved, he tries not to be dogmatic. "I would not wish to stand for a purely social or deterministic view of historical processes," he wrote. "The individual has a real part and sometimes his leadership creates public opinion, and within limits, opens new channels of tendency."[38] Turner again shows himself able to instruct us with a vivid generalization. But we must remember that his heroes were those individuals who, he maintained, represented the politics of the westward-moving pioneers from early American to modern times; he made an eloquent case for Jefferson, Jackson, and Lincoln. And we must also remember that he was always, and I stress always, talking about white male leadership.

Yet when pressed to state exactly what he stood for Turner drew back defensively and portrayed himself as a general philosopher of all American history. "But fundamentally," he wrote Carl Becker, "I have been interested in the inter-relations of economics, politics, sociology, culture in general, with the geographical factors, in explaining the United States of today by means of its history thus broadly taken."[39]

For a historian whose interests were as wide-ranging as Turner's, America was the ideal field of study:

> In America, as perhaps nowhere else in the world, we may trace the evolution of a vast population, almost under our gaze, from a handful of colonists lodged in the wilderness, in the presence of untold natural resources, up through a swift succession of changes social and industrial, to a democracy of nearly ninety million souls; from a thin line of European settlement fighting for existence on the edge of the Atlantic to a broad zone of civilization stretching across a continent and finding new problems beyond the rim of the Pacific.[40]

This Turnerian concept of colonial history is recognized, as we have seen, in the writings of Daniel J. Boorstin and other scholars. Clinton Rossiter acknowledges that he owed much to Turner for interpretations in his perceptive *Seedtime of the Republic*. In his first chapter Rossiter argued:

> If we may take the word "frontier" to mean not only the line of farthest settlement to the west, but also the primitive conditions of life and thought which in the seventeenth century extended throughout the colonies and during most of the eighteenth century

continued to prevail in many areas east of the Appalachians, we may point to at least a half-dozen indications of the decisive influence of the frontier environment.[41]

Rossiter further argued that "the all-pervading frontier" as well as other factors such as the English heritage of the colonists and the conflict between colonial and imperial interests were powerful forces that became basic themes in his book.[42]

This general view of causation in early American history was also expressed by Frederick B. Tolles in his discerning essay, "New Approaches to Research in Colonial History." Tolles stresses the need to know *"who voted"* in analyzing the attitudes "of the bulk of the colonial population." We need to know more about "the 'middling sort,'" the "voiceless," says Tolles, and we need to study more closely the hierarchical social structure of colonial society.[43] This view suggests studies in colonial history in the vein of Merle Curti's *The Making of An American Community.*[44] Curti's approach is similar to Turner's; far from centering attention exclusively on the influence of the frontier, he emphasizes the necessity of viewing colonial society as part of the most complex developmental process.

Edmund S. Morgan is another of our leading historians whose approach leads him away from the clear-cut path of traditional interpretation. In his essay "The American Revolution: Revisions in Need of Revising,"[45] Morgan reviews the familiar social and economic interpretations of the Revolution offered by Carl Becker and Charles A. Beard. He also contrasts the imperial view with the Namierian interpretation of the Revolution, which demonstrates that British statesmen of the period were too busy with local problems to control a far-flung empire. Morgan then strikes hard at the need to understand the minds of such leaders of the Revolution as Washington, Adams, Franklin, and Jefferson if we are to understand the true causes of the revolt. The crucial questions are, Morgan says, "How did Americans, living on the edge of empire, develop the breadth of vision and the attachment to principle which they displayed in that remarkable period from 1763–1789?" and "How did Americans generate the forces that carried them into a new nationality and a new human liberty?" According to

Morgan, the nationalist George Bancroft had tried to answer these questions. But the answer, Morgan says—and here we are strongly reminded of Turner—lies in the neglected field of American local institutions. "What kind of institutions produced a Jefferson, a Madison, a Washington, a John Adams? Not imperial institutions certainly."[46] Morgan's emphasis on local history and institutions, the origins of American liberty, and particularly on the interrelationships among social, political, and economic history shows some parallels with Turner's views on local history and the relations among economic, social, and political history. Certainly this approach is a far cry from that crude environmentalism objected to by Cecilia Kenyon.

This view of colonial history is also characteristic of Bernard Bailyn's analysis of early Virginia society and of Sigmund Diamond's description of the social transformation of New France.[47] Both of these writers are concerned with the interplay of social, political, and economic forces, and they stress the importance of opportunity and free land. Moreover, they are informed scholars knowledgeable about the European background.

In his essay "What Is Colonial History?" Turner concluded that both the imperial concept and the frontier concept were important in understanding the origins of colonial America. One might wish that he had taken his own conclusion more seriously and not pushed so vigorously for the frontier idea in other essays.

But Turner, like Frederick Tolles and Edmund Morgan, was often raising complex questions rather than attempting to answer them. Indeed, among Turner's papers we find a specific list of such questions that he asked during a Harvard Ph.D. examination:[48] "In a course on history of liberty in America, what topics would you treat in the colonial era?—Landmarks in history of franchise?"[49] Turner then asks about contributions made by various historians, including Beer, Osgood, Andrews, and Arthur M. Schlesinger. He also raises the questions of how Philip A. Bruce and William B. Weeden "differ" in their "treatment" of colonial economic history and of "how [to] find material available in English collections." There are further notes on "My *Old West*" and on "Immigration," but we are left with an intriguing question about the "greatest unused opportunity in colonial history."[50]

What Turner had in mind here is a matter of conjecture for us as it must have been for the candidate he was examining.

Turner liked colonial history but not for itself. For him early American history could not be divorced from the larger panorama of the American past. And the past was for him key in understanding the present. Social problems of the present, he believed, are made more understandable and perhaps more manageable if we understand the past that produced them. Turner was as unwilling to accept limitations on a specific period that he chose to study as he was to accept the bounds imposed by traditional historical scholarship. He made explicit the suggestions of the imperialists and the nationalists and then amplified those ideas by observing colonial history from the broadest possible perspective. In so doing he helped to lift much of our colonial heritage from the well of antiquarianism. Unquestionably, Turner prepared the way for the favorable reception of Beard's and Becker's social and economic interpretations of early American history. Charles Beard himself, one of Turner's most bitter critics, wrote in a 1928 letter, "Turner deserves everlasting credit for his services as the leader in restoring the consideration of economic facts to historical writing in America."[51]

As late as 1931, shortly before his death, Turner was perplexed by critics who misunderstood his views of early American history.[52] In writing to Frederick Merk, Turner summarized his views on early American history:

> I suppose that it is not unlikely that in my desire to modify current historical conceptions of American history I may have seemed to overemphasize the purely American aspects of our democracy. . . . What I was dealing with was, in the first place, the *American* character of democracy as compared with that of Europe or of European philosophers. . . . At any rate, it was not my idea that the Revolution was fundamentally a work of the West. So far as the colonial phase goes, I think it would be possible to show that in New England, for example, the interior towns and their problems had had a very important influence in modifying the form of government that the original Puritan leaders imposed;[53] and that in Virginia the development of the representative assembly, for in-

stance, was deeply shaped by the opportunity, and indeed the need, of giving concrete form to such speculations as those of Sandys and of adjusting the government to the idea of an assembly from particular plantations. These are phases of the subject which I have briefly touched upon in my class lectures and into which I have gone farther in my investigations and notes, but which I have not dealt with adequately in print. However, the data is existent.[54]

The nature of Turner's assumptions about colonial history is revealed in these comments. It is, to say the least, fascinating to observe how easily Turner's explanations for social forces and social movements can be relied upon to give a special meaning to the early development of our democratic institutions. This was the thrust of Ray A. Billington's interpretative textbook *Westward Expansion*, first published in 1949, and Turnerian concepts were fundamental in the multivolume series that Billington sponsored as histories of the frontier.[55]

What can we conclude about the Turnerian impact upon the writing of early American or colonial history? In talking about this topic with my friend colonialist Jack Greene at the April 1992 Chicago meeting of the Organization of American Historians, we both agreed that sometime in the 1960s, the Turnerian colonial histories experienced a quiet death.[56] Those already published in the Billington series on the early American frontiers, northern and southern, though carefully written by able scholars, were virtually ignored by a new generation of historians. "Nobody paid attention to them," Greene commented; and I added, "This was a time when there was a powerful impact of ethnohistory with important interpretive books on early American themes" written by Calvin Martin, Francis Jennings, and others.[57] My book, *Dispossessing the American Indian: Indians and Whites on the Colonial Frontier* (Scribners, 1972), actually attacked Turner and his frontier theory for negative views of Indians and for glorifying the fur traders' destruction of wildlife.

There is, however, a sign of life in the old body of Turnerian colonial history. Books in the 1990s with the word frontier in the title suddenly appeared—but not among publishers' exhibits of new volumes by historians. Who are these renegade scholars resurrecting these ideas that we believed had died? They are none other than the academic progeny of Turner's old friends who had invited him to speak at their national meetings, the historical geographers. Among these scholars I met a young man at the Chicago meeting who is spearheading studies of what he calls colonial "backwoodsmen." Turner, as of 1992, has risen again in a somewhat new but familiar guise, as patron saint of backwoodsmen and historical geographers.[58] Moreover, there is another sign of revival. In a lavish treatment of Turner's early West published by the Virginia Historical Society, *Away I'm Bound: Virginia and the Westward Movement,* a narrative commentary and catalog of a 1993 exhibition by David H. Fischer and James C. Kelly (see especially the first thirteen pages), it is argued that there is pictorial and documentary proof of Turner's explanation of early colonial history.

CHAPTER SIX

EXPLAINING AGRICULTURAL HISTORY

Among Turner's papers at the Huntington Library is a folder containing notes for and drafts of an address, "Agricultural History as a Field for Research."[1] Turner gave this talk at a dinner, December 28, 1922, during a meeting of the American Historical Association held in New Haven, Connecticut.[2] The invitation to speak, sponsored by the Agricultural History Society, came about six weeks before the scheduled date, and an additional three weeks passed before Turner received confirmation that the affair would be included in the printed program.[3] Further complications arose when the society decided to have another speaker precede Turner on the podium; it was also determined that the dinner would have to conclude early (by 8:30 P.M.) to permit members to hear a visiting speaker from England. As a result, Turner planned to limit his address to "five or ten minutes."[4] Nils Olsen, secretary of the society, nevertheless wrote to Turner stating that he hoped to have an allocated "time for discussion."[5]

Under the circumstances, one would expect that Turner's preparations would have been minimal, but this was not his way. Although a number of his notes are fragmentary, and indeed some introductory parts of his talk were jotted down on Hotel Taft stationery at the time of the New Haven meeting, his preparations were carefully made. More important, his material was based upon a mass of data on American economic development that he had been accumulating for decades. Turner organized his notes and fragments into two rough, handwritten manuscripts: an eight-page draft and a nineteen-page revised version including a three-page introduction.

Turner's eight-page draft contained most of the ideas that he expanded and modified in the longer revised version. Agricultural history he saw as an area of research related to the history of the frontier and section and to general American history. Thus he stressed that investigations into agricultural history must be carried on "in relation to other historical research." Agricultural history, he maintained, is an important part of financial and railroad history; it cannot be ignored in considering such varied phenomena as the colonial planter class, the emergence of the South, the origins of New England, emigration, soil exhaustion, and agrarian movements such as those initiated by the Grangers and the Populists. Agricultural history, he believed, must examine the domestic markets that have existed for various crops down through the years as well as the effects of American crops on the European markets, especially in England and Germany.

In the first draft Turner presented a short account of his own experiences as a semirural American: "I once learned how to cut grain with a cradle, bind wheat, husk corn, but my trade was type sticking."[6] He then explained how his own research on the frontier convinced him that agricultural history was part of the story of "successive waves of density of population spreading into new geographic provinces, reacting on older areas. . . . Changes in agricultural areas, crops, methods, markets, etc. were not only important but fundamental, so I set students to work." Some of those students worked under both Turner and Richard T. Ely at Wisconsin. Joseph Schafer, Benjamin Horace Hibbard, and Henry Charles Taylor, who later made outstanding contributions in the field of agricultural history, were among the group.[7]

Turner then enumerated a number of "recent things which have arrested my attention" (or "questions I could ask of this society"). He began with the general question: Is it not true that the history of America "has been a history of a people predominantly agricultural"? If one accepts this assumption, Turner argued, agricultural history helps to explain a series of important changes and movements in American history, such as "the evolution of the transportation net, the emergence of farmer political movements

and the 'farmers' Bloc,' the Progressives, the controversies surrounding the first U.S. Bank and the credit needs of planters and
farmers, the beginnings of sectionalism."

What form should studies into such areas of American history
take? Turner placed great emphasis on the need for "comparative"
studies to show, for example, how profitable or unprofitable agriculture really was, how profitable certain types of crops were in
different regions and at different times. He also recommended that
the "relative contributions" of immigrant groups to American agricultural development be assessed, especially in connection with
modifications of European farm methods. The work of researchers
in allied fields—"humanistic geographers," students of rural sociology, chemists, botanists, entomologists, economists, and geologists—should of course be consulted. Turner realized that such
studies, involving various disciplines, could best be carried out by a
team—"cooperative planning of work of investigation" was the way
he put it. Such an approach—a modern one indeed—would be well
suited to historical sociological studies on such subjects as "actual
farm life & conditions of women at different periods."

Much of the data pertinent to these studies, Turner believed,
could be usefully recorded on maps; in this way the relation
of geographical, historical, and human factors would be clarified.[8]
With the help of maps one could demonstrate the development of
agricultural specialization in the Tidewater area, in the upland
South and New England, on the Great Plains, and along the Pacific
coast. The migration of immigrants (Germans and Scandinavians,
for example) could best be charted on maps. The grazing and dry
farming areas of the plains and areas rich in timber could be pin-
pointed. Maps would also provide a useful tool for the study of
particular rural groups—the planters, the poor whites, the yeoman farmer, the Negro.

Turner concluded this first draft by underlining his implicit
point: Research in agricultural history cannot be carried on by
agricultural experts alone. The history of agriculture is not watertight and cannot be isolated from other studies; indeed, Turner
was convinced that agricultural history could not be separated
even from urban history. Research in agricultural history should
include "students of urban as well as rural life." . . . The pull from

the farm, mobile labor, markets & prices, credit, transportation, effects of manufacturing interest on [the] tariff & so on prices" are factors that influence both rural and urban society, hence the need for scholars to plan and carry out cooperative studies.

The final draft clarified the grounds for Turner's belief in the importance of research into agricultural history. The field, he claimed, was much wider than most people might suppose and broader than the statistics would seem to suggest. The 1920 census, for instance, showed that for the first time more people were occupied in manufacturing and mechanical industries than in agriculture. But this census figure was misleading, Turner maintained, because the majority of Americans still lived on farms or in small towns where they were inevitably influenced by rural attitudes and ideas. Thus, despite the trend toward urbanization, the rural influence continued to be strong in politics, as in the case of the Farmers' Bloc. To understand "American society and its ideals" one must necessarily concern oneself with agricultural history.

Turner did not for a moment suppose that agricultural history was a discipline pointing only to the past, with no implications for the future. On the contrary, he saw America's future as dependent upon agricultural developments, and he believed that the study of history could help prepare us for future developments. "How large a population is U.S. capable of sustaining on basis of self-sufficient agriculture?" he asked. If we hope to feed future generations, he argued, we should recognize "the fitness of certain areas" for agriculture and the need "to preserve a balance" in the use of land. The historian should recognize that agricultural history can be a suitable "corrective" to the emphasis on urban history. Turner himself was convinced "that a large share of history was agricultural and much of the rest was dependent upon it."

Turner, who was no "farmer by training," no "expert" in agricultural history or in "the technique or the problems of investigation," first became interested in the subject during his early years of teaching at Wisconsin:

In my courses in the social and economic history of the United States, I found it essential to go beyond the study of events and of politics and of institutions to the forces that lay behind them.

> Among these compelling forces was agriculture. In the early nine-
> ties, when I first conducted such courses we were still a [pre-]
> dominantly agricultural nation, still extending agricultural con-
> quests into the wilderness, occupying in single decades farm lands
> equal in area to nations of the Old World.

And even in the 1920s, Turner argued, in spite of increased urbanization, agriculture continued to be of great importance.

Turner then set up a list of the arguments justifying continued
research in the field: First, agricultural history provides a key to
the understanding of sectional rivalries and allows us to examine
the influence exerted by the farmer in politics. An examination of
the income tax figures for the 1920s, for instance, reveals that the
"Farmers' Bloc furnished over 82% of the total farming income."
Such facts, Turner maintained, make it clear that knowledge of
what one might call "America's agricultural past" is likely to aid
our understanding of economic and political problems.

Second, agricultural history would become increasingly important because of the food needed for a burgeoning American population. "It appears," Turner wrote, "that there must be an increase
rather than diminution of agricultural development if the U.S. is
not to become dependent upon the outside world for raw materials and food supplies." With increasing competition in the world
for such supplies, agricultural areas in the United States particularly suited to "the production of crops rather than the development of other types of industry" would be highly prized. Turner
believed that the coming population explosion would not only
bring about "a transformed agriculture" but would restore to agriculture "a large measure of its historic significance."

Turner's worries about the ability of American agriculture to
satisfy the need of a vastly expanded population have not yet
proved justified. But he was well aware that the problem was
worldwide and of the utmost gravity.[9] In 1967 the world food
panel of the president's science advisory committee issued its
highly publicized warning to the world; in 1922 Turner had already
recognized the proportions of the coming crises of the 1990s.

Third, the conditions of agriculture existing during the different
periods of American history have varied extremely and would

merit, Turner believed, careful study.[10] Indeed the whole subject of research in agricultural history should be reviewed: "There is a real contrast," Turner wrote, "between the type of study to be applied to the area before the disappearance of the frontier line and the present era." America in the 1920s, Turner claimed, was "a settled country and a different world." With the passing of the frontier, new types of agrarian legislation were required, and new economic and social developments needed to be considered. Turner told his audience that he was especially aware of some of these "transformations" because students whom he had trained in this field now held college chairs and key positions in the United States Department of Agriculture and in the Census Bureau.

Fourth, the history of agriculture and of "rural life" was of fundamental importance in what Turner called "the general history of the U.S." Unfortunately, the importance of agriculture in our history was often overlooked because of increasing "interest in urban problems and the problems of eastern labor." The investigator of agricultural history, Turner argued, should be aware of "the proportion which it bears to the total national interests."

Fifth, agricultural history research "casts new light and often gives the explanation of important aspects of American history in other fields." The researcher should be particularly conscious of interrelationships, such as the relationship between agriculture and the economic prosperity of the nation and those links between agriculture and currency and tariff problems, internal improvements, expansionist movements "such as those to Texas & Oregon," and internal movements such as migrations of New Englanders to the Midwest. Indeed, even military history could not be cut off from agricultural history, for it is well known, Turner wrote, "that an army travels on its belly." The "military history of the Civil War" could well be studied through "the census statistics by county geography for the location of crops and so on."

Sixth, many particular facets of agricultural history need further attention, Turner argued. On some five pages he compiled several lists of such topics, including "seasonal migrations of farm labor," "wages of farm hands," the "evolution of . . . the Timber farmer, Prairie farmer," "cost of transportation of crop to nearest market," "eras of home market & its collapse," "relation of government to agriculture, eg., land, cattle, laws . . . farmers' relations with credit system, sources of loans, terms—amount—time—interest etc, overlap of land & farm history, farm implements and machinery, growth and development, & by areas involved." The effect of these factors on agricultural society also deserved investigation, and "travellers' manuscripts, letters, journals, newspapers . . . the things neglected by earlier collectors; being lost in housecleanings, movings, fire" would furnish raw material for such studies. Turner was also an advocate of the "critical use of census & unpublished census data & assessors' & company clerks' data."

Turner concluded his notes by recommending agricultural history to all students of American history. The historian of America who neglects this field, Turner said, "is sure to miss important facts and misunderstand much of our development and problems."

Turner's thoughts on agricultural history as we find them set forth in these two sets of notes are of course first thoughts— undeveloped and rudimentary. Yet the three important theses that emerge from his deliberations, if they had been accepted by scholars in the field, would have resulted in a more fruitful and less restricted approach to the subject than the view that seemingly has prevailed. Turner emphasizes first that agricultural history is in no sense a self-sufficient subject, a discipline on its own; on the contrary, it is an important part of the national history, and there are no boundaries to mark the points at which agricultural history merges into economic or social or political history or any of the other areas of history that historians choose to examine. Turner's firm rejection of any claims to independence made on behalf of agricultural history was, of course, exactly to be expected. The principle he stresses here is a special application of the standard that he applied to all historical studies.

Turner was probably not the first scholar to suggest that research in agricultural history is closely related to broad themes in American agricultural development and rural life. His emphasis upon the connection between agricultural history and what he called "the general history of America" tends, however, to ignore the fact that by the late 1920s there was a solid body of agricultural history that was not labeled "agricultural." Indeed, as one example, there are sections of Francis Parkman's *France and England in North America* that provide superb agricultural history. Nevertheless, Turner's argument is still an important one today.

Turner's second major point is that the methods used by historians in the past were unnecessarily restricted. Just as boundaries had been set up between different areas of historical study, so boundaries—even weightier ones—separated the disciplines from each other. But the historian who wishes to go beyond a superficial examination of the past cannot accept these artificial barriers. Such a scholar will make use of the tools developed in other disciplines; his work may be unconventional, but it is likely to be fresh and revealing. An important example of the type of research Turner hoped for is Paul Gates's *Agriculture and the Civil War* (New York: 1965), a learned work based upon extensive research in sources of the most varied kinds. Ostensibly focused upon agriculture, the book offers an excellent history of the period; future students of this field will find it indispensable.

Turner himself, though he made use of techniques and viewpoints culled from other disciplines, did not participate in any extended group-study project. Nevertheless, he clearly recognized the direction in which historical studies were moving—away from subjective, imaginative interpretations of historical events or figures and toward objective, many-sided accounts. A team of experts in various fields, he realized, would be best equipped to shed light on a complicated historical question.

The third important point to emerge from Turner's notes remains unstated, although elsewhere in his writings he is quite explicit about it: The historian is not chained to the past; the present and the future are proper objects of professional concern. This is not a point of view that has always been accepted, as Arthur Schlesinger, Jr., makes clear in "On the Writing of Contemporary History": "Even as late as the days before the Second World War, an American professor who carried a course of lectures up to his own time was deemed rash and unorthodox."[11] Turner not only thought it consonant with his professional status to discuss the present, he also believed it his duty to apply his special knowledge and training to a consideration of the future.

Yet in his own published work, Turner was almost exclusively a historian of the nineteenth century and 1920s agricultural history was not a subject he would choose for venturing into print. His notes reveal that Turner was somewhat unsure of himself in groping for a unifying process to link agriculture, sectionalism, and economic developments. Moreover, there were complications related to food supply and growing populations. In the last decade of his life Turner was increasingly concerned about crises in world affairs, and some of the "threats" to world stability stemmed from Malthusian predictions of chaos resulting from overpopulation and lack of food.

At the same time, Turner's address on agricultural history shows how persistent he was in employing his frontier-sectional theory as an umbrella sheltering research in a given field. Agricultural history was part of his domain. And though he was not a founding father of the Agricultural History Society, Turner, as Martin Ridge has pointed out, sent his loyal students into the field to produce a stream of essays and books.[12] Four of these loyal Turnerians, Frederick Merk, Avery Craven, Solon J. Buck, and Edward E. Dale, served as presidents of the society. Additionally, the society's journal provided a forum for discussing Turner's frontier-sectionalism theory and for debating the safety-valve concept as a means for easing economic crises. Regardless of whether or not we accept Turner's inclusive generalizations about our agricultural past, we must concede that he offered penetrating commentaries on the subject. And certain of his arguments, such as the proposition that agricultural history is not a field in itself, unrelated to socioeconomic and political history, are hard to dispute even today. As for the safety-valve idea, I am a convert and always have been.[13]

PART THREE

WORLD FRONTIERS AND SECTIONS

Out of our own experience in a federation of sections . . . we can furnish a remedy to Europe for its national particularism and for the imperialism of immoderate nationalism.

——"Why Did Not the United States Become Another Europe?" Lecture (1916)

The [frontier] idea, of course, was not so much a new one as a neglected one; and I tried to show that this general advance through so many decades had profound influences both in the shaping of the society of new geographical provinces . . . and upon the American way of looking at the world. . . . my emphasis upon the phenomenon was with regard to its shaping the general course of our history.

——Turner to Isaiah Bowman (1931)

CHAPTER SEVEN

THE TWENTIETH CENTURY
Politics, Urbanization, and World Government

An intellectual transformation in Turner's life took him beyond his writings on frontier-sectionalism theory and its application to early American, midwestern, and western history and to ancillary fields such as agricultural history. World War I burst upon Turner and other patriotic Americans with tremendous intensity, and with his old friend Woodrow Wilson in the White House, Turner felt a personal obligation to help in the battle against the German kaiser. Turner's papers are filled with correspondence revealing his anxiety about what could be done and how he and other historians could lend a hand. Although he probed the sources on world issues, the notes he took and the proposals he made never reached print in his lifetime. We shall now examine Turner's preoccupation with modern world history, politics, industrialization, urbanization, and population explosions. Fascinating as Turner found these aspects, he apparently never thought them important enough to put into book form. Ironically, at Harvard and at the Huntington Library in the 1920s and early 1930s, he committed himself to a wearisome projection of his nineteenth-century frontier-sectional theories. In his publications he stressed that the importance of the American frontier in shaping American society and culture had been overlooked. Its significance could, he believed, be compared with the importance that the Mediterranean Sea had for the Greeks, "breaking the bond of custom, offering new experiences, calling out new institutions and activities."[1]

"The Development of American Society," a Phi Beta Kappa address Turner gave in summer 1908 at the University of Illinois and later published in the University's *Alumni Quarterly*, deals with the social aspects of the frontier theme. It stresses the wider implications of the frontier theory and represents an intermediate stage in Turner's thought between the original frontier essay of 1893 and his notes in 1927. Among his papers at the Huntington Library is his annotated copy of this essay with revisions in ink and red pencil, indicating that he intended to republish the piece. Modern America, he maintained, can best understand itself by "understanding its origins . . . the forces that have made the nation what it is . . . the institutions, forces and ideas that persist as controlling influences in the life of today." No single ruling idea or avenue of approach, he argued, could possibly do the immense job: "There is no single key to American history," Turner wrote. "In history as in science we are learning that a complex result is the outcome of the interplay of many forces."

Then, after writing about the complexity of a causative factor, he gradually introduced the idea of a softer, more general application of the frontier-sectional theory. The history of American society was not only complex but unique, according to Turner. "The evolution of a vast population" could be easily traced "as perhaps nowhere else in the world . . . from a thin line of European settlement fighting for existence on the edge of the Atlantic to a broad zone of civilization stretching across a continent and finding new problems beyond the rim of the Pacific." The task of the American historian, Turner continued, lay in revealing the course of this development. But at the same time these evolutionary social and economic changes were taking place, other social, economic, and political changes were occurring within the various sections. America, in fact, evolved into a "combination of sections rather than a single society."

The development of American society as Turner described it in 1908 had certain similarities to the oil-refining process in the modern petroleum industry. He used the image of a series of pipelines with different kinds of oil moving in the same direction toward the frontier line. Some of the pipes were larger than others, carrying several types of oil, none of which mixed except at the edges, but all of it flowing toward the great frontier refinery, which itself moved steadily west as a common refined product emerged from the crude elements. Yet the ultimate and specialized process of refining—the social, political, and economic shaping—was done in regional or sectional refineries over a period of time after the frontier had passed by. The larger sections—New England, the South, the middle region—and subsections (what Turner called "the Northwest and North Central" and the "Gulf Plains") worked out their own social organization that eventually was made to harmonize with the national "democratic society on a vast scale."

Foremost among the larger problems of national and sectional social adjustment were capital-labor conflicts and class rivalries. Moreover, the concentration of population in the cities and the emergence of powerful corporations suggested to Turner that the great challenge facing modern America, a situation linked to the end of the frontier era, was "to solve the problem of social justice in the spacious domain given to us."

In his presidential address to the American Historical Association in 1910, "Social Forces in American History," Turner observed that Americans, engaged in the task of the readjustment of "old ideals to new conditions," had turned more and more to government to preserve "traditional democracy." The western states in particular made demands for referendum initiatives and recalls as "substitutes for that former safeguard of democracy, the disappearing free lands." In analyzing these changes, Turner advised his fellow historians "to study the present and the recent past, not only for themselves, but also as the source of new hypotheses, new lines of inquiry, new criteria of the perspective of the remoter past." Turner spoke of history as "the lamp for conservative reform" and of "present development" as a vantage point from which to observe "what new light falls upon past events."

Turner had seen Wisconsin gradually change from an agricultural to an industrial state, a process which was to continue during his years at Harvard. Turner began to modify his initial view of the frontier soon after the essay of 1893 had been published. In 1902 he commented to his History of the West class on the role that big business had played in social development: "Rockefeller, Carnegie, and so on," Turner said, "may prove to be

Turner in 1904 at his home at 629 Francis Street, Madison, Wisconsin. (Courtesy, Henry E. Huntington Library and Art Gallery)

pioneers in the direction of social activity, for they have taught the people how to use large masses of capital for large social ends by great social organization, in sharp contrast with individual methods." But his letters during the Harvard period, especially those written to Mrs. William Hooper, show his concern over the growing influence of industrial and financial leaders on national politics. Turner was aware of the irony of an increase in financial pressures in politics at a time when party platforms were calling for reform and social justice. In discussing the various potential candidates for the presidency in 1912 (Woodrow Wilson, William H. Taft, Theodore Roosevelt, and Robert La Follette), Turner remarked on the "interesting influence of great wealth at present. . . . Every candidate, apparently, is relying on some group to finance its operations." "How," he asked, "can a popular movement, designed to afford social justice, and to regulate the present tendencies, win control over wealth, when its nutriment comes from one or other opposing financial groups?"

Turner's first book of essays, *The Frontier in American History* (1920), had been the subject of a caustic review by Charles Austin Beard, who complained of Turner's neglect of the class struggle and especially of the urban conflict between capital and labor. Turner, who was well aware that rural society was being replaced by large cities and that giant industries were taking over much individual enterprise, soon made notes for an essay, "The City, Frontier, and Section; or the Significance of the City in American History."[2] Although the notes are fragmentary, they suggest a number of provocative avenues (to this day unexplored) for the investigation of urban history.

The relationships between the passing frontier, the emerging sections, and the rise of the city interested Turner; "When and how and why did cities become densely populated?" His suggestion that urban growth paralleled the diminishing availability of free land, an application of his safety-valve theory, has been favorably noted by modern economists and sociologists. Turner begins his notes on the city with these suggestions to himself:

Do a paper on Significance of the City in American History. Examine Beard's contentions. Show relationships between Frontier,

Section and City: Capital, manufacturing, Trade, Banking and Currency; Labor; Immigration etc.

Write on the influence of the frontier phenomenon, on urban development, manufacturing, labor, immigration. In short, in successive essays, exhibit the relations between eastern phenomena and western growth. Examine Beard's contentions.

> Resources, investment of capital (free land drank up capital)
>
> Expanding market and demand
>
> Synchronize urban growth with diminishing free land—(available and "good")
>
> Examine where immigration went and why and when
>
> When do labor questions become acute

I have written and lectured more on the subject than Beard recognizes—See my book and my notes.

Use data on city growth in relation to developing section and extension of frontier; show how sectional rivalry for extending frontier, new settled regions and new resources affected urban society. When and how and why did cities become densely populated and why? How did urban (including alien) ideas, interests and ideals react on frontier and sectional items?

Extent to which the cities were built up by movement from interior rural areas to the city—Especially leaders.

See my data on "Children of Pioneers" based on "Who's Who."

Also read literature on the city—e.g. a German study—whose?—which shows how a city eats up its own children and is recruited by the young men of the country. See Clark's Nature and Nurture. Read book in Columbia Studies on Municipality by Maltby.

The city dependent upon natural resources, and markets, furnished by extending frontier, and by the talent supplied by areas recently (relatively) frontier areas. Include editors, teachers, preachers.

Its counter influence in modifying frontier and sectional traits. Urban press and patent insides and press syndicates destroy country journalist's individuality. But still leave sectionalism.[3]

Turner reworked essay after essay and in the process reexamined his frontier-sectionalism theories in the light of new events. The impact of the city and the corresponding effect on the frontier and the section crept into two of his later essays, "The West—1876 and 1926" and "Children of the Pioneers." Despite the fragmentary character of his notes, they perhaps reveal what Richard Hofstadter observed as an arrested Turner intellect,[4] that is, his lifelong pioneer bias. After the age of forty Turner confined himself to writing exhortatory works, yet at the same time, a source of his strength was his eagerness to adapt his ideas to new themes.

In "The West—1876 and 1926," published in 1926 just before he went to the Huntington Library, Turner wrote of the rise of cities in the West where business, commerce, and maritime rivalry differed little from the competition among their counterparts on the Atlantic coast. Los Angeles and Seattle had exhibited "daring initiative and community spirit" by developing waterfronts and harbors and by bringing water supplies and electricity over long distances so that these necessary facilities kept pace with the growth of the cities. The opening of Alaska, Turner said, provided a fresh pioneer and frontier spirit for the Pacific Northwest and for the country at large. He believed that community interests and public opinion in the Far West were stifling some of the earlier individualism but that initiative, optimism, and "the old love of bigness" still remained. Turner pinpoints these mixed characteristics of the modern westerner; underneath the pioneer spirit, despite the tendencies toward social and political reforms, lay "a deep conservatism . . . a union of democratic faith and innovation with a conservative subconscious." Turner's description of the West as a stronghold of conservatism has a modern ring. The political strength of conservative Republicanism of the 1960s through the 1990s in the mountain states, the Southwest, and along the Pacific coast suggests that he had judged the temper of its people correctly.

Before Turner died in 1932 he had the pleasure of knowing that his writings had a powerful impact upon American historiography and allied fields. But that a whole series of legislative enactments would be pushed through Congress the year after his death based on the theoretical framework provided by his theory on the disap-

Turner's home in Cambridge at 7 Philips Place. (Courtesy, Henry E. Huntington Library and Art Gallery)

pearance of free land was a consequence that Turner was too modest to imagine. Certainly he would have been pleased to know that his own research into the past had proved useful in bringing needed legislation to the present, for his attitude toward historical scholarship was not only highly professional but also strongly socially oriented. And indeed, few historians have influenced their times so markedly as did Turner.

His emphasis on the importance of free land in the growth of American democracy and the belief that legislative action in the present must perform the tasks that earlier conditions had automatically brought about convinced many people to support the New Deal; the measures to be enacted, it was believed, would restore by law certain equalities that had previously been provided by socioeconomic conditions in America. Members of the New Deal braintrust seemed convinced that the demise of the economic stimulus that had been generated by the frontier necessitated legislative action to promote national "pump priming." Pres. Franklin D. Roosevelt, who had been exposed to Turner's ideas at Harvard, often stressed the concept that an ordered economic society must take the place of unbridled individualism in order to preserve democracy and freedom of opportunity, the "legacy of the process of occupation of free lands." Roosevelt, in a Commonwealth address of 1932, said, "Our last frontier has long since been reached, and there is practically no more free land. . . . There is no safety-valve in the form of a Western Prairie to which those thrown out of work by the Eastern machines can go for a new start." Roosevelt was not the last president who acted under the influence of Turnerian ideas. The Fair Deal program of Harry Truman's administration and John F. Kennedy's New Frontier illustrate the continuing validity of Turner's judgment.

The free-land thesis that had had such an impact on American politics, especially the political outlook of the modern Democratic party, is forcefully stated in Turner's 1903 essay, "Contributions of the West to Democracy." In discussing the influences promoting the growth of American democracy, Turner wrote:

> Most important of all has been the fact that an area of free land has continually lain on the western border of the settled area of the United States. Whenever social conditions tended to crystalize in the East, whenever capital tended to press upon labor or political restraints to impede the freedom of the mass, there was the gate of escape to the free conditions of the frontier. These free lands promoted individualism, economic equality, freedom to rise, democracy. Men would not accept inferior wages and a permanent position of social subordination when this promised land of freedom and equality was theirs for the taking. . . . In a word, then, free lands meant free opportunities. . . . The free lands are gone. The material forces that gave vitality to Western democracy are passing away. It is in the realm of the spirit, to the domain of ideals and legislation, that we must look for Western influence upon democracy in our own days.

What portended for America after the end of the frontier? The notion that the West was, as Henry Nash Smith has noted, "the Garden of the World," an escape valve that could provide utopian outlets for America's ills, posed a dilemma. Turner was all too conscious of this dilemma and saw with some amusement that political leaders in the early 1930s were taking it upon themselves to explain that older agrarian ideals of the nineteenth century were out of date in the twentieth century. Turner had given much thought to various aspects of the problem, as his unpublished notes and essays demonstrate, but he suggested no panaceas. In a letter to one of his former students Turner gives his reaction to the use of "the frontier idea" by political leaders and various "clashing groups":

> Dear Schafer:
>   Thank you for sending me Governor LaFollette's Inaugural. My "Frontier" has been republished in a socialist magazine, in a pedagogical review, and in Bullock's *Writings in Economics* [and Bullock is of the anti-socialist group],[5] so that I am not unwilling to see myself mentioned in so handsome a way also by the Progressive governor! In point of fact, while LaFollette, Sr., was governor I found myself in agreement with his general politics, and I think that he was an important influence in shaping American tendencies in his time—although he shaped a course that I could not altogether agree with in his later years. Nor do I agree with the attitude of Senator Robert LaFollette, 2d, in his attacks upon Hoover. However to be mentioned and quoted in the opening sentence of an Inaugural is an honor that was quite unexpected.
>   The acceptance of the frontier idea, by these clashing groups, of course, leaves them open to their own respective substitutes for it now that it has gone—as a determining influence in American life. Into that problem I do not venture just now! I don't want to be anybody's patron saint! Can't fill the bill!
>   I am always very glad to hear from you and of the progress.[6]

Turner himself rarely referred to his free-land thesis as the safety valve theory; under this name, however, it became the subject of heated academic debate and provided over several decades a justification for programs of social reform. The first of these, Woodrow Wilson's "New Freedom" program of progressive legislation, was based on recognition of the end of a frontier era. Wilson was extremely fond of and much influenced by Turner, and his book on the Civil War era, *Division and Reunion*, reveals an acceptance of much of Turner's thought. Turner, for his part, returned this friendship. Their up-and-down relationship is fascinating because of the interplay of ideas between them. Their gradual separation was brought about by Wilson's rise in American politics and his declining interest in scholarship.

As early as 1892 Turner had published a rough version of some of his ideas in an essay, "Problems in American History."[7] In a letter to William E. Dodd, Turner later commented on this early version of the frontier theory: "Prior to my paper in AHA 1893 I had not read Ratzel, or Godkin or other writers who deal with this problem." He had, however, read Henry George's *Progress and Poverty* as well as Francis A. Walker's essays, which contain a clear statement of the frontier theory. Wilson's *Division and Reunion*, which Turner called "a model of brief history," was published in March 1893; its first chapter reflected Turner's ideas on western history, and Wilson had in fact received from Turner a copy of the frontier essay.

During the summer of 1893 Turner revised his "Problems" paper and produced the essay on the significance of the frontier for the Chicago session of the American Historical Association. Wilson was not at the Chicago meeting, but Turner recalled that "he was at my house some time within the year 1893 and I read it to him in the manuscript. I recall my gratitude to him for his general approval and for the word 'hither' as descriptive of the eastern edge of the frontier."

Wilson persistently tried to bring Turner to Princeton, and after the trustees of the university declined to offer a chair to Turner, Wilson became such a prominent leader of faculty opposition to the administration that he was catapulted into the office of the presidency there. The friendship between the two men managed to survive a period of coolness caused by Turner's biting review of Wilson's *History of the American People*, a lavishly illustrated five-volume publication that might more appropriately have appeared in a single volume. Turner was obviously appalled at these ornate books with their "frequent irrelevancy of illustrations." "The stream of narrative," he complained, "too frequently runs like a rivulet between illustrations." But above all Turner criticized the oversimplification in Wilson's account of the forces at work during the American Revolution:

> Here one finds a lack of attention to the important facts of economic and political significance that were so powerful in shaping the sections during that period, in preparing the way for American political parties and institutions, in shaping the conditions that affected the Revolution, and in creating forces that expressed themselves in American expansion.

Turner added, with an apparent attempt to soften his criticism, "This is the period that has suffered at the hands of all historians." Then Turner listed a page of Wilson's errors, prefacing it with this comment: "Aside from matters of judgment the author has not fallen into more errors of fact than are common to first editions."[8] In spite of more favorable comments in the latter part of the review, the overall impression was that Wilson had rushed into publication with a mass of ornate verbiage lavishly got up for a gullible public. Yet Wilson's attempt to complete his five-volume work before assuming the presidency of Princeton was no doubt partly responsible for the defects of *The History of the American People.* Merrill H. Crissey, Turner's secretary, said that the review almost broke up the long friendship, and certainly, following this incident, Turner was more cautious about writing book reviews.

Indeed, Turner's failure to publish his fascinating and critical appraisal of Von Holst's history (Turner's fifty-page manuscript in which he again stressed the complexity of historical forces) may well have stemmed from his experience in reviewing Wilson's book. After demolishing what he thought was Von Holst's one-sided approach to American history, Turner explained what made good history: accuracy, and beyond that, historical proportion but also a sense of motion reflecting the dynamic quality of American society. In describing the historian's problems, Turner wrote: "In my opinion more harm may be done by an improper perspective or by omissions, than by defects in regards to accuracy of statement."[9] Turner's criticism of his fellow historians centered on this weakness of their refusal to see the dynamic quality of history, of their insistence on compiling meaningless "bricks and mortar" or static factual data. Most of them lacked, in short, the ability that Turner possessed in full measure—to estimate the significance of historical events in relation to the time in which they occur, to later periods, and to the present.

In spite of the strains brought about by Turner's review of Wilson's book, the friendship between the two men persisted through later decades, and indeed their attitude toward history formed a strong link between them. For both men, the happenings of their own day were a vital part of their professional concerns. After Wilson became president of Princeton, the correspondence between the two men came to a virtual halt; nevertheless Turner's views on current problems remained known to Wilson. During the peace negotiations after World War I, Turner wrote a paper on the League of Nations discussing the possibility of international political parties and using American history with its sectional and political rivalries as a useful example of the problems and opportunities arising in such circumstances. A copy of this paper, "What lessons has the history of the United States for the necessary conditions of a League of Nations," reached President Wilson in December 1918, passed on to him by Turner's colleague Charles Homer Haskins.

An earlier draft opened with a description of the basic problem of the League. "The weakness of a league of nations lies in its national elements, certain of which particularly are likely to intrigue and make combinations. This is likely to result," Turner argued, in the use of force by the League, "to enforce its decrees." Turner then compared the American sections with the European nations: "The United States, which extends over a region equal to Europe has in its component sections, such as Northeast, South, Middle West, Pacific Coast, potential national elements, and yet with one tragic exception, it has kept the peace, the area of the federal system, has preserved the Pax Americana." Had the American sections "been united in a mere league even though they lacked the elements of different languages, cultures, etc. to divide them as Europe is divided, they would have been broken asunder."

What kept the sections from going their different ways? The national political parties:

> The strong point in intersectional or national political parties is that they create and maintain a community of feeling and purpose between the minority party of one section and the majority party of another. They break down sectional unity and sectional loyalty and enable the minority to find allies and a higher loyalty in national political parties. At the same time, sectional interests are safeguarded in a national system by the need each party has to conciliate the special sectional interests of its component elements, lest the party lose its national character and its national following.

Turner then turns to the international situation: "If we substitute for 'America,' 'Europe'—or 'World'; for 'section' 'nation'; for 'Congress,' or 'national convention,' the representative central power of a 'League of Nations,' we see the bearing of American experience upon the World problem." Yet the League as it was to be constituted would not really resemble the American system: "A mere league of nations means coercion of well knitted national cultures and restraint of separate national ambitions by a majority of other rival nations using force." To achieve a lasting peace on an international scale, Turner advocated that "central organization of the league of nations" be based on a structure of government "drawn from the American experience."[10]

To this end, Turner suggested a system of "representation of the people themselves rather than nations as entities." Second, he thought that the League might have "a popular legislative body as well as a council of nations." Third, the legislative body should have "a field for League legislation, preferably bearing on individuals." Although the field for legislation might be limited at first, Turner thought that through experience, it could be enlarged so that, for instance, "a declaration of war should be effective only by a majority vote of representatives of the people." He also suggested that "hours and conditions of labor, even minimum wages for all nations be matter for such action of the League's legislative body made up of popular representatives." A narrow area for legislation could be "action regarding the budget of the League." The principle involved, he felt, was "to give the legislative body of the league some tangible, though limited substantive powers."

Such a structure would lay the groundwork for the growth of international political parties to direct League policy:

> The trend toward internationalism would find an organ for action in the international political party. International political party loyalty would begin to serve as a check upon nationalism while still affording legitimate opportunity for the play of national forces and interests, just as sectional forces and interests find play in American national political parties. . . . Which is preferable? (1) a League liable to disruption on the first real clash of national interests with a new international war; or (2) a League in which there is provision for representation and legislation by the people of all nations dividing into rival international parties? Shall we mitigate the solidarity of national particularism by the solidarity of international party interests? The bearing upon the problem of drawing the teeth of secret diplomacy and of checking nationalistic imperialism is obvious.

Speaking of America, Turner asserted that

> national (intersectional) political parties have been a most important factor in limiting sectional particularism, furnishing as they did, a bond of union between men of different sections, and a basis for adjustment of sectional differences more effective than negotiation between sections.[11]

The American experience further demonstrates that the political party was "the most effective single political institution for the prevention of sectional disunion"; indeed, "the last tie that snapped before the Civil War, was the party tie."[12] If American national political parties had helped to preserve the "Pax Americana" and had helped to prevent the separate states and sections from "menacing the union, the same might be achieved on a world scale. Political parties were of the greatest importance in preventing the section from becoming a nation."[13]

Although Turner considered himself a liberal and had voted for William Jennings Bryan in 1908, he feared the potential power of left-wing parties in international politics. The American Democratic and Republican parties often enough confronted each other from opposite sides of the fence; yet in the end they usually preferred an omelet to "bad eggs separately." American political leaders of his own time seemed to him a mixed lot: Theodore Roosevelt, for instance, struck Turner as too closely allied to the financiers. Turner recognized, however, that neither of the national parties had a monopoly on progressives—or for that matter on conservatives.

Turner's fear of the influence of the Left in international politics was such that in 1918 he suggested that the stability of the world might be threatened by allowing Bolsheviks legitimate standing as a party. The "internationalization of such parties as Social Democracy, Bolsheviki, I.W.W." might result "in endangering the social order." Such parties could be used by what Turner called "national imperialists" for international penetration and propaganda. Yet Turner was not quite convinced by his own arguments. These international parties were already at work, "a menace to society as well as social peace. Would not the conversion of these revolutionary movements into political agitation under responsible parties and in the open, be preferable to secret intrigue and nationalistic penetration?" Would not "institutional recognition" have its advantages? The idea of international political parties within an international organization or League might seem, Turner said, "fantastic, at first, and it may be premature. But it demands careful thought."

At any rate, the main danger that America might face from a League of Nations with supranational parties would be an involvement in internationalist Socialist parties and in class rivalries. Turner noted: "This might result in aggravating class struggles and extending over America the destructive type of extreme socialistic proposals. . . . Would international struggles be replaced by class struggles on a world scale?"[14] An important point to consider, Turner argued, was "whether such struggles will be less harmful under world parties given a legitimate field for action, than under the conditions which foster revolutionary action and secret propaganda." To bring the international parties out in the open had certain advantages for America; moreover, it was a realistic approach to international problems.

Had the United States more to lose by supporting increased popular participation in government on an international scale, than by seeing radical socialism develop revolutionary tendencies on a national scale with secret international connection? Already the evidence of the birth of such political parties is seen in international Labor Conferences, and in less obvious ways, no doubt, in conferences of the representatives of capital. In sinister form the extension of Bolshevik and I.W.W. organizations illustrates another tendency to the internationalization of party movements. These tendencies will not die out.[15]

The threat posed by the international Socialist and Communist parties would find its counterpart on the Right in "the nationalistic rivalries of capitalism." The formation of an international conservative party, however, might ensure against the prevalence of national interests.

The rivalry of conservative and leftist parties on an international scale might eventually lead to "the growth of an international esprit de corps, international political interests, as a check upon extreme and aggressive national action." It might even be possible to develop the remaining world frontiers through international action. Nationalism would be held in check by loyalty to the international parties. "Would not war be replaced by party strife on an international scale? Would such an outcome not be preferable?"[16]

The amount of influence Turner's views had upon the peace negotiations is difficult to determine. C. H. Haskins, who was a member of the American Commission to Negotiate the Peace, received two copies of Turner's paper, one of which was found among Wilson's papers and later published in the *American Historical Review*. Unfortunately, this revised version lacks much of the liveliness of Turner's less formal writings—his drafts of papers and his letters. This final version again stresses the possibility that the violence caused by nationalism might be restricted by a growing class consciousness. In any case, the threat of the "Bolsheviki serpent" coming into the "American garden of Eden" was present with or without international parties.[17] And in connection with the class conflict abroad, Turner thought that the United States, by improving living standards for workers in other countries, would diminish the probability of revolution and increase international trade and American overseas commerce. The loss of national control over many important interests was the price America would have to pay for the League. There was the additional risk that an "ultraconservative majority" would restrain reform in certain nations. But despite national suspicions and fears, the whole scheme might be worked out by introducing a system of checks and balances in the League structure.

In the period between 1918 and 1919, Turner poured out his feelings on the international situation in letters to Mrs. William Hooper. On October 9, 1919, he commented:

> The World is certainly on a rampage, but I still expect that after the fever the patient will recover, purged of some grossness and in a higher frame of mind and body. The temperature is alarmingly high just now, it must be admitted. . . . The real question isn't imperialism, but social revolution. This I believe is in progress; but I have confidence that it will have learned the limitations of itself by the Russian object lesson, and proceed slowly and experimentally. But who knows?[18]

In another letter to Mrs. Hooper a month later Turner again voiced his opinion on the form the League should take:

> I still think the League can operate as it should only when it acquires a legislative body and acts, not as a diplomatic congress of chess playing representatives of the old conceptions of balance of power, and diplomatic cleverness, but as voicing whatever internationalism there is among the various countries. I believe Germany must be taken in, and ultimately Russia, otherwise there will be two leagues at least, with Italy and Japan, and lesser states holding a position where they can trade for concessions from each, and punish one by joining the other. So I support the League as a halfway measure, and an alternative to something worse, rather than because of belief in it as it stands in the proposed treaty. Moderate reservations by compromise, and these to include the power to withdraw and no mandates—these constitute my policy—and the policy has this value—namely that you asked me to send it to you. If you don't like it, you can burn it up in your cosy grate-fire, and there will be no damage done, will there? What a comfort![19]

Turner did not admire the role of Henry Cabot Lodge in the League's affairs:

> I shall not be surprised to see the treaty lost, so far as the League goes. The Lodge group, made up in part of men who framed the reservations to kill, not to remedy the imperfections in the League plan, refused to allow a vote on any compromise between their plan and unreserved ratification. The thoughtful part of the nation wishes "moderate reservations" and interpretations, not rejection. Probably the necessary 2/3 of the Senate wishes the same thing. But Lodge is culpable for not allowing the test. Free government requires both discussion and fair opportunity for choice between the necessary number of options to really test sentiment and purpose. . . . There is a vigorous body of friends of the League, and believers in an America that is constructive and capable of leadership instead of an America that fears "Innovation" and is timid in the presence of new conditions, and distrustful of its power among other nations in council; and there is a love of fair play. There is also a dislike of the Senate. If the President had not been stricken down by his over-exertions—and I suppose any repetition of them might cause a recurrence of the malady—he might rally these forces even now to compel a compromise. . . . Europe has some of its own imperfections and problems and past wickedness for which it must pay the penalty by itself. We needn't become European in order to play a reasonable part in the League.[20]

America's participation in the League, Turner believed, need not mean that the country be drawn into European politics and "the struggles for power." In one of his essay fragments on the League, Turner states:

> If there is to be any modification of the old world, let it come to us and follow our practices and system rather than that we should take the burden of the inheritance of the sad old world habits and experiences. We have our ideal of individuality and freedom to rise under competition as well as the ideal of co-operative democracy and efficiency in government. Nor should we abandon our right and our duty to find new ways ourselves.[21]

After the rejection of the Versailles Treaty, Turner's attention moved away from international affairs; but he never ceased to fear a new, second world war.

In 1923 Turner made notes for a series of talks on "the outcome of the Westward Movement and the transitional epoch 1800–1900."[22] Strikingly absent from these notes is the natural optimism with which Turner normally regarded the national and international problems facing his country. Overpopulation, the drift toward war, and the possibility of a "chemist's bomb" left no room for a facile cheerfulness.

These calamities, which might perhaps best be handled through a League of Nations, seemed to actualize for America after the "end of the long migration of peoples," the closing of the frontier era. In the thirty years from 1893 to 1923, interest had grown in problems of "food resources, and population, and inter[national] relations." Until 1900 the continent had been in the process of being occupied; but by 1920 the Malthusian problem of population growth and the related problem of resources could no longer be ignored. An international "war for supplies," already in progress, suggested to Turner the possibility of the "internationalization of resources." How, he wondered, would democracy be affected by such a development?

As a firm believer in his own theory, Turner concluded that the sections were in many respects the American equivalents of nations, but unlike the European nations, American sections generally had managed to live in harmony with one another. Turner thought it possible, therefore, that if the American situation could be better understood in Europe, a similar era of peace might result for that troubled continent.[23]

More specifically, Turner envisioned a changed Europe in which the individual nations would relinquish certain of their powers to a supranational government and in which political parties cutting across national boundaries would play the same binding role that national political parties have played in America. He believed that Socialists, Communists, conservatives, and liberals would contribute to an international political party system that could prevent the world from being blown to bits in a catastrophic war. To deny the existence of international political parties, according to Turner, was to ignore reality, for if the various political parties were not officially recognized by an international governing body, they would surely maintain worldwide ties through underground affiliations. It was urgent, Turner believed, that all measures be considered in a worldwide "strategy for peace."[24]

The kind of supranational government Turner had in mind would have powers of various kinds: It might set up minimum wages and conditions of labor, it might regulate international commerce, it might even have a final decision in questions of war or peace. But Turner did not believe that the League of Nations, as it was actually constituted, could forge links strong enough to hold the nations together under the pressures that were sure to grow. Turner's ideas on the ways in which international conflicts might be avoided by making use of the successful techniques tried out in the course of United States history were, of course, never put into effect.

But it can be argued that Turner's ideas on the ways in which internal conflicts might be avoided were influential in the programs for reform instituted by Franklin D. Roosevelt and his successors. Turner had recognized that with the closing of the frontier—with the disappearance of the supply of free land that until the end of the nineteenth century had been available for the discontented, the poor, and the adventurous who were prepared to try their luck at the edge of the civilized world—legislative programs would become increasingly necessary to protect and to provide opportunities for a population no longer the fortunate possessor of a reservoir for advance and compromise in the West, America's safety-valve. It can also be argued that the steady stream of measures for social and political reform in this century that has done so much to improve the quality of American life stems in some degree from the theoretical basis provided by Turner's ideas concerning ways to keep conflict in America at a minimum. Turner's self-assumed task was to show the ways in which organized society had in the past and must in the future create machinery for solving conflicts—not by violence, not by warfare, but through persistent political bargaining and compromise.

A great deal more might be said about Turner's ideas on sectional and international conflicts. Turner would be the first to agree that much more needs to be done in exploring the historical processes connected with war and modern international relations. Above all, he believed that social justice was key in establishing domestic peace in America.[25] If an international government were to be established Turner was convinced that it would have to entail some kind of political bargaining to make a portion of the richest resources available to peoples who lacked basic necessities.[26] Turner clearly recognized that insidious threats to a world order existed. World War I had jolted him from his comfortable berth in nineteenth-century frontier-sectional conflicts, and he found even greater perils in the twentieth-century Malthusian problems facing the modern world.

Bernard Bailyn in a recent address, "The Boundaries of History: The Old World and the New," delivered at the dedication of the John Carter Brown Library, offers a critique of Turner's worldwide "creative frontier." Bailyn sees New World settlements as a "periphery"; North American frontier societies were part of a "peripheral world, a diminished world," looking inward. Such is Bailyn's counterargument to Turner's earlier 1904 address at the Brown Library. Who is to say which view is correct? Bailyn's argument signifies that Turner's world-frontier views are still worth analyzing and discussing. Indeed the following chapter shows how zealously Turner attacked many of these catastrophic, insoluble issues.[27]

CHAPTER EIGHT

TURNER AND THE THREATS OF THE TWENTIETH CENTURY

Turner saw the threat of a population explosion everywhere and noted the complaints of "nordic alarmists" who spoke of a "rising tide of color." Biologists, geographers, economists, and sociologists warned of the coming difficulties. Thus Turner proposed to give "a *bomb* talk—or *Gloom*"; this talk was to include a consideration of the alternatives as he saw them: "perpetual War or [a] World State." He admired, he said, Herbert Hoover's stress on individualism, but he increasingly thought of collective action to save the planet.

Turner's notes expressed his own theories that led him to expect that the end of the frontier period of settlement would result in internal strife, to "fighting at close quarters by the strongest and by combinations to prevent extinction of pioneer types and ideas." He foresaw America's more aggressive overseas policies and the rapidly developing international political and commercial competition. At home, Americans would have to adjust to more static conditions and would have to come to grips with racism and the question of immigration. Labor and management problems, the class struggle, and the unjust distribution of wealth would loom larger on the domestic scene; Turner asked himself whether the cultured and capitalistic classes were doomed to extinction. Is "the end of the process like the beginning? . . . What a different U.S.! I have been predicting the tendency in all my work . . . an interlude? Like Slavery struggle?"

In his folder "Strategy of a Saturated Earth," Turner jotted down some conclusions about the population problem using a historical perspective. It was typical of Turner to look at the American present and then peer back to antiquity for a light that might explain the present and the future. He saw American history as a connected story of expanding life and civilization from the days of the rudest flint hatchet to the great cathedrals of Europe's Middle Ages without a serious gap. Society, art, literature, commerce, industry, religion were all part of the history of each age, and each society was influenced by that which preceded it. Thus Turner began his analysis of America's dilemma over population and food by pointing out that Stone Age man had been conscious of this challenge. Turner's notes paraphrase other writers such as Griffith Taylor:

The problem of overpopulation and deficient supply of food and raw material is not a new one for overpopulation is a relative term. The Indian like the primitive man before him forcibly resisted the advance of other tribes who coveted his hunting grounds and the cattle raiser and the farmers of civilized races who need the hunting grounds for agriculture. The German tribes who migrated into the Roman empire sought new lands for food as well as were attracted by the hope of spoils. The land that might be over populated under a cattle raising economy, would support a much larger population of grain raisers, and would hold a vastly larger manufacturing population, if its food supply would be obtained from without. Moreover, the planet is not a homogenous unit. It is divided into favorable and unfavorable geographic regions for agriculture and for the varied kinds of agriculture. It holds in certain areas the stores of coal and petroleum and iron that furnish the basis for modern industry. It is made up of regions favorably situated for transportation of needed supplies, and of lands at a disadvantage in these respects. These and like causes have from the days of Cain and Abel led men to fight for the possession of the desirable parts of the earth.

But if overpopulation is not a new problem, it is a problem that has acquired new meaning in our time. The studies which men have made of the causes of our World War, and particularly the studies which had to be made of the food supply of the earth in the course of that war and of its aftermath, have led to a multitude of works and monographs on this subject.[1]

In reading over what he called "alarmist" or "strategy" literature, Turner noted several times that the overpopulation problem held implications for racial conflict. Another complicating factor was that "a world struggle between higher civilizations with a lower birthrate and lower civilizations with a high birthrate" was a distinct possibility if the struggle did not develop between the "higher civilizations themselves for control of the sparser areas suitable to food and raw material production."

The United States would be drawn into such conflicts because of her favored position with large supplies of fertile land, minerals, and excellent climatic conditions. Turner cataloged the American "territorial control" of huge supplies of iron, coal, petroleum, copper, zinc, lead, gold, silver, sulphur, nickel, and potash and noted the United States' capacity to produce a large portion of the world's corn, cotton, wheat, and cattle. Basic to the world problem was "the strategy of control in the struggle for natural resources in relation to over population." Turner believed that the cliché "whoever rules the EurAsian 'Heartland' rules the world" was a poor analysis of the world power strategy. America's position was part of a "world ring"; in this ring the "centers of pressure" were Japan, China, and Western Europe. The United States, itself reaching a "saturation point" in its consumption of raw materials, food, and population growth, was "between these lands—itself a prize." How long could the United States enjoy its riches under these circumstances? The enormous increase of nonwhite populations in underdeveloped sections of the world suggested that a struggle would ensue between the "higher" civilizations with a lower birthrate and the "lower" civilizations with a high birthrate. How could war be avoided, and how could conflicting interests be coordinated? National boundaries often caused conflicts because they did not contribute to a balance of supplies of needed minerals, food, and productive soil. "The strategy of control," Turner noted, was one aspect of the "strategy of world questions," the struggle for natural resources in relation to overpopulation. America's problem was part of the world problem of population control, for by the year 2023, one hundred years from the time Turner was writing, the U.S. population alone might soar to 700 million persons. If all the world's acres were sown with wheat, the earth could support a population of 132 billion.[2]

An examination of Turner's notes and books in his personal library, most of which are in the Huntington Library's rare book collection or reference stacks, indicates the wide range of his reading. He was, for instance, an avid reader of the *Geographical Review,* and his copy of volume 12 shows that he marked several items. An essay by Griffith Taylor, an Australian scholar at the University of Sidney, impressed Turner with its emphasis on the favorable position of the United States with respect to temperature, minerals, rainfall, and other factors. Moreover, Taylor advanced the argument that a possible world conflict might result if "the white race" attempted to keep its "dominant position."[3] Turner also noted in the October 1922 issue a criticism of Taylor's alarmist views by a Cornell University scholar, Walter Wilcox, who questioned Taylor's facts, calling them "sweeping generalizations." Taylor had overlooked such factors as "volitional control" in the population problem and the advance of scientific agriculture in increasing the world food supply.[4] Some of these arguments were reiterated by Raymond Pearl, Johns Hopkins biologist and statistician, in an article in the same issue. Turner marked sections of the article stressing that the world's civilization was dependent upon certain production-to-population "ratios" in order to maintain its standard of living. Applied science, Pearl urged, was significant in coping with increased population, but there were only fixed amounts of certain products, such as coal. Turner noted Pearl's "curves" and "tables," indicating that he agreed with Pearl in seeing that increases in both population and standard of living could not go on indefinitely.[5]

Yet Pearl did not envision the world catastrophe as other writers had. Turner was drawn to Pearl because of their shared sympathy for the "environmentalist" point of view and because Pearl, like Turner, crossed boundaries to carry on research. Pearl had written a number of books and articles on poultry and on human biology, crowning his career with a five-year investigation that had resulted in a penetrating statistical study, *The Biology of Population Growth*.[6] Turner's personal copy of this book is heavily annotated and contains an envelope of articles, reviews, and clippings on population studies of the 1920s.[7] Pearl rejected what he called the "inevitable misery doctrine" for several reasons, one being that many heavily populated countries had high standards of living. In the "orderly evolution of human knowledge," science had found new ways to provide for "human subsistence." Moreover, and here Turner underlined the point in red pencil, "have we not overlooked to a large degree in our discussion of the population problem, the largely unknown and unplumbed adaptive potentialities of the human organism? . . . Birth control would seem to be a case in point. It is an intelligent adaptive response to an environmental force, population pressure."[8]

Turner's continued interest in the population problem after he had completed teaching his course on recent American history and had retired from Harvard motivated his reading of Pearl's book. The passages that he underlined indicate that he thought Pearl had found a real solution to the world problem in his relating birth control to the "adaptive potentialities of the human organism," what Pearl called "the crux of the whole matter." The perspective that Pearl advanced on birth control probably appealed to Turner because it represented an expansion of Turner's own theories on the growth of American society.

Moreover, Turner's notes from 1925–1926 show that he found additional evidence to support his environmentalist interpretation in an essay by Louis Israel Dublin, chief statistician to the Metropolitan Life Insurance Company, who in a 1926 article in the *Atlantic* declared that the "fallacious propaganda for birth control" overlooked "the influence of environment and tradition on our conduct and achievement." Dublin maintained that alarmists were putting forth a thinly disguised argument for "a race of supermen who presumably would spring only from the upper social and economic strata."[9] Dublin, born in Lithuania, was familiar with the humble origins of emigrant families and dismissed racist birth control literature that proclaimed the "Nordic myth" of superiority.[10] As late as 1928 Turner was clipping items from the *Los Angeles Times* and the *Pasadena Star News* that showed the "alarmists" to be in error. The "lengthening of life span," reports of declining birth-rates, and renewed interest in birth control added new dimensions to the population problem and made it seem less urgent.[11] Some of these clippings forecast "a hungry world," and Turner was concerned with that problem throughout his later life. In his 1923 folder, "Alarmist Criticism," he assessed the "limitations" of using "alarmists' data." He wrote of a tendency for scholars working in natural sciences such as biology and geography to break into new fields with too much confidence in the quantitative side and in the time factor. Yet, Turner added, "If their curves are too much based on insufficient data, and their generalizations seem at times incautious, and if the discrepancies between them are considerable they do accurately describe a *trend* of vital significance, unless conditions are revolutionized—of which there is no adequate prospect in sight."[12] Discoveries and inventions might lead to uses of "inferior soils" for food production. People might develop vegetarian diets. Birth control programs, he regretfully noted, would probably be used by the "best classes," resulting in an "inferior race." And there was the additional problem of dealing with and "adjusting" to various types of rivalries among races, nations, and classes.

In summarizing his arguments for the restraint of population growth, Turner spoke of the only alternatives: famine, pestilence, a "friendly comet," or "the flash of the earth by a chemical compound," a reference to the dreaded "chemist's bomb," which he feared would be used in a world war. If birth control were used, two problems arose:

> (1) The highly developed, cultured and prosperous classes—the bearers of the gains of civilization—already have small or no families—hardly perpetuating themselves. (2) At the other end, the poor and ignorant, and to a lesser degree (because of death rate) the slums multiply rapidly. How to restrain fecundity of such classes.[13]

Turner queried "the moral result." In another fragment, he noted the opposition of the Catholic church; Turner, a Unitarian, had no religious scruples over birth control. The population problem also had an effect on international relations, Turner noted, since excess population was "food for cannon." This "rivalry for superior numbers" he questioned: "*Are* numbers desirable—or quality?"

Turner was unsure about the reaction of America's middle class to birth control. The "plain people," he wrote, are "honest, natural, moral, substantial, reachable by the doctrine, but should they respond?" Middle-class approval would be necessary for any birth control program to succeed. Black and white rivalry, Turner thought, had been exaggerated, and there was in America a new "mulatto element." Turner's notes give the impression that he thought of the "infusing of the mulatto" as a favorable development for improving relations between Caucasians and Negroes. One of the last fragmentary notations Turner made on the problem of controlling lower-class reproduction (he was still teaching his course on recent U.S. history) was "Problem of breeding for the fit, sterilization of the unfit—selection. Not workable."[14]

When Turner told his students in 1923 that he was offering a class in recent United States history because he wanted to know more about the period, he was motivated by the challenge of studying this problem of population growth and birth control. It was characteristic of Turner to take on a big problem; in fact the problem was so large that he gradually had to scale down his research on it in order to complete his book on the United States during the era 1830–1850. Yet it is important to know that Turner undertook the study of population control and left a record of his investigations and tentative conclusions even though he made no serious attempt to write on the subject.

His annotated books show that he profited from Harold Wright's *Population*,[15] Edward M. East's *Mankind at the Crossroads*,[16] and Warren S. Thompson's *Population: A Study in Malthusianism*[17] in addition to writers such as Raymond Pearl. Turner's study of population and food supply seems to be linked to his general interest in social history and economics. Thompson's conclusion that "Malthus was essentially correct" was heavily marked by Turner.[18] East, a biologist and a colleague of Turner's at Harvard, stressed in his study that population increase in the United States would go "beyond the maximum agricultural possibilities," a passage Turner underlined.[19] Yet East's somewhat frantic predictions were modified by Turner, who noted the importance of invention and discovery and the capacity of human beings to adjust to environmental change. Wright stressed that the complexity of the problem involved "the most intricate system of cooperation between individuals, classes, nations and races." Under these circumstances, Wright maintained that the issue of population control could not be dealt with "by the method of legislative enactment."[20] Turner's underlinings reveal that he was selecting conclusions that blended with his own.

Turner was also influenced by the two-volume textbook written by his Harvard colleague Frank William Taussig, who called himself a "political economist."[21] Turner's notes in his copy of Taussig's *Principles of Economics* noted Taussig's argument that "some parts of Malthus's teachings have been sustained" and that Darwin, impressed by Malthus, came to "a wider conclusion" that though elephants could double their population every one hundred years and cats could "bring forth sixfold twice or thrice a year," man, Turner wrote *"can* double population every twenty-five years." Another of Taussig's conclusions important to Turner was that "high birth rate goes down with high death rate in general hard conditions," an indication that Malthus's warnings, Taussig noted, were "applicable." Turner jotted down the exception to this generalization, "except in countries with abundant land," a point that had application in the United States. Turner concluded, "Resources as well as population are concentrated in regions, and the struggle will be between the nations which feel the pinch." Civilization in modern times was disinclined to occupy many areas in the tropics and the polar zones, and there was "a growing reluctance of newer countries to receive immigrants." The United States, for example, had restricted immigration. New immigrants added to the increasing population in America and would complicate the problem of dwindling natural resources, for by 1923, Turner wrote, "We have nearly cleaned up the original 800 million acres of virgin timber."[22]

We build machines to help us feed, cloth, and shelter our increasing population, Turner noted, but the machines cause problems by dividing us into groups and classes. We have given the name "machine" to our ruling bodies, calculate our "internal consumption" by "calories," and talk in terms of "scientific management." Thus Turner believed we had come to the point where "we must match our wits against the machines."[23]

But the machines, despite their widespread influence over contemporary society, could not solve the problem. For instance, Harold Wright's *Population* reemphasized the importance of population pressures in nations such as Great Britain, which had to depend on the New World for some of its food supply and also had to improve its industrial "capacity."[24] This point essentially restated the view of John Maynard Keynes, who, in his preface to Wright's book, noted that population was "the greatest of all social questions."[25] Keynes maintained that a transition period of human history was in sight when man would endeavor "to assume conscious control in his own hands, away from the blind instinct of mere survival."[26] An influential essay by Keynes that Turner read and marked heavily, "Is Britain Overpopulated?" defined overpopulation with a question: "Is not a country overpopulated when its standards are lower than what they would be if its numbers were less?" Although Keynes thought England's problem might be solved in part by emigration as "a palliative," he concluded: "It is not safe to leave the question of numbers unregulated, in the mere hope that we may be rescued by one of these conceivable but as yet unrealized improvements." Turner also heavily underlined the passage that followed:

> And even if we do realize them, is it not discouraging that they should only operate to compensate an increase of numbers, when they might, if there had been no increase, have availed to improve the lot of the average man?

The improvements that Keynes mentioned to "put off the evil day," such as greater accumulation of capital, swifter progress in science, "a raising of the acquired and inborn endowments of the average man, more common sense, intelligence, and public spirit," were only conceivable. He asked,

> Does it not seem that the greater part of man's achievements are already swallowed up in the support of mere numbers? Malthus's

Devil is indeed a terrible Devil because he undermines our faith in the real value of our social purposes.[27]

Thus the problem was tied up with economics, sociology, history, geography, politics, and a maze of forces and contradictions. But it could not be overlooked, and the dilemma remained.

John Maynard Keynes and Raymond Pearl both contributed to Turner's thoughts on the problem, each man stressing its complexity and its importance. Keynes, the British economist viewing the pressures the British Isles were facing, was less inclined to perceive any ameliorative prospects of environmental adjustment than was the biologist-statistician from Johns Hopkins. But both scholars agreed that some measures were necessary to control overpopulation. And Turner agreed as his notations again and again attest. It is a tragedy that he was unable to explore this problem with the concentrated research that could have produced a published essay. As it is, there are only notes, accumulated reference articles and clippings, and a collection of books with marginalia. Moreover, we are not always sure that Turner himself is speaking in these notes taken from a plethora of authors.

In 1925 when Harry Elmer Barnes completed his two books in history and the social sciences, *The New History and the Social Studies* and *The History and Prospects of the Social Sciences,*[28] Turner devoured them, eagerly searching for his own name. (When he checked the index references, he carefully noted by penciled page notes where the index was incomplete and where his name had been included in the texts.) In his *New History* Barnes pointed out that an exaggerated view of North and South sectionalism had been set forth by writers such as J. W. Draper in *The History of the Civil War:*

> It is, however, with the work of Frederick Jackson Turner and his more capable disciples that the development of a really dynamic historical geography of the United States is properly associated. By this thorough knowledge of the physical geography of the country, and his envisaging of American history as a process of conquering

the continent through an ever expanding frontier society, and as the achievement of welding together in a workable unity a group of diverse sectional societies and cultures produced by the variegated geography of the country, he has introduced more vitality and realism into the study of American history than any other American historian of this or any earlier generation.[29]

Turner welcomed this fine tribute as an exchange of letters between Barnes and Turner revealed. Barnes had written in his preface:

The new history consists primarily in reconstructing from the past the products of man's multiform activities as a member of changing and developing social groups and cultural complexes. Hence, it can completely pursue its objectives only when the historian is adequately grounded in the various social sciences which are necessary to clarify the nature of the diverse and complicated social and cultural situations in which man has been placed in the past.[30]

It should be noted further that Barnes interpreted Turner's view as the legacy of conquest. This is a fascinating rejoinder to Patricia Limerick's view of Turner's frontier. In many respects, Turner went beyond the "New History" in his quest for understanding American social history. He believed that the methods of natural science could be applied in the analysis of historical forces. The historian must be "breaking line fences, as hyphenated sciences do, Thermodynamics, Geo-physics, Geo-Botany, Geo History, Demography, Economics, Politics, Society, Religion . . . Ecological basis." Such disciplines could help in furthering an understanding of political parties.[31] The complexity of forces reached to Puritan times, and the historian should always guard against oversimplification. The "New History" of the Puritans is revealed in a comment that Turner made in the early 1890s in one of his manuscript lectures:

The American Puritans did not simply continue English political institutions under the changed conditions of the American environment, as was the case among the English colonies of the South and Middle regions. They came to America to put in practice a religious system and this religious system gave rise to new political forms, as in our own time economic demands change political institutions.[32]

Even the American "Hill Billies," Turner wrote, were the product of a complex of forces, among which were "inferior soils for ordinary agriculture." These people occupied "the rejected farm areas" of eastern America and could be studied in terms of "relations of land and people."[33]

Turner in his last years was clearly involved in the currents of sociopolitical and economic change. One has the feeling that, as his retirement approached, he saw that his pet ideas on frontier and sectional history might easily be bypassed, given the flood of new developments at home and abroad. We can see the Anglo-Saxon bias as he probes questions of birth control and the rise of Third World populations. He never did perceive, as William McNeill has argued in books and in public addresses, that the expanding frontiers of Europe into new lands were accompanied by labor shortages. This need to exploit the land with cheap labor brought about, as McNeill has convincingly maintained, the exploitation of native people in the form of slavery. Even in the colonies white indentured servants as well as slaves were used to fill this need for labor.[34]

But Turner, locked into his frontier-sectionalism ideas, tried in vain to see the twentieth century through the rose-colored glasses of his ruling theories.[35] We can even say that Turner was in some respects an opponent of African American history if that history was presented in the form of the struggle against slavery. That theme is rubbish, Turner argued in attacking Herman Von Holst, who saw the nineteenth century as a constitutional battle centering on the issue that we now call civil rights.

So it was that when Turner entered the world of the twentieth century, he tended to stagger under the weight of the intellectual baggage of his old theories. Yet Turner's ideas on world frontiers continued to be debated, and in this debate, as we shall see, William McNeill has his innings.

CHAPTER NINE

TURNER'S SHADOW ON WORLD FRONTIERS

Reading William H. McNeill's collection of lectures, *The Great Frontier: Freedom and Hierarchy in Modern Times*, is like embarking on a tour where one can observe through fleeting impressions patterns of expansion on remote frontiers.[1] From time to time one would wish to remain at a given place to observe details, but this is not possible. Frontier after frontier appears and disappears, sometimes in blurred images. In two lectures originally given at Baylor University, McNeill, a distinguished scholar of world history, tells briefly what global frontiers have meant to him. His arguments are clear, some of them set forth in ideas that have been filtered through his earlier books. But in this collection McNeill explicates an interpretation he has not emphasized in his other writings: the conception of the history of the world in terms of Europe's expanding frontiers.

A catalyst for his thinking is the frontier theory of the venerable Frederick Jackson Turner. McNeill also pays homage to one of Turner's disciples, Walter Prescott Webb, who wrote a much discussed volume on global frontiers called *The Great Frontier*. McNeill borrows from both Turner and Webb (including the title of Webb's book) but maintains that both men gave us an incomplete concept of the "reality" of the past.[2]

McNeill entitles his lectures simply "To 1750" and "After 1750." Even if one is not acquainted with his earlier books, one can discern that he deals with themes previously explored. He cites himself, especially his *Plagues and Peoples* (1976), to set forth basic propositions. He asserts, for instance, that cultural differentiation brings about continual change, a theme that emerges from his *Rise of the West, A History of the Human Community*.[3]

McNeill develops the fundamental argument that cultural variations were characteristic of the earth's landscape. Uniformity never existed, although there is simple evidence of high skills concentrated in a few centers. Factors that controlled the spreading of skills from civilized centers (McNeil does not precisely define his meaning of "civilization") were climate, disease barriers, and techniques of agricultural production. With generations succeeding one another, peoples from civilized centers moved to new places. McNeill, in short, shows us new perspectives on Turnerian frontiers, particularly those beyond our borders.

Europeans who occupied new areas already have experienced and developed immunities to certain diseases, giving them an epidemiological advantage over many non-Europeans. For example, lethal infections from Europe and Asia carried by immune Europeans proved to be real killers of indigenous New World Indian peoples. Indians died by the millions from the onslaught of smallpox, flu, measles, tuberculosis, diphtheria, and other infections. Those allegedly "empty" lands of the New World seized by the Puritans, for instance, had few native peoples because of the destruction of Indians by these epidemic diseases. There were similar epidemiological plagues decimating native peoples in Oceana, the Canadian Arctic, and South Africa, some of the disasters occurring as late as the 1940s.

Although the advance of the great European frontier ravaged native peoples with lethal diseases, native depopulation in contact zones was also caused by the introduction of guns, alcohol, and agricultural and industrial technology. When the Spaniards exhausted Indian labor to exploit mining wealth, they imported black slaves from Africa who proved to be a labor force largely resistant to certain diseases.[4] In North America, the British tried to enslave Indians for agricultural labor, but this policy proved to be unsuccessful (a complex story that McNeill has not developed).[5] Instead, the Tidewater colonial planters, in order to produce a "marketable wealth," developed a social hierarchy based upon a subordinated black slave-labor force. Gangs of indentured servants were also imported.

The importation of a labor force to the frontiers resulted from the basic need to exploit the land in a remote area where there was a shortage of labor. A society based upon masters, servants, and slaves produced a polarized social structure. Land ownership by the masters gave them control over a labor force that in time often became tied to the place where the labor was performed. By the 1750s the great frontiers of distant continents developed a group of managers and owners who dominated "an enslaved, enserfed, or debt-ridden work force."[6]

Changes in Europe brought about corresponding transformations on the global frontiers. After Europe achieved a certain equilibrium in surviving the Napoleonic wars, there was an increasing movement of disease-experienced individuals to remote global areas, to Oceana, to Australia, to Africa, and to North and South America. With the new technology of transportation revolutionized by railroads and steamships, the old legally enforced subordination of non-European labor cadres underwent radical modifications. The United States finally resorted to armed force to abolish slavery. In other areas, the British Empire for example, compensation was paid to slave owners. Mormons created a unique pattern of frontier penetration and settlement by doing the labor themselves and were successful because of their remarkable self-discipline.

The expansion of Europe's great overseas frontiers gradually diminished after 1914, McNeill concludes. World War I halted the flood of immigrants, and in the 1920s a series of quota systems appeared in the frontier areas, limiting migration.[7] Moreover, in Europe there were modifications in sexual habits and a lowering of family numbers and birthrates, trends that have continued. Fortunately for tribal peoples and other non-Europeans on the frontiers the late nineteenth and twentieth centuries brought a discernible repair to the early demographic disasters; widespread epidemics gradually disappeared.

Throughout the frontier expansion there were patterns of exploration and settlement in successive stages that were described by

Turner and Webb, both of whom overlooked the impact of diseases. Because of their "romantic delusion," McNeill argues that Webb and Turner also failed to recognize the issues of slavery and forced labor on the frontier. He then asks how such an oversight can be explained. McNeill speculates that both historians had "a cherished ideal of American liberty and equality" and that both men, throughout their lives, retained a nostalgia for their youth. When Turner and Webb were young men, they lived in communities that still had the trappings of a frontier society; as a result, their view of the reality of frontier history was skewed.[8]

McNeill, however, does concede that both Turner and Webb made a certain contribution to historical scholarship. Webb at least comprehended that American frontier expansion was part of a global process, and Turner sounded a "trumpet call" in stressing the significance of the frontier.[9] McNeill gives attention to both historians at the beginning and end of his lectures because he believes that their "romantic" pretensions should be put to rest.

Certainly McNeill has given a readable description and analysis of the great frontier. The significance of disease as a factor in European expansion is now recognized by historians, and surely the subordination and exploitation of a frontier labor force must be seen as a worldwide phenomenon in the heyday of European expansion into colonial empires. McNeill, however, is not the first to provide this graphic insight into the evils of colonialism; the enslavement or virtual enslavement of colonial peoples is a recurrent theme in contemporary historical scholarship.

Because McNeill's book may strongly influence the writing of international history and the concept of world frontiers, there are good reasons for setting forth other reservations critics might have. Admirers of Turner and Webb could well be disturbed by McNeill's neglect of the larger corpus of frontier scholarship (American and international), and McNeill apparently is unaware of many of the books written by Turner and Webb that supplement and modify their interpretations of frontier history. Unfortunately, McNeill's judgment of Turner's theories is based on a booklet by Margaret Walsh, an economic historian; an outdated study by Billington, *The American Frontier Thesis: Attack and Defense*; and an assessment of American frontier literature written some forty years ago. McNeill has limited his reading of Turner to one book of essays, *The Frontier in American History.*[10]

Although it appears that McNeill has dipped far enough into Turnerian literature to make a judgment about its worth, he nevertheless falls into the trap of setting up a straw man to demolish one essay that represents only a portion of what Turner later called the complexity of "the frontier process." This frontier process was an intricate and involved frontier sectionalism and is part of a multiple-causation concept of history in which Turner emphasized the slavery issue. McNeill censures Turner for disregarding slavery, but this allegation is not altogether true. Turner viewed slavery in terms of politics and sectional rivalry that formed patterns of regional and national political development. If Turner passed over the history of black-labor exploitation it was because his interpretations were tinged with Anglo-Saxon and Social Darwinist hues.

Similarly, Webb supporters may complain that McNeill sets up another straw man in selecting only one of Webb's books, *The Great Frontier,* as an object for criticism. McNeill passes over Webb's substantial contributions to environmental history set forth in *The Great Plains,* and he neglects Webb's other volumes that deal with sectional rivalry and controversies over water in frontier arid regions.[11]

Undoubtedly the most important book by Turner that McNeill ignores is *The Significance of Sections in American History.* There are, in addition, two other volumes of Turner's essays that have been in print for decades and are often consulted by scholars interested in the subtleties of Turner's theorizing. McNeill seemingly had little time to explore these studies before setting forth his criticism.[12] Moreover, McNeill has not consulted the literature attacking Turner on the themes of imperialism and world frontiers, the very subject of his own book.[13]

Critics of McNeill's methodology can point to the problem of selecting one or two "landmark" works on Turner to represent the man and his interpretations (McNeill uses this term to cite a book that gives him a basis for generalization). A deeper penetration of the literature on Turner discloses that his theory on sections has been applied to the international sphere.[14] Another deficiency in the landmark technique is that besides providing the reader with limited views of scholarship, such emphasis upon one book or essay fails on occasion to recognize scholars who have performed the basic research in a given field. For example, in tracing the impact of disease frontiers, McNeill neglects to credit the research of Sherburne F. Cook, Woodrow Borah, and Henry Dobyns (though he mentions them in *Plagues and Peoples*). Cook's and Borah's investigations in historical demography on California Indians and on native people in the Mexican highlands and the Caribbean are fundamental to any account of the spread of European disease epidemics on world frontiers.[15] Furthermore, scholars investigating the history of European commercial-industrial expansion into Third World frontiers may well be disappointed with McNeill's reluctance to mention the environmental factor of resource exhaustion and industrial pollution. McNeill's environmental blind spot might be pardoned if there were no visible evidence, no data, no literature on the subject. But even in the 1920s Turner was concerned with the severe problems of resource exhaustion, environmental chaos, and possible overpopulation and with the specter of war that might involve what he called a "chemist's bomb."[16]

Turner's interest in this topic was little known, but a host of writers have sounded the alarm. The names are familiar to readers in environmental history: George Perkins Marsh, John Muir, Aldo Leopold, Fairfield Osborn; more recently, Rachel Carson, Barry Commoner, Rene Dubois, Lewis Mumford, and Roderick Nash have added their voices. The abundance of environmental literature on world frontiers is further supplemented by three excellent new journals, *Environmental History Review, Environmental Ethics,* and the strident but authoritative *Sierra* published by the Sierra Club. And one may add to these sources the thousands of books, essays, notices, and bulletins coming from the presses of Common Cause, Friends of the Earth, and multiple wilderness and wildlife societies and organizations concerned with a global population explosion.[17]

Other critics may lament McNeill's missing a remarkable book of 1972 on global modeling of environmental frontiers, *Limits of Growth*. This book, assessing escalating damage from resource exhaustion and environmental pollution on global frontiers, was sponsored by a group of concerned scholars united in an organization called the Club of Rome. Although *Limits of Growth* was both hotly attacked and defended, it served notice that alarm signals were pointing toward world catastrophe. Among the book's supporters was Robert L. Heilbronner, who had serious concerns about the interrelationships among resource exhaustion, global pollution, population pressures, and the danger of nuclear war.[18] The debate resulted in a second volume by Club of Rome members in 1982, *Groping in the Dark, The First Decade of Global Modeling,* by Donella Meadows, John Richardson, and Gerhart Bruckmann. This unusual book is based upon international conference proceedings. A basic argument set forth is that computer models can reexamine paradigmatic assumptions such as "growth is good and bigger is better."[19]

Other literature on environmental frontiers, controversial, interdisciplinary, and voluminous, is more than visible. Critics of McNeill's reconstruction of *The Great Frontier,* recognizing his "remarkable omission of the environmental factor" may well conclude that he, as well as Turner and Webb, suffers from the imperfection of giving readers a limited view of "frontier reality." It is ironic that although Webb and Turner ignored certain aspects of this frontier reality they gave attention to the type of environmental history that stresses the impact of the land upon the individual and upon the society as a whole.

Turner's interpretations, far from being put to rest by McNeill and other critics, were the subject of a session of the American Historical Association (where McNeill presided), "Frederick Jackson Turner Remembered." Although his theories may well be criticized, paradoxically, as one book points out, Turner's message was phrased so well that his ideas live on as a "beckoning archetype" in the American self-consciousness. Ronald Carpenter's *The Eloquence of Frederick Jackson Turner* traces the development of Turner's oratorical style. Carpenter, a specialist in speech and rhetoric, convincingly argues that Turner became one of the most effective practitioners of his time by imitating polished orators in constructing "chain of impact" statements.[20]

One of Turner's devices was to use "parallelism." Some of his most effective parallel constructions were used time and again, for instance, "stand at Cumberland Gap" and "stand at South Pass," or "It was western New York" and "It was western Virginia."[21] As he worked his way through oration after oration and moved on to the creation of academic speeches and addresses, Turner practiced the use of antithesis in developing an epigrammatic style. To argue his own original approach to American history, he wrote, "Our early history is the study of European germs developing in American environment. Too exclusive attention has been paid by institutional students to Germanic origins, too little to American factors." He used antithesis again to illustrate the transformation of the European as he entered an American environment: "It takes him from the railroad car and puts him in the birch canoe. It strips off the garments of civilization and arrays him in the hunting shirt and moccasion."[22] Carpenter, in assessing Turner's stylistic techniques, concludes that Turner's early essays were in fact addresses, orations, or eulogies in which literary and rhetorical devices were carefully developed and perfected. These essay-orations included such eloquent pieces as "The University of the Future," "American Colonization," and "The Significance of the Frontier in American History." Certainly this insight into Turner's style provides a deeper understanding of his success as historian-persuader who influenced generations of writers.

Still another volume illustrating Turner's continuing impact on historical frontier studies is *The Frontier in History: North America and Southern Africa Compared*. This excellent symposium on comparative frontier history relies on Turner as a point of reference to demonstrate how his theory promulgated the theme of equalitarianism among frontiersmen. At the same time (as McNeill also points out) the frontiersmen declined to extend equal status to nonwhites: the Indians, Mexicans, and blacks. Not only do the editors of this well-documented book begin their introductory essay with reference to Turner, they also close with an epilogue pinpointing a key reason for Turner's power as a theorizer about the frontier experience:

> The irony of Frederick Jackson Turner's lasting eminence as a frontier historian is that he thought he was describing a zone, a process, a period, and an outcome that were unique to the American experience. What he was actually describing—however inade-

quately and one-sidedly—was one example of the many frontiers generated by the capitalist system and European settlers, which in turn constitutes a particular process that takes place whenever one people intrudes into terrain occupied by another.

Turner's work, the editors conclude, can be seen as part of the "universal and still ongoing process."[23]

The details of the ongoing process are given in essays by leading authorities on various aspects of the frontier advance. On each frontier, there are specific phases, social changes, politics, and missionary penetrations. In assessing the overall results of the European invasions, the editors find that some native peoples survived better than others. The Bantu-speaking peoples of southern Africa, for example, survived the collision of cultures with less damage than the American Indians because the Bantu were more numerous and were better able to resist European diseases and because they could fall back upon diverse patterns of subsistence. North American Indians who outlived the assault were thought to be a "useless" people to be shoved away onto reservations. In contrast, southern Africa "reserves" were created for black people where they could be tapped as a source for cheap labor.[24]

Certainly this carefully researched volume demonstrates that comparative study lends insight into national and international frontier history. And throughout, the editors and the individual authors frequently return to the time-honored Frederick Jackson Turner as a point of reference. He was, as McNeill pointed out, the writer who sounded the "trumpet call" on the significance of historic frontiers.[25] Turner cast a long shadow on frontier historiography. Of course, many scholars besides Turner took up the theme of a closing frontier. Among historians and other scholars there was concern about the termination of an era of expansion and individualism that portended an unhappy future.[26]

There was also an uneasiness of mind among these historians over the impending vacuum created by Turner's death in 1932. A complexity of problems existed, not easily observed outside the power structure of academe, that involved more than Turner's networking or his help with job prospects, fellowships, and opportunities for publication. Turner was gone; who was to become his primary disciple and the spokesperson for western history? Who had the best pipeline to Turner's message, and when and how could this be controlled?

Turner had handed over his classes at Harvard to Frederick Merk, who dominated the field in giving lectures and training graduate students. Turner's message, which I call the "realwestern" history, became a hotly contested prize. Here was the heart of Turner's teaching, and it caused, as we shall see, a virtual battle for the possession of another man's work. As this story unfolds, we can only conjecture as to who owned what in the bitter contest between Frederick Merk and Ray Billington for the proprietary rights to the "realwestern" history.

PART FOUR

HARDENING THE TRAIL
The Ruling Theory Perpetuated

I don't dream of being a trust magnate in the historical domain—
I wouldn't hog anything if I could.

> Turner to Max Farrand (1909)

You do not ask me to give you anything in the way of interpretation of American history that is legitimately my own. If I did
so I should be debarred from its use in my own productions. . . .
I should not stand in the way of your doing your own piece of
work and it would be wrong to historical scholarship if I should
be in this position.

> ——Turner to Max Farrand (1917)

CHAPTER TEN

THE "REALWESTERN" HISTORY
Its Impact upon Generations of Students

Turner had a favorite dinnertime joke for student guests at his home. At the telling of the story he would placate his daughter, who obviously had heard the story before, by saying that "she has a different opinion." "Women's minds," he said, "tend to be like the Platte River—a mile wide and an inch deep." He had another pet tale that he liked to repeat in letters about a woman student at the University of California at Berkeley who boasted that she had "sat at the talented feet of Professor Henry Morse Stevens." A friend of Turner's, Stevens also enjoyed this illustration of how a woman enjoyed sitting at his "talented feet."[1] We can be reasonably sure that these examples of Turner's humor are related to the fact that women were virtually ignored in his version of western history, which as a teaching field is here identified as the "realwestern" history.

As a teacher, what did Turner say in his lectures and write about in his work? We have as evidence the detailed notes taken by some of the most able students in his classes. Much of what he said flowered in the classrooms of Frederick Merk, his protégé, after Turner's retirement from Harvard in 1924. At the University of Wisconsin the field also bloomed, with some variations, in the teachings of Frederic L. Paxson but it withered under persistent attacks while Turner wrote and studied at the Huntington Library. Criticism mounted and the popularity of Turner's theories sank to new lows after his death in 1932. But in the 1940s the "realwestern" history had a rebirth with the appearance of a talented disciple, Ray Allen Billington.

My intention here is to show that Billington, the leading practitioner of the "realwestern" history after the 1950s, borrowed much from Turner and Merk. He also made a significant (to use Turner's favorite term) contribution to the field by restating his ideas within the cast of the growing body of historical scholarship about western America. He thus gave Turnerian history new respectability as a viable and indeed an exciting area of study. Billington did this almost singlehandedly by first writing a remarkable textbook, *Westward Expansion, A History of the American Frontier* (New York, 1949), a narrative of frontier advance. This text was followed by *The Far Western Frontier, 1830–1860* (New York, 1956), *America's Frontier Heritage* (New York, 1966), *The Genesis of the Frontier Thesis* (San Marino, Calif., 1971), and a prize-winning biography, *Frederick Jackson Turner, Historian, Scholar, Teacher* (New York, 1973). These studies, accompanied by a continuing stream of other books and essays, culminated in his twenty-fifth book, *Land of Savagery— Land of Promise: The European Image of the American Frontier* (New York, 1980). These publications appeared at a time when the Turner frontier theory was still being attacked and even regarded as "old hat" history. Billington seems to have gradually turned the tide, especially after the enthusiastic reception of the series, *History of the American Frontier*, launched in the 1950s. One of Billington's admirers has summed up his career: "All would acknowledge his mentorship as the most productive and dynamic scholar of frontier and Western history in this century."[2] Much of this praise was probably deeply rooted in the admiration western historians had for his penetrating textbook, *Westward Expansion*.

For many years this extraordinary book appeared to be a masterful narrative setting forth Turner's lectures in a manner that Turner himself might have employed had he possessed Billington's skills as a captivating and engaging storyteller. There can be little doubt that had Turner read *Westward Expansion*, he would have been impressed with Billington's dramatic style. Anyone who has read Turner's many letters detailing his literary problems will be convinced that Turner could have never written a frontier

Ray A. Billington, ca. 1945, at Northwestern at the time he was working on the first edition of Westward Expansion. (Courtesy, Henry E. Huntington Library and Art Gallery)

narration in Billington's fashion. Turner himself acknowledged that he was not a "saga" narrator; moreover, he confessed that he was simply unable to finish a textbook. One problem was his inability to "crystalize any portion." Although one suspects that Turner was bored with textbook writing, he went to great lengths to rationalize his failure to keep his publishing commitments. "My methods," he wrote to his publisher, "require me to see how I wish to organize the field as an entirety before working out the details."[3] Billington's methods, as we shall see, were quite dissimilar.

There was a fundamental difference between the two men revealed in the fact that Turner was more creative, analytical, and social-science oriented than Billington. True, Billington studied cultural themes, but he never had the data-processing orientation or the tenacity for research of the master. Indeed Billington, in an autobiographical essay noted by Martin Ridge, frankly stated that he had never consulted manuscript sources before he began work on his biography of Turner's in the 1960s. He had limited himself previously to printed materials. Billington thought of himself as a Turnerian, but in many respects he missed Turner's message.

The wide acceptance of the "realwestern" history, the version of western history set forth by Turner (especially in lectures), was also enjoyed by his followers in the immediate period after Turner's rise to national visibility in the late 1890s. The "realwestern" history reached a high point in 1910 with his election to the presidency of the American Historical Association and was undoubtedly based upon the unique qualities that his frontier-sectionalism theory embodied. There was little opposition to his view that the beckoning frontier buoyed up confidence in the new American destiny, free from the burdens of ancestral European systems of governance. The West was an "ever-renewable" place that made possible the concept of transcending the Old World inheritance. We could leave our European past behind us and concentrate on the development of a new nation based upon distinct regional or sectional characteristics. The older past was so far removed that there was no need to battle it. As Turner argued, each frontier offered "a new field of opportunity . . . a gate of escape from the bondage of the past";

hence each reflected scorn of older society, impatience with its restraints and ideas and indifference to its lessons."[4]

This conception of the frontier, Turner managed to convince his readers, was the basis for understanding the emerging national character. In his classroom lectures, Turner portrayed his heroes of the frontier—Thomas Jefferson, Andrew Jackson, and Abraham Lincoln—as impressive modernists, independent of earlier precedents and British parenthood. In Turner's theorizing, which was decried by his friend the colonialist Charles M. Andrews, America was particularly an orphaned nation; Andrews reminded Turner that his conception of colonial history virtually ignored the Revolutionaries' reliance upon British methods of governance and common law.[5]

Turner persisted, however, and ultimately, as his student admirers and disciples have argued, he helped to release Americans from their fealty to a golden age of the past. His was a frontier-sectional theory that stressed progress, early settlement, the forging into the wilderness, and the occupation of new territories. If America became imperialistic or acquisitive in the process, those tendencies could be set aside in favor of the cultural development and the sheer prosperity that came with the sea-to-sea occupation of the continent.[6]

Thus, as Turner reaffirmed in his correspondence with his former students, especially in several long autobiographical letters preserved among his papers, he created a new view of American history that gave a fresh interpretation to the origins of American institutions. He reexamined the worn-out germ theory to show that our inheritance was not at all dependent upon European germs of culture.[7] He reacted strongly to the orthodox credo professed among the eastern guild of historical scholars, which implied that beneficent developments had come to pass in our history without any real break from our European past. He did this without attacking Herbert Baxter Adams, his own mentor, and there is no mention of this difference of opinion in Turner's correspondence until long after Adams's death. In Turner's view, the West was ignored. It was necessary to turn the orthodox credo upside down, to suggest that continuity be replaced with discontinuity, to supplant the old harmonious inheritance with a conflicting frontier revisionism.

Ironically, Turner's new credo, the "realwestern" history that was to supersede the old, became in itself another orthodoxy. Although it gave birth to a new nationalist interpretation based on the impact the frontier had upon a growing America, Turnerian thought ultimately turned increasingly inward, away from urban developments and foreign problems, and tended to concentrate almost entirely upon the internal history of the westward advance. This trend is indicated in the mass of research notes at the Huntington Library, the basis of Turner's last work on sections and the nation.

Although not stated in so many words, Turner's work clearly implied that the Yankee, white male pioneers were the agents of real progress. A central theme in Turnerian "realwestern" history was found in the writings of one of Turner's disciples, Ulrich Phillips, whose work stressed a southern history seen in terms of frontier-sectional white supremacy. Even worse, Phillips trivialized issues relating to the conflict between races and classes of people, and southern historical orthodoxy under his leadership became a chorus celebrating prosperity, process, and development combined with sectional division and reconciliation. Ulrich Phillips's work came to represent a new political conservatism eulogizing the white planter society.[8]

Looking back on his career, Turner wrote that historians of the 1890s were enveloped by "the romantic side" of the frontier or the "shadow of the slavery struggle." There were those scholars who treated the West as "fighting" material for the Civil War or "ground for exploration history." Here he saw an "opportunity." "My . . . Frontier paper," he wrote, "was a programme, and in some degree a protest against eastern neglect . . . and against western antiquarian spirit."[9]

"Meantime," he recalled, "out of a course on The Economic and Social History of the U.S. . . . I evolved the course in the History of the West, the first, I think, in the country. . . . It seemed," he added with some pride, "to 'take.'" Emphasis in his lectures, he said, was on "our social and economical development, and the frontier advance."[10] From the beginning Turner recalled that he linked the frontier and the evolving sections, and although the emphasis on sectionalism is lacking in his 1893 essay, he fused the two as part of the frontier "process."

"I saw at once," he said, "that the frontier passed into successive and varied regions, and that new sections evolved in the relations between these geographic regions, and that the kinds of people and society which entered them adjusted to the new environment. . . . Uncle Sam's psychology," he asserted, was based on a "federation of sections."[11] At the same time, he argued, "The frontier was a moving section . . . a form of society, determined by reaction between the wilderness and the edge of expanding settlement."[12]

Here indeed was an exciting but complex "programme" of study. Incorporated into an undergraduate course, it was first offered in 1895–1896 as History 7 (later History 17a and b), "The History of the American West." Turner's lectures contained threads of economic, social, and constitutional history carried over from earlier classes, but the main fabric was frontier advance. "The 'West' with which I dealt," he wrote a former student, "was a *process* rather than a fixed geographical region; it began with the Atlantic coast, and it emphasized the way in which the East colonized the West, and how the 'West' as it stood in any given period affected the development and ideas of the older areas to the East."[13]

Turner, in commenting on his role as a teacher-historian, accented time and again the complexity of his approach to American history. In his autobiographical letters he tells us that he is concerned with the whole of the American past and that the frontier experience was actually part of a social "process" that became a major part, if not the major part, of American history. Repeatedly he told his students that the frontier was an American heritage. Not only did the turmoil of the frontier serve to forge bonds to blend peoples together, but it colored our national character with recognizable traits.[14]

Turner implied, although he did not emphasize and argue the point, that the frontier process encouraged an aggressive nationalism fed by local levels of self-government that molded a Yankee democratic spirit.[15] It was not Turner's practice to down-

Turner's American history seminar, 1893–1894, in the alcove of the Wisconsin Historical Library located in the state capitol. The women in the seminar were probably studying for an M.A. degree, which would qualify them to work in libraries or to teach in noncollege positions. Not in the photograph is Louise Phelps Kellogg, who earned her Ph.D. in 1901 under Turner and worked as an editor and as an assistant to Reuben Gold Thwaites. Other women who very probably earned their doctorates under Turner are difficult to pinpoint because they were not clearly identified by Turner in his correspondence and all we have are graduate records at the University of Wisconsin and Harvard University. (Courtesy, State Historical Society of Wisconsin)

play the negative aspects of the frontier advance because in his eyes it meant progress: forward movement in our history, growth, improvement, reform, and, as he argued in one of his most important essays, "development of society." The moving frontier thus possessed an unstated but clearly implied concept of progress. Seen on his classroom teaching maps, it was a "thin red line, . . . the dynamic element in American history."[16]

The "realwestern" history as revealed in Turner's essays and lectures was "dynamic," progressive, and male-Anglo-Saxon ori-

ented. It was based on the records of "the men of the frontier" as
Turner wrote. These "men on the frontier had closer resemblances
to the Middle region than . . . to other sections." Their "ideas and
needs" had an impact on "the nationalizing of political parties, an
example of which was the Whig Party.[17]

A closer examination of Turner's frontier process revealed that
there was a conglomeration of factors involved in addition to frontier politics and parties. Among these was a special "tone of
frontier democracy."[18] There were also cultural changes among
pioneers, diplomatic events, socioeconomic factors, and sectional
forces that appeared along the cutting edge of settlement. Frontier
history was tied to sectional rivalry and development. Turner
claimed, in an understatement, to approach history from "somewhat different angles than my predecessors. . . . I have found it
necessary to consider the history as a whole, not as the history of
the West by itself."[19] Telling his classroom students that although
he was forced at times to make a "summary statement," he did so
only after "the examination of the historical evidence, the analysis
of the problem, often complex."[20] Added to this approach was a
quiet but persistent theme of westward conquest, a theme that
appears occasionally in his lectures as well as in his published
writings. In a review essay, "The Westward Course of Empire," he
wrote stirringly of the "interesting picture of the American advance," "a fresh horizon of American ambition" (following the
War of 1812), and "the trans-Mississippi empire."[21]

We may be at a loss to explain how American history with such
density and intricacy could be taught effectively in a lecture
course. His themes were so compounded with entangling elements that Turner spoke about the challenges in working out, as
he said, "my own salvation."[22] He seems to have solved his problem, however, by going around it. Notes taken in his classes tell us
that he emphasized his interpretations in a series of factual lectures that chronologically traced the westward movement of the
pioneers. The lecture topics were attuned to familiar political, economic, and diplomatic turning points. These in turn traced the
early American frontier's expansion to the fall line and Piedmont

frontiers, from there to the "old" northwest and southwest, and finally to nineteenth-century waves of exploration and settlement. Culminating in the great compromises of the period and the census report of 1890, Turner's lectures, with their incorporation of maps and lantern slides, offered more than ample data to document a great surge of westward expansion.[23]

Turner's "West," as confirmed by his notes and lectures, concentrated on the great geographical province of the Midwest, America's heartland of agriculture, commerce, and industry. He seems to have become convinced that the nineteenth-century Midwest was a kind of governor determining the swing of his nation's political pendulum. That this area became a producer, processor, distributor, and consumer undoubtedly served as a stimulus to his studies of sectionalism. Here he found the dependable pulse of the American spirit he liked to talk about, and he and his students could examine the "evolution" of society from sources in the Draper Collection at the State Historical Society of Wisconsin and elsewhere.

Most of all Turner found a real sense of satisfaction in charting historical changes by pinpointing Midwest geology, geography, and politics. As late as 1928, teaching at the California Institute of Technology, he lectured on the unusual results of his map studies of elections. "Observe," he said, showing a lantern slide, "how in the election of 1856, the counties that voted in favor of Frémont almost exactly coincided with . . . [the] second glacial ice sheet. This was the land of the basin of the Great Lakes and the prairies."[24] When speaking on data compiled from maps, Turner remained cautious about conclusions. In a lecture on political maps he spoke about the hazards of overlooking the fact that "the dominant influence at one period may not be the same as that in a later period, though the political result is the same in each case."

Here again Turner offered an apparently convincing case for his impartial stance in making judgments. "One must," he told his students, "adopt the use of the geologist's use of the multiple hypothesis to explain complex areas."[25] There was, however, a bit of unintentional equivocation here, for Turner was not actually relying on the geologist's use of the multiple working hypotheses since he confused the use of interdisciplinary data with that scientific concept. And it is to be noted that Turner, as well as his admirers and students, promoted this misconception. Turner, for instance, did not use the word "working" to state his purpose in adopting the scientific method. This is key in understanding the promotion of his ruling theories under the guise of applying scientific methodology. Thus his devoted student Frederick Merk in turn perpetuated many of Turner's misconceptions in the "realwestern" history.

CHAPTER ELEVEN

THE EMERGENCE OF FREDERICK MERK

Evidence indicates that Turner's detailed, map-oriented lectures, a basis for the topical organization of the Turner-Merk *List of References on the History of the West,* became the "realwestern history" that helped to shape generations of teachers in the field. Themes from these lectures were later incorporated into Frederic L. Paxson's Pulitzer Prize–winning *History of the American Frontier* (New York, 1924), a book based upon his scheme for a western history course at the University of Wisconsin, where he succeeded Turner in 1910 when Turner moved to Harvard.[1]

After leaving Wisconsin Turner continued to teach his western history course at Harvard, and his lectures were practically unchanged. Despite his intense study of the field, he offered little new factual data or interpretation to his undergraduates. This observation can be determined by comparing sets of notes taken by his students at both universities. And lectures given by Frederick Merk, who followed Turner at Harvard, have so much of Turner in them that they might have been given by the master himself.[2] Merk's *History of the Westward Movement,* according to a number of his former students including Rodman Paul and Francis Paul Prucha, was primarily a printed version of Merk's classroom lectures, many of them with clear echoes of Turner. Prucha remembers Merk's continued use of the *List of References* as late as 1948–1949. This work had been originally published almost a quarter of a century earlier when Merk began to share the teaching of the history of the West with his mentor.[3]

Merk did of course prepare original lectures and poured a stream of data into them from his own investigations. It is evident that his lectures carried on his story of western development far into the twentieth century, beyond the closing of the frontier in 1893, a date stressed by Turner. Merk's published lectures include discussions on dry farming, mining, and land-planning through the era of World World II.[4] His bibliographical notes show that although he consulted references through the 1970s, he still relied on Turnerian standbys such as Ellen C. Semple's *American History and Its Geographical Conditions* (Boston, 1903), a work that repeated the now discredited geographical-barrier hypothesis. Merk, never a specialist in colonial history, was probably unaware of a well-reasoned and documented article by H. Roy Merrens giving a modern geographer's critique of the outmoded concept of "geographical determinism" that coupled early frontier settlement with fall-line urban growth and the Appalachian barrier.[5]

Merrens's essay had been published in 1965, but the respected geographer Ralph H. Brown had earlier revised Semple's pseudo-scientific geographical theories in his influential 1948 volume, *Historical Geography of the United States,* which devoted almost a third of its space to a consideration of geographical changes along the Atlantic seaboard in the seventeenth and eighteenth centuries. Brown had especially made a point of downplaying geographical determinism by heading a brief section on early settlement with "Expansion Not Seriously Obstructed by Geographical Features."[6] More significantly, Brown attached no particular importance to the fall line or line of falls. Furthermore, Semple is ignored in the bibliographical notes and in the text.

Neither Brown nor Merrens argued that a fall line did not exist or that the Piedmont was not a distinct area separate from the Tidewater; they asserted that the barrier lines for frontier settlement did not exist. The frontier advance was highly irregular. Indeed, there is no historical geographical evidence to support the concept of a step-by-step occupation of the wilderness areas as conditioned by geographical factors.

Ironically, Turner himself was one of the very few historians of his time who had close academic associations with geographers. The turn-of-the-century view most geographers held was Tur-

Frederick Merk in the Harvard Yard, ca. 1957. (From the author's collection)

nerian; indeed, he was one of the scholars who helped to create the mindset of determinism. Turner even suggested that one could go too far in looking for causative factors in analyzing the role of geographical determinants. He was largely responsible for convening a conference of historians and geographers who, according to Turner, gained "insights by looking into . . . common ground . . . by looking at past events in terms of a rigid hypothesis of the creative role of the physical environment."[7]

In his lectures Merk does not seem to question the Turnerian fall line–Appalachian barrier theories, stressing at the same time that the fall line was also "an insulator between the sections."[8] In true "realwestern" fashion this theme of fall line–Appalachian geographical determinism was also set forth by Ray Allen Billington, who described the "tumbling cataracts two hundred feet high" and the "westward march" that was checked by "forbidding mountain ranges," a "barrier, the unifying influence of the Great Valley."[9]

Prucha also remembers Merk's continued use of an environmental-determinist discourse on settlers who occupied western "physiographic provinces." A favorite simile of Merk's was that westward-moving pioneers "poured into these provinces like liquid flowing into a mold to find its own level and shape."[10] This imagery is repeated in Merk's statement from a lecture arguing that the frontier was an area of "distinct regions or provinces. Each region constituted a separate set of conditions for the settler; each developed a different civilization. They were giant molds, which shaped the people flowing into them."[11] In discussing the Revolutionary era, Merk continued the same theme by arguing that "the Piedmont was insulated from the Tidewater. [There was] little communication between the two. [There was a] break in all the rivers. Another insulator—[the] belt of sandy sterile soil between the Piedmont and Tidewater."[12]

There can be little question that geographical determinism and the Turnerian barrier to westward movement continued as an interpretation for a second generation of "realwestern" historians. The barrier argument, growing from the geographical-provinces interpretation, is key in environmental determinism in the sense that the frontiersmen were, as Merk stated, forced to adjust to specific environmental circumstances and thus had to create a "different civilization." The overwhelming emphasis in Turner's own History of the West course was on this "physiographic" argument. Turner, for instance, gave a series of lectures, "The Relation of Physiography to the History of the West," in which he described western physiographic provinces as being "comparable to groups of European states." Among these "regions" or "provinces" were those areas that played an important part in tracing frontier advances: "the Atlantic Plain," the "plateaus" of New England, the Piedmont, and the "Alleghenies and the Great Valley." From this setting Turner could move to "the physiographic basis of sect[ionalism] in Amer. Hist."[13] Turner's lectures, as one might expect from an examination of his papers at the Huntington Library and from other sources such as Frank J. Klingberg's notes, were largely extensions of his published essays on the frontier and section.

One of these essays, nearly overlooked in his published and partly published essays, is a piece in which he sets forth his geographical-environment determinist theme almost as if he had delivered it from the lecturer's podium. This essay, an address and very probably an offshoot from classroom lectures, is entitled "The Development of American Society." In it Turner portrays America as "a human sea . . . that has been ever adjusting itself to new shore lines, new beds."[14] The first printed version of this article was published in 1906 and most certainly was familiar to Merk, who became over the years an authority on his mentor's writings and doctrines and used them as reference works for lectures and for advising students.

There is another aspect of Turner's impact upon Merk—the matter of Indian history. In many respects, specialists in this field have found that the manner in which Indians are treated is a visible litmus test to identify the traditional Turnerian views on "real-western" history. Turner's insensitivity to women and Indian people is also reflected in his attitude toward other minorities such as Mexican Americans and blacks. His frontier theory describing environmental influences on pioneer men came close to celebrating a Yankee pioneer cult of masculinity.[15]

Turner's "realwestern" history emphasizes the consequence of the Anglo-American progressive advance. Hence there is no room to portray Indian societies in their desperate struggle for survival in the face of adversity. Indian tribes might be given some importance if their survival techniques were adopted by the pioneers in the wilderness, but Indians were not recognized in the "realwestern" history as having a culture worth protecting or preserving. Pioneers overcame these "savages" in the westward march of white society. Turner's investigations relating to Indians were almost entirely confined to their accidental appearance in historical accounts recorded by pioneers who fought them off in a seemingly unending series of violent conflicts; thus Turner discovered in his sources stereotypes of the Indian. Although he might have corrected his distorted lens by reading in what had become a sophisticated field of ethnology in the early twentieth-century literature, Turner never took the opportunity to do so. In the entire collection of Turner's research notes and reference works there is not a single instance of his having curiosity or concern about expanding his diverse interdisciplinary studies to include anthropology. He liked to mention that he had encouraged a former student, Emma H. Blair, to undertake the editing of a series of journals relating to Indians, but that appears to have been his one excursion into Indian studies. One might expect there would be correspondence between Turner and leading anthropologists of his day in his papers. But here, too, is a void. Although it is difficult to find historians of note who versed themselves in this new ethnology in the early twentieth century, it is important to single out Turner because he wrote about Indians in his doctoral dissertation and in later books.

Turner's unfriendly attitude toward native people resulted in a version of western history that has given us what has been called "the white man's Indians."[16] In Turner's view Indians were a mere background for fur-trade studies or for atmosphere, as a foil to accompany the pioneer advance into the wilderness. They were part of the "realwestern" environmental factor that became so important in explaining how Europeans adjusted to and conquered a new land. They were a slight modifying influence on the frontier as another kind of "barrier." For Turner, the word "native" meant Yankee pioneer. Indian trails were a "fissure" bringing about a decline of "primitive Indian life." Indians were, however, important as a "consolidating agent" helping to bring about intercolonial congresses to consider measures of frontier defense. They helped, too, in "developing the stalwart and rugged qualities of the frontiersman." At the same time "savages" could be "troublesome" to pioneers crossing the fall line, and although they might well serve as a "buffer state" they still, as the Massachusetts minister Solomon Stoddard suggested, should be hunted down with dogs "as they do bears." Indeed, if Indians "act like wolves" they "are to be dealt with as wolves."[17] In a review essay Turner offered the defeatist argument that it was "too late to study Indian life in its unmodified form," which seemingly excused him from looking into the world of anthropology. More to the point, his attitudes toward Indians are revealed in a letter to his friend Charles Van Hise about naming points in the Grand Canyon after Indian tribes. "It would be a great mistake," he wrote, "to call the Grand View point . . . which is well established by name—by the name Paiute—the most degrated [sic] & disgusting and low aggregation of grasshopper eating savages that disgrace the West."[18]

Merk, who had the intellectual heritage of hearing and reading Turnerian "realwestern" Indian history, tended to do little more than repeat it. Secretive about his relationship with Turner, he reluctantly surrendered a few of Turner's letters to the Huntington Library collection, and at Harvard he closed the use of his papers for an apparently indefinite period. In dealing with the subject, he followed his master when he told his students that he had an excuse: "I don't know much about Indians"; and he virtually ignored them in his long and copious lectures.[19] Indians are scarcely mentioned in Rodman Paul's notes taken in Merk's classes in 1936 or in Francis Paul Prucha's notes in 1948. Merk, however, did make amends for his tendency to neglect Indians—in *History of the Westward Movement* he began his lectures with a fourteen-page overview of Indian "background" and "culture." Henceforth, Indians are mentioned in connection with such topics as treaties, wars, rationing, and loss of land. One of Merk's last advanced students, Otey M. Scruggs, his assistant in the "wagon wheels" lecture course, recalled Merk's loyalty to the "westering" process, his negative treatment of women and minorities, and his jokes about backward Indians. Scruggs, now a professor at Syracuse University writes:

> As for recollections of Professor Merk, what can one say about him and Turnerism? He was a Turnerian. The course was organized so as to stress frontier and sections, especially the first semester of it, but really throughout.
>
> In the process of their great nationalistic enterprise of expansion westward (and Merk was a nationalist-progressive-New Deal believer in an active central government) whites made a lot of mistakes with the land, screwing up streams, forests, plains (enter the Dust Bowl), pushing aside Native Americans, Chicanos, Britons in Oregon. In Merk's view there seems to have been a certain inevitability about it all, given the frontier stress on "rugged individualism." He certainly disapproved of much that went on here, but in the end, inevitability enters again, it all turns out for the best in the sense that the greatest nation on earth emerged from the westering process. I don't know that this makes him some sort of Anglophile. It is conceivable that he subscribed to some form of Anglo-Saxonism, for he does talk as Turner did about the movement as spreading "civilization" over the continent. Much of this might be implicit in his approach: the Indians were doomed because they clung to their ways (culture) yet they were not prepared to deal with such a "civilizing" measure as the Dawes Act and so got ripped off. I recall one of his pieces of humor in a lecture on the Oklahoma tribes who got jilted out of their land (oil) and used the money to buy the biggest cars they could lay their hands on: hearses! It was amusing the way he told it, but I am not quite sure what emotion he was trying to evoke—humor, pity, contempt? He did, however, in a later lecture, deal with sympathy and I think approval with the Indian Reorganization Act of 1934. But of course, that act involved something quite different than where Native Americans are at today. In sum, non-Caucasian groups were really passive actors in the drama that had whites at center stage. Without

flat-out saying it, I believe it isn't too far-fetched to say that the spear-carriers (blacks, Indians, Mexicans) were to him part of that "frontier" waiting to be "civilized."

As for women, Merk had nothing to say. They were on the western pilgrimage for the ride. He assigned *Giants in the Earth*, and as you know women (or at least one woman) play a powerful role in the book. We get a glimpse of what westering did to those women, but I don't recall Merk saying anything about all this. But then who in the profession has anything to say about women in Merk's day? Or a long time afterwards?[20]

Scruggs, who has written prize-winning essays on minority history, was especially aware of Merk's attitude toward people of color who were "waiting to be civilized." And although Merk followed Turner in having little to say about women, Scruggs correctly points out that nobody else in the field made an issue of gender in those days.

Yet on issues of racism and environmental despoliation and even on issues of conservation, the Turner-Merk message was out of date even for its own time. Much of that misshapen legacy was passed on to Frederic L. Paxson and then to textbook writers such as John Hicks and Ray A. Billington. These writers also echoed the Turnerian stereotypes of Indians that Turner found in the writings of early pioneers.[21]

Perhaps the best index of Merk's treatment of Indian people is his assertion that they were a people who were "rising steadily on the ladder of civilization." Their "cornfields were cultivated in common . . . families had private gardens," and "traders who had married into tribes owned fenced gardens of considerable size." Merk saw progress in "notable advances in education and in tribal economy" as Indians "made use of implements and techniques of civilization. Spinning wheels and looms were operated by women, trained by missionaries." He points out how alarming "the advances toward civilization were" to those people who had "designs on Indian lands." And this alarm, he implies, was a fundamental cause of Indian removal. The debate on the removal was "on sectional lines." Merk correctly stresses the fact that Indians were not to be removed to a "desert" area; the removal land in the West had good hunting and agricultural potential.[22]

Henry May, one of Merk's students of the 1930s who had little curiosity about western deserts or Indians, has left us with a touching if not a patronizing memory of his teacher. Described as "a frail and saintly man" whose voice rose "almost to a squeak" in attacking student papers that he considered "truncated," Merk could be even "less gentle." May recalled that in the "true Merk-Turner style," he "made maps charting the relation between poor soils and Democratic votes." When rebel students composed essays on Charles A. Beard, they "greatly upset Mr. Merk," who saw them endorsing a quasi-Marxist idea of history. Beard was also a threat because he claimed that writing history was an act of faith and thus there was really no objective historical writing. When students tried "to corner Mr. Merk" to query him on "what history was or why he thought it was important, he could not understand them." Merk "loved to get the facts straight—the precise topic did not matter at all." According to May, Merk "loved history for itself and for what he could do with it."[23]

Most intriguing about this judgment of Merk is the jumble that comes with it. Merk did verily "love to get the facts straight." This he did very well in his books, *The Oregon Question* and *Manifest Destiny and Mission*. But there was another Merk, the steadfast devotee of the "realwestern" history with its admixture of dogma, stereotypes, and reality.[24] The "realwestern" saga of jumbled history continues to unfold as we examine other Turnerian themes.

CHAPTER TWELVE

REVERSE ENVIRONMENTALISM AND OTHER TEACHING THEMES

There are still other characteristics of the "realwestern" history that can be traced in Turner, Merk, and Billington. They ignored, or virtually ignored, the most destructive influences upon the land by westering farmers, cattlemen, miners, and lumbermen. Although it is true that American historians, except for James C. Malin, tended to overlook environmental themes before the 1960s, it is nevertheless important to point out that Turner's writings were aggressively hostile to ideas of environmental conservation. Merk relented on this point. In his very last years, Merk, according to Otey Scruggs, lashed out at "uncontrolled individualism" and suggested the need for "a strong dose of government control" to avoid "the rape of a continent." Yet this was not a subject that Merk wrote about, and his advanced students of earlier decades, such as Rodman Paul and Paul Prucha, do not dwell on his concern for the environment. Merk in fact supported frontier expansionism. Like Turner, Merk lectured on the theme of Yankee male conquest in a victory over the wilderness, Indians, and Mexican Americans, a theme underscored with the ever-present paternal view of women as passive companions on a trek.[1]

But let us look at the environmentalism issue more closely. When Turner, Merk, and Billington gave their students heroic portraits of pioneers made rugged by environmental challenges, they became advocates for and promoters of a reverse environmentalism that tended to sanctify exploitation of resources in fur trading, timber cutting, mining, and destructive uses of the land by

170

ranchers and farmers. Turner's focus on blacks was centered on his theories about slavery and sectionalism. Blacks were important as property in slave-owning sections of the South that in turn promoted slavery. Consequently he castigated Hermann Von Holst, whose monumental *Constitutional History of the United States* was primarily concerned with constitutional as well as with moral aspects of the struggle against slavery. Von Holst overlooked the story of the white pioneers in the West, the frontier "processes" of social change.

Turner's lectures stressed the "process" of taming the wilderness land by generations of pioneers, and American "traits" of character were traced to this experience.[2] The idea was contested, however, by the ecologist Aldo Leopold, a founding father of the Wilderness Society. He became a neighbor of Turner's on Van Hise Avenue in Madison in 1924, living only two doors away, but he apparently could not convince his older friend that he could be wrong about his historical treatment of land occupation. During this year, when preparing the essay "Wilderness as a Form of Land Use," Leopold scolded Turner for his misjudgments: "If we have such a thing as American culture," he wrote, "is it not a bit beside the point for us to be so solicitous about preserving those institutions without giving so much as a thought to preserving the environment which produced them and which may be one of our effective means of keeping them alive?"

Leopold, himself a professor at the University of Wisconsin with a loyal following of students, the founding father of biosphere thinking, and the author of several influential essays, was irritated by Turner's insensitivity to conservation issues. With a mind like a razor, he sliced through Turner's "realwestern" history to exhibit the shortsightedness of Turner's reverse environmentalism. Why ignore the very land that gave us such a rich frontier legacy? This upside-down environmentalism resulted in part from Turner's blind spot in passing by writers such as George Perkins Marsh and John Muir. Just how blind Turner really was to issues of soil exhaustion and other abuses of the land can be judged from his discussion of agricultural history.

Amazingly, he seems to have completely ignored *The Conservation of Natural Resources*, written in 1910 by a lifelong friend,

Turner (left) *and his friend Charles Van Hise* (right) *on the trail in 1908.* (Both photographs from the Dorothy Turner photo album; courtesy, Henry E. Huntington Library and Art Gallery)

geologist Charles Van Hise. Among Turner's preserved books is a copy of this volume with Turner's marginalia, but the book seems to have been like a glass balloon, present but invisible. Turner did enroll in a class on physical geology taught by Van Hise at the university, and undoubtedly conservation issues were mentioned. The class must have had some influence, for we see in Turner's papers that late in life he actually did recognize that there was such a thing as pollution in the lakes around Madison.[3]

A leading anthropologist, Joseph G. Jorgenson, tells us much of what Leopold had already said about the catastrophic ecological results of the American westward march. In a volume on western Indians, he gives a thorough analysis of the comparative environments, languages, and cultures of 172 tribes that fought the frontier advance.[4] Some of this kind of information was of course available in Turner's lifetime. Lewis H. Morgan wrote in the 1850s, Adolph Bandelier published on the southwestern Indians throughout the 1890s and the early 1900s, and Franz Boas, anthropologist and ethnologist, introduced an entirely new way of thinking about native people, and the problems of soil exhaustion in the southern cotton fields were simply left out.

Billington's textbook faithfully passed on to students the "real-western" history: the misrepresentations of Indians and other minorities and the upside-down concepts of land use. Merk used a similar approach although in one case he did single out mention of "Negroes as migrant farm laborers."[5] And Billington in his fourth edition made an effort to correct the traditional distortions present in Turnerian Indian history.[6]

Frederick Merk over a period of years treated his students to virtual duplications of Turner's lectures.[7] These "realwestern" history lectures were once more altered, this time as a narrative to appear in Billington's 1949 *Westward Expansion*. Billington also borrowed from Paxson's text (he had been a student in Paxson's classes at the University of Wisconsin) and combined this material with Merk's lectures to create a flowing narrative for modern readers. In 1978 Merk published *History of the Westward Movement*, a final revision of his lifelong lecture course on the West. Thus, the "realwestern" history arising from the Turnerian tradition has stayed with us in textbook form through the works of Paxson, Merk, and Billington.

There is more to this story, especially in the controversial details, but first let us return to Turner himself. A key to his teaching is found in his remarks about gaining an "independent and thorough knowledge of American history by taking up successive years, successive periods of American history, beginning with American colonization."[8] This method of study filled his time as well as his reference file of thirteen drawers containing thousands of notes relating to all aspects of American history and the frontier-sectional development of America.[9] At the same time, then, that he taught the history of the West, Turner carried on an ambitious program of studying and teaching general American history, epoch by epoch. This complex teaching program was concentrated in seminar work with advanced students. He taught an early advanced course, "History of the Old Northwest, 1830–40," and when he was preparing his volume *The Rise of the New West* for the American Nation series in 1906, he studied the era 1819–1829 and gave a lecture course on the period. In his last year at Harvard he prepared a course on America covering the years 1880–1920, spending time on an offering that he would not teach again.[10]

At Wisconsin Turner had by 1900 established his position not only as the leading authority in his field but also as a professor who had certain perquisites. More and more in the early 1900s, as he received invitations to teach and indeed for permanent transfers to other universities, he was able to consolidate his position within his department. After turning down an offer from the University of Chicago in 1900 Turner was given the title "Director of the School of Economics and Political Science" and was provided "Stenographic Service for Director Turner." He was also to have two graduate scholarships and two fellowships in history for students as well as a salary of $3,500 for himself and a leave of absence for 1900–1901.[11]

In his correspondence with friends at Stanford, Berkeley, and later at Yale and Harvard, Turner wrote about his courses and teaching, emphasizing that Wisconsin had made life agreeable for him, especially by permitting "the semester's leave for research." Moreover, his seminar graduate students "bring to me the spoils of the rich library day after day."[12] When he was asked to teach at Berkeley, he told Pres. Benjamin I. Wheeler exactly what the content of his courses would be in summer session offerings. He would for the summer of 1906, he wrote, teach one course, "The Advance of the American Frontier"; this would involve a "course of lectures interpreting the history of the West from the point of view of the movement of population from the Atlantic to the Pacific." He added, "Attention will be given to the colonization of physiographic provinces of the United States, and, in general, to the economic, political, and social causes and results of the westward movement." This description, as much as any other, specifically pinpoints Turner's History of the West course (and it dovetails with notes taken by students in his classes at about that time). Turner wanted to teach another course at Berkeley, one on the history of America during the presidencies of "Monroe and John Quincy Adams." Here, he noted, attention would be given to "the importance of sectional development" especially related to economic, political, and social "conditions."[13]

Turner's descriptions of his teaching programs at Wisconsin showed that not only had he surfaced as a leading faculty member who was able to arrange his own lecture courses and leaves of absence but that by the early 1900s he was very much in demand as a visiting lecturer. Other leading universities were interested in what he had to say, especially about the history of the frontier and the West. Turner tended to think of frontiers in connection with his place of residence, and Wisconsin was still regarded as the western part of America. Later, at Harvard, he gave much attention to the New England past, and still later at the Huntington Library, while working on larger projects involving sectional American history, he considered possible essays on the Far West, including California.[14] One suspects, however, that throughout his life he retained the mental image of Wisconsin as the West.[15] Turner, writing to Carl Becker, recalled, "The frontier, . . . you see, was real to me, and when I studied history I did not keep my personal experiences in a watertight compartment away from my studies."[16] The "watertight compartment" of the library was thus not a factor that controlled Turner's teaching. He was, as he wrote time and again, himself a product of the frontier, the pioneer life of Wisconsin.

Turner's teaching was based largely upon the accumulation of a corpus of data showing westward advance as well as on factors such as his own personal manner of looking at frontier history. His main course, the History of the West, which emphasized "the advance of settlement" and the results of this movement, was only one of several courses that he offered at Wisconsin and at Harvard; he also lectured on American colonization, on the history of liberty, and on specific epochs. Although after 1895–1896 he consistently offered History of the West, he did not give a separate course on sectionalism but incorporated this theme into that class.[17] That these lectures had a powerful impact upon the profession is an understatement. Young historians from all over the nation crowded into his classes to "work with Turner."[18]

A personable, outgoing man, Turner was an eager professional who quickly climbed the ladders of the academic marketplace to take on key committee assignments within the new American Historical Association, partly as a result of his old Johns Hopkins University connections. Turner maintained lifelong contact with Hopkins friends, especially Charles Homer Haskins and Woodrow Wilson.[19] Haskins was largely responsible for engineering an offer for Turner to begin teaching at Harvard in 1910.[20] He was convinced that Turner would have better teaching opportunities at Harvard in that he would be freed "from the constant interruptions he never escaped at Madison."[21] In time, J. Franklin Jameson, editor of *American Historical Review,* extended favors to Turner including an appointment as "research associate" in Jameson's department at the Carnegie Institution. Although Turner had not known Jameson at Johns Hopkins, they later established a lifelong friendship that survived a bitter American Historical Association "reform" movement with elements of rebellion against Turner himself, an establishment historian who shared governance of the editorial board of the *Review.*[22] Turner's papers are filled with details of the uproar surrounding the "revolt" against the powerful clique that Turner and his friends had built to dominate and control the *Review.*

As a major leader in his field, Turner commanded a network of followers and supporters. As a classroom and seminar teacher and as an innovative scholar, he brought about revisionism in his area of concentration, particularly in teaching. Turner himself was of course a catalyst. Even more important, he became the patriarch of a theory as well as the paternal guide to a veritable legion of loyalists.

Turner had become famous in his mature years as a leading historian, but recent investigation demonstrates that he added prestige to the "realwestern" history in another way by disciplining potential rival scholars through critical book reviews. Martin Ridge, in an important essay, has demonstrated that as early as the middle 1890s Turner, in a series of hostile reviews, claimed that Philip Alexander Bruce, a historian of early Virginia, set forth "the point of view of an antiquarian" and that Justin Winsor failed to consult "manuscript sources." James Schouler and Hermann Von Holst also were targets for his critical bow. Even Francis Parkman

(left, from the author's collection) *Carl Lotus Becker, one of Turner's most distinguished students and a lifelong friend;* (right, courtesy, Henry E. Huntington Library and Art Gallery) *Max Farrand, another longtime friend and disciple, ca. 1933.*

was antiquarian in the sense that he lived before the time of writing "institutional" history. In his reviews, Turner, with an intimidating knowledge of sources revealing an acquaintance with a vast area of primary materials, fended off many would-be critics.[23] Here was another aspect of the way in which Turner built a foundation for himself and his work. With his edifice solidly in place, it was almost astonishing to him that there would be scholars with the temerity to launch attacks on his lifetime of work while he was still in a position of strength at Harvard in the early 1920s.

Turner's prestige as the founding father of western history was such that he was able to pick his teaching successor at Harvard, Frederick Merk. Even more important, Turner was able to weather a storm of increasing criticism, beginning with an assault on the whole concept of a frontier theory by Charles A. Beard in a 1920 review of *The Frontier in American History.* Beard censured Turner's handling of socioeconomic American history because of his neglect of the "conflict between capitalism and organized labor." In a later correspondence with Turner, Beard expanded on his criticism: "Slavery would have been slavery and capitalism in essence even if there had been no free land."[24]

Turner was truly frustrated with such well-reasoned criticism. His reaction to Beard's attack brought forth a halfhearted attempt to show that the expanding frontier was supposedly responsible for the development of cities in the West. But one suspects that even for Turner himself his arguments were not convincing. It is not surprising that his abortive essay "City, Frontier, and Section, or the Significance of the City in American History" was a series of incomplete notes and remained unfinished, never to be resurrected in defense of the frontier theory.[25]

At the time of Beard's attack, a prelude of things to come, Turner's correspondence with family members, students, former students, and fellow historians shows a degree of genuine anxiety about the future of his reputation. Although copies of *The Frontier in American History* continued to proliferate in the historical marketplace, Turner's apprehensions (despite a tone of optimism in writing to his daughter) about Beard's behavior could be explained by the fact that "the ex-Columbia professor" was "radical in tendency . . . chiefly interested in urban problems."[26]

Particularly noteworthy about Turner's reaction to Beard's chastisement (unfortunately we do not have Turner's side of the correspondence) is that Turner remained unreconstructed as to his frontier-sectional theories. If Beard censured his frontier theory, Turner would react by showing that the frontier was in fact a father of cities and urban growth. The Turnerian view, as Turner himself later acknowledged, was one that he struggled with to make his case.[27] In fact, one could assert that Turner's entire career was devoted to an unflinching statement and restatement, especially in classroom lectures, of the frontier-sectional theories. They appear in his 1893 essay, in drafts and revisions of his essays, and in longer published pieces on such topics as social forces, sections and the nation, and the development of American society.[28] There can be little doubt that Turner was a monocausationist as far as his frontier-sectionalism theories were concerned, despite his persistent lip service to "multiple hypotheses" and his penchant for confusing comparative, interdisciplinary studies with scientific methodology.[29]

CHAPTER THIRTEEN

MERK TAKES THE FLAG

In maintaining the bastion of western history in later years, Turner relied more and more on Frederick Merk, who in turn adopted Turner's lecture patterns and theories. A graduate of the University of Wisconsin, Merk left the editorial staff of the State Historical Society in Madison to follow his mentor to Harvard. In 1921 Merk accepted Turner's invitation to share lectures at Harvard on what was then called "History of the Westward Movement." Turner taught the early years of the frontier advance, the first half of the course, and Merk took over the second. After Turner's retirement in 1924, Merk wrote that "the course as a whole fell on me."[1] Born in 1877, Merk came to regard Turner as a father figure even though Merk was only sixteen years younger. Among Turner's students he was probably closest to his master.

Quiet, industrious, ambitious, and extremely conscientious as a teacher, Merk prepared himself to take over the field of western history at Harvard, one of the most coveted positions in the nation.[2] Turner depended upon this agreeable young man for consultation and for comfort as a fellow member of a field under siege. In these years Merk apparently became so close to his mentor that Turner came to regard him as the son he had never seen grow to maturity and achieve professional success.[3] It was through Turner's unflinching support that Merk obtained a foothold in the Harvard history department that eventually led to a part-time and then to a full-fledged position after Turner's retirement. In writing to Turner about their special "communion" Merk declared: "You would say something, in a sentence or two [in History 17 lectures], with particular emphasis, with 'that lifted flash of an eye' . . . I used to glory in the thought that I was in a kind of secret communion with you, that you were giving out something that only a few were privileged to see, and this spurred me on."[4]

Even after Turner retired, Merk seems to have remained his closest correspondent. Merk had not only succeeded him at Harvard but had also shared summer-session work in Utah. As late as 1927 Turner, as he always did in correspondence when the occasion offered itself, was promoting Merk's virtues as a teacher-researcher. "Merk or [and?] Schlesinger of Harvard," he wrote "have great promise as researchers and interpreters . . . if they could be furnished means to break away for at least part of the time from college or university routine."[5] As he moved into Turner's position, Merk felt more cramped and confined by his growing teaching duties, the demands put upon him by Harvard for committee work and other assignments, and the problems of putting the results of research work into print. Although Harvard maintained him on the faculty, he was unable to publish more than a handful of essays, a volume of documents on Wisconsin economic history, and one book, *History of the Labor Movement in Wisconsin during the Civil War*, before 1950 when he wrote *Albert Gallatin and the Oregon Problem: A Study in Anglo-American Diplomacy*, which was published by Harvard University Press. His other major works did not surface until more than a decade later. There seems to be little question that Merk, uneasy about his slow rate of productivity, toyed with the idea of resigning in 1930.[6]

A turning point in Merk's career came after other individuals assumed at least part of his nonteaching assignments. Turner seemed always to be at Merk's side, following every aspect of his development in the profession, and urged him, in one letter, to avoid administrative work "at the expense of choking off your research interests."[7] It was undoubtedly Turner's enormous prestige at Harvard that created the protective mantle for his protégé, allowing Merk to work at a deliberate pace in preparing books that would in time give him a scholarly reputation of his own.[8]

At the time that Harvard relieved Merk of his collateral duties (one suspects that Turner somehow had a hand in persuading the history department chair, Arthur M. Schlesinger, to give Merk relief, although that bit of evidence if it did exist does not now appear in Turner's papers), Merk unexpectedly wrote to Turner about a new development that had changed his mind about his priorities: "I have had a very happy course [of studies] with a graduate student of Radcliffe, Lois Bannister. . . . She and I have met on common ground in our admiration for your writings . . . and I have just persuaded her to let me give her a diamond ring."[9]

Merk was indeed such a confirmed Turnerian that admiration for his mentor's writings was fused with his own personal life and future marriage and family. He wrote to his student Rodman Paul, "You will find that there are great rewards in a late marriage"; moreover, Merk never again thought of giving up teaching "because having children to educate is great stimulus to continue teaching!"[10]

It was only after retirement in 1957 that Merk, with the assistance of his wife (who had earned her doctorate at Harvard under her husband's direction) was able to complete articles and booklength manuscripts for publication. Though he embarked on individual research projects in Oregon diplomacy, in manifest-destiny studies, and in fur-trade accounts, his teaching remained closely tied to his mentor's guidelines, and even as late as 1962 he occupied himself in an essay defending the Turner safety-valve doctrine long after the storm of debate over this aspect of Turnerian thought had subsided.[11] Merk was among those scholars who had offered sympathy to Turner after John C. Almack wrote a polemic on the frontier theory, "The Shibboleth of the Frontier," which appeared in *Historical Outlook* (May 25, 1925). Almack, with a certain persuasiveness, asserted that Turnerian theory was contrary to the facts because cultural advance had its origins in urban areas and not in backward pioneer settlements, which actually delayed progress.

Writing to Merk, Turner went to some length to defend himself. He was particularly annoyed that Almack, an education professor at Stanford, by virtue of his being merely a "normal school graduate," could have such a forum. His background, Turner continued, "may help some in understanding" the depth of his "misconstruction."[12] Meanwhile, Turner continued to compile a list of all the favorable appraisals of the frontier theory that he could find in textbooks, encyclopedias, and learned articles; later, he enlisted the help of his secretary Merrill H. Crissey in a search to find further acceptance of his work. For example, Turner refers to an article by Frederic L. Paxson in the *Encyclopedia Britannica* and to a favorable mention by Vernon L. Parrington in the third volume of *Main Currents in American Thought*.[13] Turner also must have been encouraged by reports from his publishers that *The Frontier in American History* had caused so much controversy that it was selling about 800 copies each year, after reaching a high of 1,345 in 1921.[14] (It was in 1921 that Turner finally paid off a note of $500 to his publishers from royalties received from that book; the debt had been longstanding, an advance made fifteen years earlier for a textbook he was never able to complete.)

A most formidable attack on Turner's work came in 1930 from a Harvard instructor in government, Benjamin Wright. He argued, as Almack had, that backwoods democracy had played only a minor role in America's development. Armed with statistics, Wright penetrated visible chinks in the armor of Turner's theories;[15] moreover, the criticism was echoed by the prominent geographer Isaiah Bowman, who implied that Turner, not mentioned by name, was in "error."[16]

Again it was Merk whose sympathetic friendship supported Turner in his response to Wright's assault. "I think Mr. Wright," Turner told Merk, "fails to realize that what I was dealing with was, in the first place, the *American* character of democracy as compared with that of Europe or of European philosophers." In answer to Bowman's argument that Turner was in "error" claiming that the frontier ended in 1890, Turner wrote Merk that of course the frontier "'did not end with a bang' in 1890."[17]

Turner's last two books, *The Significance of Sections in American History* and *The United States, 1830-1850: The Nation and Its Sections*, both published after Turner's death in 1932, kept alive the Turnerian tradition. *The Significance of Sections*, setting forth his familiar frontier-sectional themes, was received with almost reverent enthusiasm. Frederic L. Paxson set the tone by praising Turner as "the historian's historian" who had "kept writing and his readers kept trailing."[18]

But scarcely two years after Paxson's tribute appeared, John D.

Hicks, one of Paxson's former students and a writer who quietly incorporated the frontier theory into two popular American history textbooks, in a critical review of *The United States, 1830–1850*, opened the entire field of Turnerian thought to reappraisal.[19] In a masterfully written review, in which Hicks seemed to sit back and allow other schools of thought to ponder Turner's long-awaited last book, he announced that "there will be many who will find much to criticize about the book. . . . The most obvious charge," Hicks wrote, was that there was little that was "new." Moreover, Hicks declared that "belligerent Turnerians" would be disappointed because Turner did not "take up the cudgels on his own behalf" to argue his case. Hicks lamented that the book appeared in the midst of a now persistent "dispute between the Turnerians and the anti-Turnerians . . . unhappily a bad omen." It was necessary, Hicks concluded after surveying the Turnerian battleground, for the "present generation to open its eyes" to enjoy "perspectives on the past that Turner and the men of his day never had."[20]

Hicks, in a leading history publication, felt at liberty to speak with some harshness about the decline of Turnerian thought and the need to reevaluate American history. Never "anti-Turner" or even "belligerent," Hicks, in personal conversations and in other writings, was a friendly supporter of frontier interpretations and sectional analysis; but as he observed in 1935, Turner's star was waning.[21] It is not surprising that the long-sustained enthusiasm for interest in the field, both as a teaching area and as a research discipline, had begun to languish. Merk and Paxson were among those scholars who still held forth, but a champion with a dynamic flair was needed to carry the Turnerian banner. Someone had to be the fervent missionary as Turner had been, but there was no one who could popularize or in this case revitalize the field in quite the same way that the old master had done. Turner was more than an ordinary speaker and writer; he was an eloquent and persuasive historian.[22] And he was a master academic politician who held his own against powerful rivals such as Edward Channing at Harvard.

In the hothouse world of academic politics, Turner had taken on all comers. Turner's death in 1932 clearly left the field without an able and powerful spokesman. The approaching retirement of Paxson in the 1950s was a loss to western history, but not as great as it would have been earlier. Although he had written on the West and the frontier in several volumes and had acquired an international reputation in the field after his *History of the American Frontier, 1763–1893* won a Pulitzer Prize, Paxson increasingly devoted his teaching and research work to general histories of recent America, especially during the era of World War I.[23] Moreover, Paxson's orientation toward recent history made his version of frontier history a capsule portrait, virtually ignoring the Turnerian emphasis on the colonial frontier and ending abruptly in 1893. Although Paxson reprinted a "student edition" of his frontier history, he brought out no new editions and his book was soon considered dated as other publications appeared. And as a director of doctoral students, he trained fewer and fewer specialists in frontier history.[24] But Paxson himself seems to have recognized that Turnerian frontier history was declining in popularity as he turned increasingly to teaching and publishing in recent American history.

Merk, who did not retire until 1956, became known as a celebrated teacher at Harvard, training students in western history and ancillary fields such as the history of American foreign relations. His main undergraduate course, Wagon Wheels, continued to follow Turnerian footpaths. Although he took no grandstand role in defending Turner against the ever-present bubbling of criticism, he did on occasion show his dander. When a younger scholar, a student of his own protégé Paul Gates, attacked Turner in a speech at Harvard's Henry Adams Club, Merk objected. Lee Benson argued that Turner borrowed heavily from the Italian economist Achille Loria, and even worse, that Turner was guilty of "a mistransference fallacy," that is, he uncritically adopted laws or principles from one discipline and applied them to another. Although Benson's arguments had validity, they were not accepted by Merk. If we analyze Merk's lectures, we can see that he willingly accepted Turner's "transferences" from economics, geology, geography, and other fields. By comparing classroom notes taken by Merk's students with lecture notes taken decades earlier in Turner's classes, we can see how closely Merk followed Turner's interpretations.[25]

Merk, almost without revision, faithfully repeated Turner's historical chronology. He identified the same geographical landmarks and turning points (i.e., the Cumberland Gap and the South Pass) in tracing details of westward migration. There is the same correlation of political and social data on "physiographical" maps in setting frontier-sectional themes. In the rainbow of his career Merk added descriptions of agricultural and mining land use.

Merk's lectures, as might be expected, brought the history of the West beyond the year 1893. He gave his students a fascinating example of mining developments in a description of "froth flotation" in the copper industry that made possible exploitation of "lean" western mines.[26] It was Merk, then, through his lectures and through his own research on manifest destiny and foreign policy, not to mention his training of doctoral candidates, who kept interest alive in the field. Although he read detailed lectures from what appeared to be books of notes, Merk still gave an eloquent and inspiring performance on the podium, rising up, lifting his head and facing the audience to emphasize a point.[27] Although Turner had other eminent students who supported him, they were not "realwestern" historians. These students, such as Carl Becker, Avery Craven, Herbert Bolton, and Merle Curti, had made their reputation in fields other than the history of the West. Nevertheless, each of these historians wrote affectionately about the impact of Turner and his teachings.[28] Paul Prucha and other scholars who were Merk's students remember with affection and admiration Merk's detailed, analytical lectures, including the maps, charts, and other data that were the basis of his text, *The History of the Westward Movement*.

Merk's "Contents" in his textbook, substantially a recapitulation of his lectures, were similar to Turner's with the exception that he carried his story far beyond the Turnerian ending of the 1890s (although some of Turner's syllabi show that he took his story to the 1920s). The close resemblance of Turner's lectures to Merk's (and later to Merk's text) can be demonstrated by looking at copies of notes taken in Turner's classes. Merk's description, for instance, of the Piedmont and Great Valley settlement of the eighteenth-century frontier is similar to Turner's as evidenced by Frank J. Klingberg's notes taken in Turner's Wisconsin classes: "The people who came into this region were made up of people from all parts of the British Isles, French Huguenots and Germans. But the three most important strains were the German and the Scotch Irish and the English." Turner then declares that "the Germans found the best soils and soon became the leading farmers in their several communities." This description is strikingly similar to Merk's portrait of the Germans as "excellent farmers [who] knew good soils and how to preserve them."[29]

Other parallels can be seen, for example, in lecture headings. In other notes taken in Turner's classes there is a section called "The French Barrier"; sometimes this section is also called "The French and Indian Barrier." This identical heading is used by Merk in his text of 1978. There are, of course, major differences in language and in the occasional juggling of chronology, but in the main, as Merk acknowledged in the preface of his text, Turner himself was the "initiator" of the course.[30] Indeed, one can see how Turner assumed a kind of immortality for Merk, who even used some of his maps. This is not to say that Merk did not dig deeper and expand but merely that his research never veered very far from the traditional westward movement. He worked in the related fields of expansion, foreign relations, politics, slavery, and manifest destiny. In his research on the controversial Oregon boundary question, Merk sought to prove that peaceful negotiations served as a good case study in finding solutions to international problems that could lead to war. As an example of the opposite kind of policy, Merk, in his lectures and in arguments developed in a book published by the Harvard Press in 1971, *Fruits of Propaganda in the Tyler Administration*, maintained that John C. Calhoun promoted a reckless, conspiratorial policy in promoting the annexation of Texas.[31]

As a fledgling academic at Harvard, Merk always had Turner's support, but he did not have the prestige to step in and command the kind of power Turner had held. Networking was not Merk's style, and it comes as no surprise that the Turnerian web of western historians weakened and then fell apart after Turner's death. Billington was well aware of the changing of the guard. He had a sixth sense about the realities of academic power politics, as he was later to prove. When he hitched his star to the fading galaxy of western history, he knowingly identified himself with a field that had lost its master and much of its luster. But Billington never looked back

once he had made his decision, for he envisioned new opportunities instead of problems. He would not take on Turner's critics;
he would ignore them and preach the gospel as if the sun of
western history had never gone down. In both teaching and research his energy and his enthusiasm were concentrated on his
new field of study. Even Turner's critics came to admire Billington
for his gracious reviews of their works and for the warm personal
hospitality he offered from his home in Evanston.

CHAPTER FOURTEEN

THE BILLINGTON ERA

In the early 1930s the Harvard history department was in a phase of growth that was to bring it continuing distinction. Under the sheltering elms of the Yard, students attended Frederick Jackson Turner's Wagon Wheels course, now taught by Frederick Merk and occasionally by James Hedges, one of Turner's last students, then completing his doctoral work. Ray Billington, a visible onlooker, had nearly finished his Ph.D. dissertation under Arthur M. Schlesinger. Billington was also attending meetings of Merk's western history seminar and auditing undergraduate classes in western history.

Billington was a midwesterner. His early life has been chronicled by Martin Ridge, his former student, who wrote that Billington from boyhood had been a writer, publishing poems, essays, and articles in a high school newspaper. Born in Bay City, Michigan, and brought up in Detroit, he attended the University of Michigan, where, as an editor of the *Michigan Daily,* he "scandalized" the university and was expelled, as Ridge has noted. The offense was not too great to keep him from entering the University of Wisconsin, where he earned his B.A.; he then returned to Michigan for a master's degree. From 1924 to 1927 he embarked on a career as a journalist, writing hundreds of reports for the *Detroit News* and the *Detroit Free Press.*[1]

By 1927 Billington had proved himself as a seasoned stylist who could write with brilliant clarity. But he was bored and left a promising career in journalism to enter a doctoral program in history at

Harvard. Here he began his studies in sociointellectual history. Later, in 1938, he published his dissertation, an analysis of religious persecution in the history of Protestant-Catholic conflicts, *The Protestant Crusade, 1800–1860, A Study of the Origins of Nativism.*

In the halls of the Harvard College Library it was hard to miss the blue-eyed, effervescent Billington, with his ready smile and enormous enthusiasm. Merk saw him and liked him, and an early friendship bloomed. According to Martin Ridge, Billington in the late 1940s taught western history at Harvard at Merk's invitation. This was before the appearance of Billington's *Westward Expansion.*[2] After examining an apparent pilot copy of the book, Merk was enraged, and, according to Billington himself (Billington told versions of this story at social occasions), considered legal action to protect what he considered to be the theft of his lectures.

A key to understanding the complexities and emotional trauma connected with the transfer of Turner's lectures from Merk to Billington is found in Billington's voluminous corrrespondence with Merle Curti, distinguished University of Wisconsin historian, Pulitzer Prize winner, and former Turner student. The extraordinary power that the well-liked, soft-spoken Curti wielded in two academic associations, the American Historical Association and the Mississippi Valley Historical Association, was gradually extended to Billington, his protégé. It is clear from Billington's letters that Curti engineered Billington's advance from Smith College to Northwestern University, and he was largely if not entirely responsible for Billington's election to the Harmsworth Professorship at Oxford.

Curti also helped to arrange a remarkable feat of academic politics: Billington would succeed to the presidency of the Mississippi Valley Historical Association at a time when he would not directly have to follow Merk in office, forcing Merk to have the unpleasant task of introducing him at the presidential banquet. With Curti's help, Billington on occasion actually stacked nominating committees to arrange for the election of particular favorites to the association's presidency. Between them the two historians were able to marshal a shower of letters to support a particular candidate. Incredible as it may seem, Billington almost singlehandedly brought about the firing of an editor of the association's *Review.* He then presided over the appointment of a new editor of his choice who would edit the journal at a place he deemed appropriate.[3] At a later date Billington wove another powerful network in the Western History Association (of which he was one of the founders). Although Turner's networking in the American Historical Association was formidable, Billington was even more skillful. It is clear from Billington's correspondence that he and Curti generated approval from the Mississippi Valley Historical Association members to lead a reform movement. At no time was Billington without Curti's advice and support.

So it was when Merk sought to prevent the publication of *Westward Expansion* that Billington in spring 1949 turned to Curti at the University of Wisconsin. In a letter of March 23, 1949, Billington described a sequence of events at Harvard that had apparently resulted in a temporary pacification of Merk. At the instigation of Curti, a prominent member of the Harvard history department prevailed on a recalcitrant Merk to avoid the publicity of a conflict that would sully both parties. Would Merk accept a compromise in which Billington would make a brief statement in the book's preface acknowledging his debt to Merk? Billington in addition would give tribute to Frederic Paxson and to James Hedges. The mediator, Prof. Paul Buck, actually wrote a "compromise," adding that he hoped Billington would accept it since Merk, referred to by Buck as an aged man of sixty-two, was overly sensitive about injuries whether they were imagined or real.

Merk grudgingly accepted the agreement as did Billington and approved publication by Macmillan for a college edition on March 29. For Billington the "imbroglio" was at most an unpleasant episode, but he looked on the bright side. Merk's assault, he told Curti, was in reality a sign of praise. As for Curti himself, he had been "damned helpful." If the entire affair could be forgotten all would be well. It was important to stop "any leak of it reaching the profession." Members of the Harvard history department could be trusted to keep quiet because they would be concerned with "protecting Harvard's fair name."[4]

Reading the 1949 preface to *Westward Expansion* reveals that Billington was as good as his word. Even more revealing, Hedges is named as a collaborator, and there is a separate dedication, "To

(left, courtesy, Henry E. Huntington Library and Art Gallery) *Turner in front of the great bronze door of the Huntington Library, ca. 1927*; (right, from the author's collection) *Ray Billington standing in the same place, ca. 1967.*

Frederick Merk, whose inspirational teaching and meticulous scholarship perpetuated the traditions of Frederick Jackson Turner." According to those individuals who heard Billington recount the episode, Merk was the one at fault in his "unreasonable" behavior. Not surprisingly, Merk was not placated by Billington's dedication.

Some background to this angry dispute over the Turnerian legacy may be traced to the Macmillan Company. According to Richard Leopold, Billington's longtime associate, Macmillan apparently encouraged academic rivalry. The company first offered the textbook contract to Merk and when he declined awarded it to Hedges, who in turn sought out Billington. Hedges, who had a reputation as a procrastinator, was delayed in finishing his contributions as a coauthor. Meanwhile, Billington began at once, writing and rewriting. He received a Guggenheim grant in 1943 that enabled him to leave his lecture podium and devote an entire year to working on the book. Billington, now in his late thirties and married with two children, had a slight hand injury and was not obliged to enter military service. He had begun his academic career at Clark University, then moved to Smith College, and by 1944 had arrived at Northwestern where he was eventually to hold the William Smith Mason Professorship of History. Throughout World War II and afterward Billington concentrated on the writing of *Westward Expansion*.[5]

Homer C. Hockett, loyal to his former teacher, wrote critically in a review of *Westward Expansion*, stating that Billington repeated material that was well known and failed to appraise the significance of events in terms of causes, consequences, and interpretation. Turner's book, Hockett wrote, could have been written only by Turner: "Only Ulysses could draw Ulysses' bow."[6]

Yet one can contend that Billington did indeed bend Turner's bow in magisterial style. How did he do it? In his autobiographical accounts Billington recalled how he worked nine years on a volume that became a labor of "true love—the frontier." Here was a "once-in-a-lifetime opportunity" to be a coauthor of a text on western history based on "the outlines developed by Turner for his History of the West." Eventually, Hedges found that "textbook writing was not for him," and Billington took over the project.[7]

Turner's role had been to lead a school of thought that was now losing its direction, but Billington was to make a difference. Not content to follow smaller trails, he saw himself as the pathfinder for western history. As an eloquent lecturer enthusiastic about the exploits of frontiersmen, Billington attracted large classes and devoted graduate students at Northwestern University. Among them were Martin Ridge, Richard Oglesby, Alfred Young, Lawrence Towner, Edward Lurie, and George McGovern.[8]

By the mid-1950s Billington had established himself as a primary spokesman for reviving the frontier theory as a mainstream interpretation of American history. He changed his professional identification in writing book reviews, gradually concentrating on western history. (While teaching at Northwestern in 1949 he had reviewed a volume on "church history" and a biography of John Bach McMaster for the *American Historical Review*.[9]) He took this new direction in 1951 when he accepted an invitation to review a volume on the exploration of the Colorado River and a frontier study of the Northwest. In his reviews Billington showed that he was a no-nonsense enthusiast for the "neglected" field of frontier history.[10] Billington's final venture into nonwestern history appears to have been in 1953 when he edited *The Journal of Charlotte Forten*, a free Negro woman of the 1850s.[11] Immensely productive, Billington in these years wrote a secondary-school textbook and began working on a two-volume outline of U.S. history, which later became a widely used reference work for college students.

By the 1960s he had established himself as a nationally known scholar of Turnerian theories by closely identifying himself with the master. Early in that decade he decided to leave Northwestern to accept the post that had been held by Turner, senior research associate at the Huntington Library in San Marino, California. Billington's correspondence with Curti indicates that Curti had helped to bring about his appointment.[12] After the library opened Turner's papers for scholars, Billington took advantage of the magnificent opportunity to study Turner's correspondence, lecture notes, and research materials. Unlike Turner, Billington did not see himself as a theorist. He would be a disciple commenting on and seeking to expand Turner's frontier theory. He often spoke of himself as a "Turnerian" and gave offprints of articles to scholars who could be classified as "fellow-Turnerians."[13] Paul Zall, Research Scholar at the Huntington Library, recalls that Billington was "much concerned with theories of self-reliance, independence . . . in turning our attention to . . . public . . . preconceptions." Billington had a lifelong interest in the persistent traits of frontiersmen that Turner had often described. So much talk about "traits" at the library provoked a coffee-hour comment that "one could inherit blue eyes, but not blue laws." Good Turnerians could not always see the humor of such observations.[14]

An analysis of Billington's main publications show that he increasingly became a defender, supporter, and vindicator of Turner's frontier theory. Along the way, however, he missed the larger view of Turner as a social historian and the interrelationships between the frontier and the section. Thus, although Billington avoided the one-issue controversy over the validity of Turner's conception of a frontier in American history, he nevertheless became the chief exponent of a kind of one-sided view of Turner's frontier theory, or frontier hypothesis. As Billington contended in the preface of his textbook's fourth edition, sectionalism was relatively insignificant when compared to the frontier hypothesis.

Seemingly unruffled by critical reviews of his textbook or his biography of Turner, Billington did not counterattack. Instead, his publications became a statement and a restatement of certain frontier-school doctrines. For instance, he maintained that character traits induced by a frontier social environment could be transmitted over space and time, and he advanced this theme in his *Frontier Heritage*. Robert Berkhofer, reviewing the book in *Agricultural History*, responded that "Billington would seem from the viewpoint of the last decade's thinking to be squeezing new data and new assumptions about human behavior into an old conceptual framework to the distortion of both description and explanation."[15] Instead of defending himself on the issue of transmitted character traits, Billington, when Berkhofer visited the Huntington Library, responded to his critic with charm rather than with argument. Like Turner, Billington was a most agreeable man with a mission.

Billington's self-appointed task, he said, was "to restore Turner and his theories to their rightful place in interpreting the past." According to Billington the defense was two-pronged. First, he would deal with the assertion that Turner was unscientific in his themes by pointing out that he was "far better versed in geographical and biological sciences than most of his generation." Second, Billington would argue that Turner was correct in asserting that the "frontier environment had in some manner altered the behavioral patterns of pioneers, and those altered patterns had persisted in lessening degree down to the present."[16]

It was upon such arguments that Billington reassembled the primacy of Turner's message. Yet at the same time Billington retreated from the task of proving his points; instead, he repeated and paraphrased what Turner had said. In a sense he played Huxley to Turner's Darwin and became "Turner's bulldog" in the process. A stream of printed pages issued from Billington's typewriter, each one increasingly stressing his version of a frontier theory, with a cleavage separating it from the bothersome issue of sectionalism. Seasoned scholars in the field were often silent because they found it hard to disagree with the amiable Billington. There was, however, vocal controversy about his vigorous support of amateurs in the Western History Association.[17]

These western history buffs, whether they romanticized the cow-country days or Custer's last stand, regarded Billington as their hero. He entered their circles as a speaker or as a presiding "sheriff" at "westerner" dinner clubs. With a seemingly never-ending series of anecdotes, limericks, toasts, and cordiality, he brought his friendly lay enthusiasts into the inner circle of the new scholarly organization he had been instrumental in founding, the Western History Association. Largely for their benefit, the association published for a number of years a popular magazine, *American West*, as well as a scholarly journal, *Western Historical Quarterly*. The latter became the mainstay of western history, which by the 1960s was in the midst of a renaissance that has continued.

The loyalty and interest of Turner's former students and in turn their students and disciples, along with Billington's enthusiastic efforts, resulted in an unexpected expansion of the field. By the 1960s hundreds of new scholars were including western history classes in their teaching schedules and were directing candidates for Ph.D.'s in the subject. A number of Billington's books and dozens of his essays collectively formed an imposing monument to the frontier theme that dominated his thinking. Although somewhat repetitious, his writing found publishers eager to sustain his drumbeat on such topics as the frontier hypothesis, the frontier thesis, the frontier heritage, and the far-western frontier.[18]

One can scarcely underestimate Billington's impact as a professional in his field. In conversation, in social groups, and in lectures he generated a fervor, an inspiring zeal that convinced his listeners of the fascinations of western history. He often reminisced about his academic adventures, spicing his accounts with a sense of humor that left his male audiences slapping their knees. At Northwestern, however, his classes in the Vietnam era unexpectedly dwindled in size, and occasionally he found inattentive students boldly reading newspapers at the back of the room. Their offending presence in his lecture hall, he said, was one of the reasons he left Northwestern.

Disciples and former students followed Billington's every move. They remembered how his stamp of approval on their early books had been trumpeted in academic reviews. Few historians (except for Turner) have been so popular as leaders in western history. Not surprisingly, he served as president of the Westerners International, a worldwide organization of western clubs. In 1959 he was elected president of the American Studies Association and three years later president of the Organization of American Historians.[19] In the late 1950s and early 1960s he headed that organization's energetic executive committee, which threw out the name Mississippi Valley Historical Association. The Billington network expanded to the extent that western history under his leadership became a prestigious field.

A prolific correspondent, he wrote thousands of letters, banging them out on an old Corona typewriter, and he wielded considerable authority. Hundreds of young people hung on his every word, partly because he was a key person to write confidential letters on such matters as promotion, fellowships, or research grants. He was also an important referee for academic books and could readily promise fellowships at the Huntington Library. One of the major honors he conferred was in the form of an invitation to write a volume in his *Histories of the American Frontier* series, which appeared under the imprint of Henry Holt Company, Turner's old publishers.

These developments soon eclipsed Frederick Merk's place in the Turnerian sun. What was his reaction to the continued printing of new editions of Billington's textbook? Merk was not pleased. Rodman Paul, Merk's student and a lifelong friend of Billington, often remembered his embarrassment at being in the middle of such an acrimonious controversy. Merk remained angry and talked quietly about a breach of trust and of literary piracy. Again he seriously considered litigation. Even though Billington had dedicated his book to him, Merk was still not appeased. Time heals old wounds, but for Merk, this tribute to his "inspirational teaching" had overtones of self-interest.[20]

Yet Billington did indeed write an original narrative; it is difficult to show that Merk's lectures were appropriated and placed in his book. One can easily compare Merk's lectures as they appear in *History of the Western Movement* and notes taken in his classes by Rodman Paul and Francis Paul Prucha with Billington's *Westward Expansion*. Merk's lectures and Billington's text are distinctly different. They are of course similar in the sense that they are both Turnerian; even chapter headings are taken from Turner. And both contain themes of the frontier-sectional theory and underlying characteristics of the "realwestern" history, although Merk tends to be more analytical. The central question arises, is Billington's *Westward Expansion* the book Turner would have written? Most critics would agree that it is not. Although Billington adopted Turner's chronology and his emphasis on the frontier, he was less concerned with analysis, interpretation, demography, the social sciences in general, and sectionalism. In a sense, Billington's text was more similar to Paxon's survey of 1924 than to the views and writings of Turner.

Before we leave this simmering controversy over the control of Turner's legacy, two points should be emphasized. First, Merk himself borrowed unmercifully from Turner for his own lectures. This can be determined by comparing notes from Turner's lectures with equally detailed notes taken in Merk's classes.[21] Evidence shows that Merk often repeated the very language found in Turner's lectures; indeed some of Merk's lectures are so imitative that either person could have been speaking. If Billington modeled his textbook on Merk's lectures and the Turner-Merk syllabus, he was not alone in borrowing interpretations, thoughts, and language from the master. The second point to emphasize is that even though the unfortunate "realwestern" racist, sexist, paternalistic, and reverse environmentalism themes stand out, a wider and significant view of Turner's life and work still merits appreciation and understanding and is discussed in the Epilogue.

Billington in his last years tried to cope with some of these troublesome issues in lectures and through revisions of his text-book. For instance, at the request of Macmillan and of Billington himself, Paul Prucha and I excised many of the references to "savage" or "barbaric Indians" from the fourth edition.[22] For this 1974 edition, still containing the dedication to Merk, he stream-lined the material on the frontier theme through substantial dele-tions. In his preface he was specific about cutting chapters that "dealt with the sectionalism of the pre–Civil War era rather than the frontier's advance and [that] probably should not have been included in the first place."[23]

Regarding minorities, he declared, "Today authors are obligated to let Negroes or Mexican-Americans or Indians speak loudly from their pages. Yet I cannot resist a lingering hope that the tide will turn again, and that all men will be recognized as part of a family of mankind, all equal, all deserving of recognition for their exploits or ideas, rather than because of race, color, or nationality."[24] His argument implied that he had been writing all along about minor-ities but that he did not identify them as such. Billington was never able to catch up with the women's movement and the new social history that blossomed in the 1980s (he died in 1981). We must remember, however, that he anticipated the women's movement in his editing of Charlotte Forten's journal, a tribute to a woman significant in black history. He also spoke on environmental mat-ters in public lectures and on the habits of wastefulness in frontier history.

When on January 2, 1960, the Huntington Library finally opened the Turner collection to all qualified scholars, Billington quickly established his turf. He kept a proprietary eye on large sections of Turner's correspondence, including autobiographical letters and the "Dear Lady" mass of correspondence to Mrs. Alice Forbes Hooper, all of which he later edited and published.[25] More impor-tant, he at last had his chance to write Turner's biography and to tell a story of academic pioneering on the frontiers of historiogra-phy. The result, a prize-winning biography of 1973, *Frederick Jack-son Turner, Historian, Scholar, Teacher*, gave a fresh and vivid picture of Turner's life and work as well as Billington's own views on the frontier. This approach to western history is now questioned by a group of young scholars. One of them, Richard White, is the author of an exciting 1991 textbook, *"It's Your Misfortune and None of My Own," A History of the American West.* Can it replace the Turnerian legacy? Part Five is devoted to forming an answer to that question.

PART FIVE

NEW TRAILS AND NEW CHALLENGES BY THE NEW WESTERNERS

Turner's remarkable intellectual edifice for American history did not long survive him. Once the attack began, much of the frontier thesis crumbled quickly. His evidentiary foundations were weak, his claims too sweeping, and the comparative basis of the thesis was virtually nonexistent. Eventually testing of Turner's generalizations has reduced most of them to rubble.

——Richard White, "Frederick Jackson Turner" (1988)

And those reporters always appear when Patty is there.

——Richard W. Etulain, "The New Western History" (1990)

CHAPTER FIFTEEN

THE CHALLENGE OF RICHARD WHITE TO THE TURNERIAN LEGACY

With the appearance of Richard White's book, *"It's Your Misfortune and None of My Own," A History of the American West,* published in late 1991 by the University of Oklahoma Press, a new era in western history began. A focus on White's book is necessary because it is the ultimate anti-Turnerian volume to make its way into print. White assumes the role of virtuoso who as if by magic causes Turner—the man and his ideas—to disappear from western history. Why and how does he do this? What theoretical scaffolding does he use to accomplish this remarkable feat of historical writing?

Recently at a Huntington Library conference on western history I had the opportunity to ask White directly. "Well," he said, "in writing the book I had several problems in dealing with Turner. If I agreed with Turner, if I disagreed, if I accepted part of his writings, I'd have to make my case, but I didn't want to write a book about Turner. The best way was to leave him out of the book altogether." These may not be White's exact words, but having locked them into my mind at the time, I'd say this is an approximation of what he said, and it makes sense. When William Cronon wrote about Chicago in *Nature's Metropolis*,[1] another important contribution to western history, he found himself talking a lot about Turner and, in my judgment, had problems. In White's case, there are also problems, but at least they do not concern what Turner wrote or said or where he contradicted himself.

203

Ray Billington (seated) *and Wilbur Jacobs* (standing) *in the manuscript department of the Huntington Library, ca. 1960, surrounded by boxes and file drawers containing Turner's papers.* (From the author's collection)

The best way to answer the questions about White's approach is through an intensive examination of his book. In a close reading of *"It's Your Misfortune,"* we find a stunning volume on the Great West with both omissions and commissions and with the shadow of Turner hovering in the background. The more one reads this anti-Turner book, the better it becomes. One must, as it were, get out of the Turner closet to have a genuine appreciation of White's accomplishment. One initial impression is that the old West that Frederick Jackson Turner saw as a cornucopia looks more like a test tube than a horn of plenty. Obscured is the old frontier spirit of buoyancy, optimism, and confidence that exploded into a national ethos of social strength.

Richard White shows us how that spirit masked another kind of West, one that often suffered from a virulent malady of socio-economic and environmental distemper. At first glance this book seems to be an audacious improvisation of western history, but upon further examination we find a first-rate revisionist textbook. Since there is so much that is new, one yearns for an annotated bibliography to reveal where White got his information.

There can be no question about the singular importance of this "new" book (the word "new" is on the jacket but not on the title page). The title, *"It's Your Misfortune and None of My Own,"* is taken from a cowboy song (sung to the dogies) that echoes throughout the book and that illustrates White's argument that the parade of cattlemen and other western immigrants used the land with little concern for those people who followed. The West they invaded is a specific place bounded by particular "physical entities—the Missouri River and the Pacific Ocean" (p. 3). Thus cowboys of Hawaii (and there were some) must join the mainland or find themselves in a homeland that is neither West nor East. A formidable 644 pages, the book is all-embracing in scope. In well-written, densely packed chapters organized around specific topics, White takes us from the times of the early Spanish explorers in the 1500s to the years of the Ronald Reagan presidency. An immediate impression is that it is hard to find anything that is left out. White avoids the limitations of narrative history by analyzing and interpreting the mass of facts he presents; he can thus create layers of history, one upon another.

His twenty-one chapters are organized around six thrusts of interpretation: origins of the West, the federal government in the nineteenth century, the West's transformation and development, bureaucratic changes in centers of power, further transformation of the West, and finally the modern West to the 1980s. I believe that the text and index could be converted into a database for a computerized encyclopedia of the West.

How can an author mesh all this information into one book? White can because he is a gifted scholar who has cut himself off from Turner and from dated Turnerisms. Since "the West" is clearly defined as a place, there is no need to speak of a westward-moving frontier as described by Turner or his modern disciple, the late Ray A. Billington. Nor does White name (in the text or index) Turner, Billington, or Martin Ridge, coauthor of the memorable textbook *Western Expansion*, revised by Ridge in 1982. The very word "frontier" is excised, except when unavoidable—for instance, when it is in the title of certain books coming out of the Billington series on frontier history listed as collateral reading.

Nor does White specify Turner's influential studies on sectionalism, although he occasionally refers to the West as a section to distinguish it from the East. He also leans on "sectionalism" (p. 74), and "safety valve" (p. 75) and mentions regions or subsections of the West (p. 344). In these terms and ideas Turner is ever lurking, even when given the silent treatment. But for all the virtues of White's pathbreaking work, it lacks the Turnerian regenerative spirit. Traditional frontier histories, as old as Frederic L. Paxson's and Robert E. Riegel's and as recent as Billington's, carry with them an image of reborn frontiers along with a sense of excitement and expectation; Billington almost made the reader a participant in his vivid frontier narratives. White's history, in contrast, is of necessity locked into an edifice of essays, the central floors of which are formidable treatises on the nineteenth-century West.

How then does White conceive the Great West in history? My impression is that White might have organized his book around subsections, or regions, and still avoided referring to Turner. He could have built his book around an exciting scheme of several pioneering regions and used modern regionalism studies as models. In such a scheme White could have masked the ghost of Turner's frontier-sectionalism theory.[2] Instead, he sees the true West as a great spatial area having its origins somewhere along the Missouri River, with Independence as a virginal source of Anglo-American emigration. Relying on a seemingly immaculate-conception theory of immigration history, White gives us oceans of data on immigrants and their descendants. The early chapters are exceptions because they concern Spaniards penetrating from what is now Mexico to begin their conquest of Indian peoples. But White quickly moves on to a series of treatises, often encompassing shorter ones, which account for the nineteenth-century flood of peoples and for federal government polices.

In my judgment, certain problems are inherent in neglecting regionalism in western history. If the West is treated as a kind of monolithic place without clear distinctions among, for instance, the Southwest, California (Northern and Southern), the Great Basin, and the Northwest, there is a risk of a skewed historical portrait. Indeed, this may be the major weakness of *"It's Your Misfortune,"* one that White has tried to cope with by giving a regional flavor to immigrants as they occupied their homelands.

Let us look at the book more closely. In the fields that I know best, Indian and environmental history, White's factual and statistical data are relevant, and the analysis and interpretations are a breath of fresh air after reading those chronicles of heroic conquest that have characterized much of traditional western history. We find, for example, the phrase "ecological disaster" (p. 223) in a penetrating commentary on cattle ranching, with its overstocking and fence-building in the 1880s. But it is important to show that White's extraordinary textbook confronts some of the problems that the older "western civilization" texts encountered when the author faces a vast edifice of factual data. In White's case, it is useful to point out his omissions because these are sometimes the very marrow of information that should have been included. Turner never faced that problem because, as he wrote in his letters, he could not complete a textbook manuscript. Billington created a textbook following Turnerian outlines, but he, as we have seen, gave us a jaded version of western history. White, in contrast, makes the best effort although he confines his account to a geographical area.

In environmental history, to keep abreast is sometimes to fall behind, especially in the modern era. We find no mention in White's book of ecofeminism so clearly defined by Carolyn Merchant. Overlooked are the noteworthy essays of Aldo Leopold, written in the era of 1920–1940, setting forth biocentric ideas (i.e., "thinking like a mountain"). Not unexpectedly White neglects the significant concepts of "deep ecology" that emerged in the 1970s (identified by Norwegian philosopher Arne Ness) that are, in some respects, cross-grained to White's traditional environmentalism. Nor does White discuss the environmental movement of the 1960s and its leaders such as David Brower, and even more important, the powerful Sierra Club. We miss the story of the New Yorker Henry Bergh whose American Society for the Prevention of Cruelty to Animals had branches in San Francisco and other cities in the 1880s. Organizations in New England promoted the rapid spread of antivivisection societies (precursors of the powerful animal-rights movement) throughout California's cities in the 1930s, with Pasadena as a western hotbed of protest under the leadership of Nona I. Jacobs.

In spite of White's accomplishment (he gently protests that he could not tell everything), there are other significant blanks. White gives space to Kit Carson but not to Rachel Carson or Sally Carrighar. Although he presents an accurate picture of the social turmoil of the 1960s and the riots over U.S. involvement in Vietnam, there is no mention of the subsequent change in immigration policies that brought millions of Asians into California and other parts of the West. He omits the saga of the rise of great western universities and their impact upon society. It is not an exaggeration to say, I think, that in the West education was the stem that wound the watch of social development. Also neglected is the western renaissance of popular religion. Where, for instance, are William Seymour, the black preacher of the early 1900s, and his Pentecostal Holy Rollers of Los Angeles?[3] They had a major influence on Aimee Semple McPherson and on modern TV evangelists.

When White took on the task of writing a non-Turnerian textbook of western history, he confronted an entire arena of American history that had not heretofore been examined. Omissions notwithstanding, we should be grateful for White's masterly accounts of the reckless conquest of the nineteenth-century West. Here, of course, he echoes the theme in Patricia Limerick's *Legacy of Conquest*. Limerick has skillfully mastered the art of using illustrative examples of blocks of history to make her point, and White, in writing a textbook, could have buttressed the conquest story with a chapter on western literature and the arts. What about Edward Abbey, Robert Marshall, and Joseph Wood Krutch and the arresting western tales of Bret Harte and Jack London? Although White briefly discusses the popular-culture writers Zane Grey and Louis L'Amour and the dramas "Little House on the Prairie" and *High Noon*, he neglects serious commentaries on writers such as Gertrude Atherton, Carey McWilliams, Mark Twain, Wallace Stegner, and others. Those authors whom White quotes he classifies as writers whose subject was "the imagined West." Willa

Cather is so categorized; White acknowledges only her supposed influence on Laura I. Wilder and the Little House books. He seems even to have misunderstood Twain's tongue-in-cheek humor over Brigham Young (p. 169). I remember John Walton Caughey's notable textbook on California, which still can serve as a model for treating western American literature. Another worthy example is Walton Bean and James J. Rawls's *California, An Interpretive History,* which includes astute evaluations of writers such as Frank Norris and Henry George and bibliographical essays at chapter endings. Perhaps the best reference work is *A Literary History of the American West* (1987), edited by Thomas Lyon and others.

On the positive side we can observe that White's discussion of William Henry Jackson's photographic illusions of a mythic West is to the point; yet at the same time White misses a chance to comment on the controversial assessments of Albert Bierstadt's classic paintings. His mere mention of Frederic Remington's "bloodthirsty racism" may steer the reader away from the eyewitness excitement of Remington's memorable horse-and-gun action paintings.

One of my favorite chapters in the book is "Social Conflict"; here are drunken young gunmen who carom recklessly around the western landscape. Man Eater, a brawler who chewed off his opponent's ears and noses, was more formidable than the others who relied on mere fists, feet, and guns. We also learn that there were effective gun control laws in certain cattle towns and that among the vigilantes were decent men as well as villains. Texas Rangers had their heroes (read Walter Prescott Webb), but White tells us that they also had a sort of war "against all Hispanics" (p. 335). White overlooks the part the Rangers played in the extermination campaigns against Texas Indians, however. These bloody campaigns help to explain why there are almost no reservations in modern Texas (the one or two exceptions are so small that they are invisible on White's Indian reservation map [p. 100]).

There are still untold chapters about maltreatment of Indians, and White certainly cannot be faulted for leaving out what has been ignored by his peers.[4] But let us see how some of these stories vanish in *"It's Your Misfortune."* What about those tribes in the east and to the south of the Great Lakes who were forced to move westward? In discussing Indian removal, White mentions the Cherokee and the "Five Civilized Tribes" (ethnohistorians I know do not like the latter term), but how can he overlook the terrors that the Delaware people experienced before they ended up as Parkman saw them, as dangerous, hungry scavengers on the prairies? With respect to Indian removal as well as to other topics (such as American political history), I am troubled by White's tendency to disconnect at the Missouri; nevertheless, he gives us an excellent treatment of tribal peoples and their white conquerors west of that river. I have read, for instance, no better brief account of brutal "Indian hunting" and slavery, and I know of no more valuable summary of what happened to Indians caught in the miserable Indian education programs and in the termination and relocation projects. Though his discussion of the mission period in California is tantalizingly brief, it is to the point in citing A. L. Kroeber on the precipitous decline in mission tribal population. One might wish that in addition White had commented on Father Junipero Serra's Indian policies (Serra is not named) and on the raging controversy of the last decade over Serra's prospective canonization.

What can we say in making an overall evaluation of *"It's Your Misfortune"*? On the up side, White's work justly could be named the best western history to be concerned solely with events west of the Missouri; on the downside, we miss much on modern western history. Moreover, the history of our nation seems oddly empty when a saga of American occupation of the territories east of the Missouri is missing and when American westward movements are truncated. Western history told as a Turnerian story of the whole nation in movement has, for me, more interest and significance.

A related issue is a kind of conundrum about White: Is he a western historian or an early North American frontier historian? As much as any scholar on the West, perhaps more than any other, he has written about the penetration of eastern settlement from the first day of the European invasion of the new continent. By a marvelous coincidence, in 1991 he also published a carefully researched study of genuine originality, *The Middle Ground: Indians, Empires, and Republics in the Great Lakes Region, 1650–1815*. In his

Francis Parkman persona White thus becomes the historian of early French-Canadian frontiers and of interactions between Europeans and tribal peoples. As a good long-haired man himself, he has a sympathetic understanding of those long-haired peoples of the *pays d'en haut*.

In *The Middle Ground* White writes eloquently about northeastern Indians, their culture, their intermarriages, and the fur trade that swept over eastern North America to penetrate the lands just east of the Missouri by the early 1800s. By following the paths of the fur trade in both his books, we can see how the eastern trade led west. My initial feeling in comparing White's two books is that I would like to see more about the devastating ecological impact of the fur trade on wildlife. White does comment briefly on this point (*"It's Your Misfortune,"* pp. 216–19), and he graphically describes the bison slaughtering, but his emphasis tends to be on the fur traders' intermarriages, adventures, and explorations and on the trade as a wide-ranging business. Failure to evaluate the long-term ecological consequences also weakens his treatment of western mining and miners although he does comment on the environmental mess left by some mining companies. We need more on the continuing environmental destruction in modern surface mining that began in the 1940s and 1950s.

Despite omissions, particularly in a modern history of the West, we can conclude that White is a successful pioneer on the frontiers of western-history textbook writing. One is impressed with how closely his book follows the contours of the new western history.[5] White's textbook generally orchestrates what has become a national debate on the "new" versus the "old."[6]

But there is still another resource that helps us envision western history writing in the 1990s: the 1992 issue of *American History and Life*.[7] We find in it the cumulative abstracted historical literature on the "Western States," totaling some one hundred entries including the states of Hawaii and Alaska. Scattered throughout this issue of historical abstracts are some forty references to "frontier and pioneer life," but many of the western states entries also deal with "frontier" topics. As in White's book, the corpus on the western states' West tends to be in one place, but scholarship on the "frontier" sprawls across the historiographical landscape. The division of opinion about the West is graphically portrayed in Walter Nugent's "Where Is the American West? Report on a Survey; Western Historians, Journalists, and Writers Comment on the West's Boundaries," *Montana, the Magazine of Western History* 42 (Summer 1992):2–23. Nugent argues that his survey centers on the western debates about "place" or progress (p. 2). In answering survey questions Janet Fireman and Judith Austin stress "sense of place" or "impact of place" (pp. 18, 20); William Cronon maintains that the Midwest is West (p. 12); and Allan Bogue, like Turner, writes that he follows the census (p. 14). Other respondents provide a variety of fascinating replies. According to Nugent's charts, most writers place the eastern boundary of the West at the Missouri River, but historians move it back eastward to the Mississippi. Those authors writing on the West and the frontier are still divided in their opinions of what is East and what is West. We can say, I believe, that despite White's exemplary and wide-ranging book, Turner is still on the burner.

CHAPTER SIXTEEN

TURNERIAN ECHOES IN WILLIAM CRONON'S *NATURE'S METROPOLIS*

In writing about William Cronon and Turner I find that my perceptions have come full circle and echo my viewpoints from my first two volumes on Turner, *Frederick Jackson Turner's Legacy* and *The Historical World of Frederick Jackson Turner*.[1] In the first four parts of this third volume, I have offered criticisms of the Turner legacy, but in analyzing the work of the new western historians I must at the same time assess important contributions that Turner has made to our thinking, particularly the way in which they underlie Cronon's *Nature's Metropolis*. At the same time, I join others in acknowledging the tremendous debt we owe new western historians for transforming our perspectives.

In the previous chapter we have examined new western historian Richard White's efforts to erase Turner simply by leaving him out of a leading textbook in western American history. White generated gains and losses by this strategy, yet he did prove that a major work in western history need not have Turnerian mudsills. Using a contrary strategy in another significant book, this one spotlighting the emerging urban frontier of the Midwest, William Cronon, also recognized as a champion among the new western historians, incorporates Turner into his story. In his prize-winning volume, *Nature's Metropolis: Chicago and the Great West*, Cronon successfully blends images of his own life and Turner's. He tells of growing up in Madison, Wisconsin, and living in the very shadow of Turner, which seemed to hover over the history department of the university.[2]

A skilled writer, a former Rhodes Scholar, and the recipient of a

213

Cartoon of Turner as a computer historian. (Courtesy, Kerry Soper)

MacArthur fellowship and the Francis Parkman prize, Cronon has served as the inspiring and vigorous president of the American Society of Environmental History. The author of two notable books, *Changes in the Land: Indians, Colonists, and the Ecology of New England* and *Nature's Metropolis*,[3] he has now been recognized by his appointment to the Frederick Jackson Turner Chair of History at the University of Wisconsin. At a reception in his honor at a recent meeting of the Organization of American Historians, Cronon told me that he has been asked to give the Merle Curti series of lectures at the University of Wisconsin, and he will take this opportunity to tell more about the influence of the frontier theme on American history.

A natural outcome of his Wisconsin associations is that Cronon blossomed into a Turnerian who respects, but wishes to modify, the Turner legacy. Cronon accomplished this feat by degrees, first in a series of scintillating essays whose purpose was, he said, to "get Turner out of my system."[4] These essays had the desired results, for his monumental book retains both bright images and corrective shadows of the Turnerian patrimony.

Cartoon of Turner reflecting on criticism of 100 years. (Drawn by the author)

Cronon grew up near the Madison campus of the University of Wisconsin, where his father is an eminent scholar in the department of history. Other new western historians, however, have been less exposed to Turner. Three distinguished scholars, Patricia Limerick, Richard White, and Donald Worster, have been less than kind to the Turnerian heritage. If Cronon sees himself as a kindred critic of the Turnerian legacy and therefore distances himself from the others, he nevertheless exhibits intellectual ties with these three. He takes pains to single them out for elaborate statements of praise and indebtedness to them in his prefatory statements in *Nature's Metropolis*.[5]

Cronon's literary design in *Nature's Metropolis*, although partly based upon Turner's stages of frontier advance that appear and reappear as perplexing semiplots, relies on a master theme that is similar to a Parkmanesque literary device. As Francis Parkman turned to Edward Gibbon as a model in creating a major dramatic theme to tell of the rise and fall of New France, so does Cronon reflect Parkman as he chronicles the ascent and decline of nineteenth-century Chicago as a gateway city of commercial enterprise. Because business stratagems and commercial stories serve to confine the boundaries of his narrative plan, perhaps there are few alternatives to the basic storyline of economic growth and decay. Cronon makes no effort to argue baseline Turnerian concepts of frontier-sectional politics and cultural history. His narrative gives no account of the impact of the frontier upon national character, regional politics, or the rise of the Midwest with Chicago as the regional center. Yet he stirs a watery swirl of urban-history theory, and a reading of this literature suggests that Cronon's arguments can be contested. Cronon shuffles around Turner's shadow implying that Turner wrongly named Chicago as "center place" city instead of "gateway city," but such manipulation of narrative plot does not prevent Cronon from giving shaded life to the frontier theory.

Nature's Metropolis, in a 502-page narrative-bout with Turner, is divided into three sections. Part 1, "To Be a Central City," begins with the wilderness hinterland and traces its transformation by the railroads and commerce. Part 2, "Nature and the Market," a noteworthy account of the rise of the grain, lumber, and meat businesses, lays the basis for an exciting climax in Part 3, "The Geography of Capital," stressing the interrelationships of city and country and concluding with an account of the 1893 Chicago World's Fair, where the youthful Turner presented his essay. Throughout, the narrative traces the intertwining destinies of city and country in terms of the extraordinarily complex and intricate exchange of commodities and money.

Cronon, like Francis Parkman, has proven himself to be a remarkable storyteller, notwithstanding subject matter as dull as bankruptcy records. Cronon has given us clues to the better telling of various kinds of historical stories in a prize-winning essay, "A

Place for Stories: Nature, History, and Narrative."[6] In it, for example, he juxtaposes contradictory "stories" that are based upon similar data, contrasting different interpretations of the Dust Bowl that had been gleaned from a common documentary base. The opposing authors even agreed upon "most of their facts," but one praises heroic farmers who battled dust storms and the other argues that the Dust Bowl was "one of the worst ecological blunders in history." As for Turner, in Cronon's view, he told a story of "heroic pioneers": "Making Indians the foil for its story of progress," Turner's "frontier plot made their conquest seem natural."[7]

In *Nature's Metropolis* Cronon follows just this kind of novelistic scheme, whether he contrasts Turner's ideas to the gateway concept or reveals sunny booster images that suddenly shatter when they are put under the lens of ecological perspectives. Cronon shows us that this style of narrative invigorates the reader's expectations. One might judge that if Turner had had Cronon's novelistic skills (Turner said he was not a "saga man" when he failed to complete a textbook), he might have been able to execute his sectional writings on a level with his immensely successful frontier essay of 1893.[8]

Consider the contrasts in Cronon's and Turner's stories as they are plotted out in *Nature's Metropolis*. Turner's plots are fixed in a ruling-theory format; they revolve around the growth and development of frontiers and sections, with minimum references to towns and cities although Turner concentrated on Chicago's powerful role as a sectional center. But Cronon, like urban history writer Richard Wade, spearheads the city with the frontier as backdrop. At the outset Cronon and Turner cast contradictory shades of meaning, and this incongruity becomes a kind of subplot in Cronon's story. Turner's frontier theory slithers in and out of the narrative as a kind of foil.[9] The reader is carried along by a feeling of suspense that builds until a subclimax is reached when the substitute thesis of the "gateway city" unfolds. In the developing masterplot to justify the gateway interpretation, Turner's shadow persists, at times barely visible, sometimes identified with a nineteenth-century economist-geographer who is gently but firmly discredited. In the climactic conclusion, virtuosic detail is used to brighten shades of agreement and disagreement with the beclouded Turnerian legacy.

The pleasant ending is that "good old Freddie Turner," as Carl Becker remembered him, has an appreciative admirer among the new western historians. Cronon's narrative of discovery in urban-frontier history tells us, with some alteration, that there is indeed a middle ground from which the Turnerian legacy in American history may be appraised.

Because the narrative design in *Nature's Metropolis* is partly based upon exposing to the reader dramatic dissimilarities in viewpoints, Cronon sets the scene by telling us that the Turnerian term "free land" in fact now has a very different meaning. "Free land" in ecological parlance is actually "unexploited natural abundance."[10] This assertion releases a flood of reasoning to expose disharmony in Turner's thought:

> Chicago and other cities of the Great West grew within the ecological context of what the historian Frederick Jackson Turner would have called "frontier" conditions. Despite all the ambiguities and contradictions that have bedeviled Turner's frontier thesis for the past century, it still holds a key insight into what happened at Chicago in the years following 1833. The "free land" that defined Turner's frontier was important not because it was "empty" or "virgin" or "free for the taking,"—the Indians, at least, knew it was none of those things—but because its abundance offered to human labor rewards commensurate with the effort expended to achieve them. . . . Unexploited natural abundance was central to the meaning of Turner's frontier. . . . Much of what made the land valuable in the first place had little to do with the exploitation of *people*. The exploitation of *nature* came first.[11]

In alerting us to the idea of "the exploitation of *nature*," Cronon implies a certain paradoxical decadence in Turner's free-land concept, a mini-subplot that must be dealt with later in his own narrative. At the same time, there are good reasons why Cronon does not enumerate other of Turner's shortcomings criticized by new western historians, such as the neglect of people of color and of women or his waspish views of history. In discussing population booms Cronon talks about German and English people and, like

most economic historians, leans toward a Pollyanna view of population increases (as opposed to biologists, who tend to be Cas-
sandras contending that population growth can lead to disaster).
In discussing the crowded world of Chicago and its environs,
Cronon mentions no African Americans although there must have
been black slaves in pre–Civil War southern cities as well as in St.
Louis, a gateway city he discusses. Understandably the welfare of
blacks cannot easily be brought into Cronon's commercial history.
Nor will the design of his literary scheme permit him to be caught
in nonessential discussions about other people of color or the
treatment of women. The formal elegance of his case (and this was
perhaps also true of Turner) makes it in some sense unexceptional.

Although he talks about population growth, he passes over the
literature on the subject (by immigration and population historians, biologists, anthropologists, and nutrition experts) that helps
to explain booms and boomers.[12] Yet the environmentalist wants
to hear Cronon's assessment of the direct jolt of population explosions upon ecological resources, and Cronon deals with this only
indirectly. Economic historians for years have equated business
booms with population growth, but as Thomas Malthus taught,
population increase does not always lead to economic expansion
and commercial success. Garrett Hardin, biologist and Malthusian
scholar, demonstrates that the invasion of the wilderness "commons" by the "explosion" of European peoples is a vital but neglected narrative of our past.[13] One of Cronon's minor literary
stratagems is to provide an emerging story of city entrepreneurs
and developers who initiated a continual barrage of unsavory impacts on the wilderness and then upon country people. It was the
urban phalanx of boom that eventually determined the price and
extent of the refashioning and exploiting of "first nature." Cronon
names the altered new land "second nature."

In consequence, his story traces the pattern of business history
in urban-country-ecological-geographical-economic happenings.
This approach does not entirely differ from Turner's explanation of
events by means of the frontier theory, where there is a brief
account of the social evolution of towns and cities from frontier
trading posts to modern urban centers. But Cronon repeatedly
tells us in his subplot on Turner that the city grew much faster

than Turner envisioned. This anti-Turner stratagem gradually becomes clear in the sketches of the rise of gateway cities such as St.
Louis and its successor, the metropolis of Chicago.

During the whole course of his narrative Cronon keeps the
reader's eye on the lateral east-west boundaries of financial exchange. He takes pains to separate his story from what he believes
to be Turner's story, and indeed there is some difference between
Cronon's Turner and the frontier-sectional Turner. Is there room for
confusion? Not exactly, because the literary scheme of putting
Turner in the outback of events is smoothly woven into the narrative; it is done so skillfully that there seems to be no room for
questioning the sequence of events as presented. Cronon has mastered the cobbling of many components, yet he gives the impression of a single guiding hand. A mass of factual data is continually
cited to signal the gradient ascent of the gateway-city interpretation.

Turner's papers at the Huntington Library, particularly his collection of handmade maps held together with old-fashioned safety
pins, show him to be a pioneer in the collection of various types
of databases. Such data was cited as proof of the validity of the
frontier-sectional interpretation. Incrementally, Turner's target was
the section,[14] and, like Cronon, he was fascinated by fiscal details.
He turned to financial registers to chart regional industrial and
commercial growth. He discovered what was happening to the
tariff. He saw positive indicators of voting strategies for New England, the Middle West, the South, and other sections. One can
feel confident that Cronon's research methodology in tracing the
history of Chicago's financial ascent would have appealed to Turner. He would have probably approved of Cronon's history of
"commodification," especially the story of accounting in "the geography of capital" as revealed in bankruptcy cases. But he most
certainly would have tried to tie Cronon's data into some kind of
sectional pattern.[15]

This kind of business history is, to be sure, not the most fascinating subject matter for a narrative even though it underlies the
drama of the colorful city of Chicago. One of Ray A. Billington's
most notable accomplishments was the detailed demonstration of
Turner's sectional themes about the Midwest and Chicago for the

first edition of his textbook *Westward Expansion.*[16] Skilled narrator that he was, Billington finally decided to delete these "dry" chapters, a term Billington used himself, because the story element was so laden with facts and business history data and so uninteresting that it was avoided by students. Billington once told me that he had to bow to publishers and delete or modify most of the analytical sectional narrative; at stake was the very life of his text.

Cronon has adroitly argued that modern environmental history is the natural modification of Turner's environmental viewpoint.[17] We may ask specifically about the environmental rumble that led to Cronon's acknowledgement of Turner's impact. As mentioned in earlier chapters, the environmental influence of the rugged frontier helped to mold the character and the sociopolitical outlook of the frontier people as they and their descendants pushed off to occupy successive frontiers. The pioneers carried the seeds of democracy and representative government and set up new societies in the terminal moraine of the frontier. These new societies evolved into sections, almost like miniature nations in their distinctive characteristics. The successive waves of occupation had a profound impact upon the sections and the towns and cities that appeared in their wake. There was and continued to be modifications in the natural landscape as the sections emerged from what Turner called "geographical provinces." Within the sections each town, settlement, village went through a sequence of evolutionary-social stages, from pioneer trading posts to modern towns and cities. Here Turner gave us an environmental-geographical view with firm outlines of geographical determinism. Yet at the same time he provided the foundations for regional studies that throw light upon the origins of the American nation. Cronon extracts part of this scheme of argument but at the same time treats Turner's view of urban origins as a demonstration of the weaknesses of the central-place theory of Chicago's birth.

Clearly, Turner gave little consideration to the disastrous walloping given the soil, the flora, the fauna, and the Indians, too, by fur traders, fur companies, farmers, cattlemen, miners, timber cutters, railroaders, and speculator-boosters; these types were his heroes in books and essays on the frontier and the section. It was the challenge of the conquest of the land that helped to build the inventive, democratic, enterprising individual. So much for the Turnerian tale of reverse environmentalism.

Cronon silently corrects Turner with elaborate descriptions of the ruthless transformation of the wilderness by business forces. This corrective emerges as a parallel plot, the economic changes wrought by second nature over wilderness, or first nature. Chicago's massive expansion to exploit first nature was part of a capitalistic network formed by the gateway city and its links to the Northeast and the Far West. Time and again we are told how virgin wilderness of "first nature" is seized by pioneers who changed, modified, and exploited the land so that it became "second nature." Cronon repeatedly tells us about business inroads, which he sees as the primary cause of ecological mischief, but as we have seen, he backs off from analyzing the population issue because it might steer the reader away from the overall literary design, which contrasts two kinds of nature. Unlike Turner, Cronon is therefore not interested in alarmist ecopopulation literature by biologists that might bear on his evidence or his conclusions. And Turner himself, though he made inroads in research on population issues and demonstrated an acute fear of future overpopulation, barely mentions the subject in his historical writings except to pour out lavish praise on the northern European peoples who settled the frontiers.

On other topics in *Nature's Metropolis* Turner is everywhere present as a shadow. It is almost inevitable that echoes of Turner can be heard in Cronon's work as well as in the works of practically all new western historians. Points of view tend to blend the old and the new. William Cronon is, perhaps, the most conspicuous example of this tendency because he returns more than others to Turner's (and to Ray A. Billington's) sectional boosterism.[18] In addition, Cronon builds upon recurring themes of other Chicago-area historians, especially Bessie Pierce, who wrote on the soaring heights of commercial success reached by the windy city as a railroad-commercial-meatpacking booster center.[19]

Cronon creates another predominant though minor ploy in response to an added environmental rumble, this one as provocative as Turner's. To actuate a controversial theory on the origins of western cities, Cronon spins a subplot around Johann Heinrich von Thünen, a nineteenth-century farmer-economist and the author of a monumental work, *Der isolierte Staat*, published in three volumes in Hamburg between 1826 and 1863.[20] Von Thünen in a historic economic model analyzed belts of agriculture surrounding a city situated on a fertile plain that was not served by a canal or riverway. His model city, in the center of concentric areas of agriculture, was bounded first by a belt of garden and dairy farms, the second had orchards and grains with crop rotation, and finally a third belt had livestock grazing.[21] This last belt was bordered by a wilderness, an area that has been compared to Turner's wilderness frontier.

Von Thünen was primarily an economist who focused on rental costs in the various belts, which, he argued, would depend upon wagon-transport charges. Rent charges (or land values) were differential as a result of location. *The Isolated State* was a profound work of economic theory that modern economists cite as a prototype for concepts of marginal productivity, mathematical economics, and econometrics, and only recently has the work been examined in light of wilderness frontiers and the theory of central-place cities. In any case, there is some doubt if von Thünen's model of a city on a large central plain (with no adjacent waterways) surrounded by concentric circles of agricultural production can be used as a model to explain Chicago, a city largely dependent upon the presence of a great freshwater lake. In a strict sense, von Thünen's belts in a Chicago model would float far out in the waters of Lake Michigan. Nevertheless, there are comparisons, and von Thünen's city with its agricultural belts does have a resemblance to Turner's frontier zones of expansion.

By bringing von Thünen's model into his narrative, Cronon deftly paints a contrasting image to his gateway interpretation to distance himself from Turner. Readers, somewhat to their surprise, are told that von Thünen's erroneous interpretation about central-place cities resembles Turner's. But to support Cronon, a case can be made that there are similarities, and even today at national meetings of geographers an occasional paper suggests that Turner was influenced by von Thünen's ideas. Cronon does not make this case, nor can I. In my examination of Turner's papers, along with other Turnerian scholars such as Al Bogue and David Wrobel who have probed the Huntington Library collection, no evidence has been found to justify Turner's indebtedness to von Thünen.

For Cronon, a story about von Thünen's environmental belts of settlement is useful as a foil so that he can enlarge a subplot climax telling us that both Turner and von Thünen are in error. We then have a kind of fermata in Cronon's story as he disavows both writers—but not quite. Later in the narrative both men make surprise appearances as ailing but productive thinkers representative of their own times. What about Turner? The drama is extended when his shadowy persona hovers over the entire narrative. His frontier "stages" actually represent, Cronon tells us, "the expanding edge of the booster's urban empire."[22]

At the same time, however, Turner must be firmly shoved aside. Cronon explains: "The hierarchy of the city, town, and country that appeared too quickly in the great West during the second half of the nineteenth century represented a new phase of frontier expansion, far more rapid than anything Frederick Jackson Turner described." And worse, Turner, like poor old von Thünen, set forth the central-place theory, which is, as Cronon declares, "profoundly static and ahistorical."[23]

Having erased the Turnerian image for the moment, Cronon then turns to that fascinating economic-geographic-ecological concept of the gateway city.[24] There is, as Cronon amply demonstrates, nothing static or ahistorical about this kind of viewpoint. There was action involving Chicago all over the Northeast and laterally to the Great West, as he shows in his analysis of railroads and in riveting bankruptcy cases, with massively detailed treatment of the commercial interchange surrounding wheat, hogs, cattle, sheep, and other products. People were there, but we are not told much about them except that they were English or German. A few individuals surface in Cronon's narrative, such as the slaughterhouse king, Philip Armour, and several sad entrepreneurs who lost their shirts in bankruptcies because they lived far beyond their means.

The anti-Turner presentation of the bankruptcy cases buttresses the gateway theme adopted, Cronon says, from the writings of a

Canadian geographer, A. F. Burghart. These cases, as well as other financial records, provide evidence that St. Louis and later Chicago produced elongated gateway patterns of commercial impact. Chicago's patterns measured well over a thousand miles in a westerly direction but a shorter distance eastward. The city, the Great West, and the Northeast were lashed together by rails and commerce in a kind of horizontal maze of tracks (demonstrated by railtrack maps in *Nature's Metropolis*), with a bulging nucleus around the southern end of Lake Michigan at Chicago.[25] In describing the gateway city, Cronon, however, states that "there was nothing *central* about it."[26] Yet these very railtrack maps also seem to indicate that Chicago had a vaguely rotund shape as a central hub of the entire Midwest. Indeed, as Indiana historians have complained, the east-west orientation argued in Cronon's books says nothing about Chicago's influence upon the southern areas of the Midwest. Indiana did not find its way into his massive book because it did not fit the gateway theme. One could argue that Chicago was as much a central-place city as a gateway city, but Cronon with his narrative design stresses a dichotomy of opposites.

Near the grand climax of his suspenseful narrative Cronon, not mincing words, tells us why the gateway-city concept is the only way to explain Chicago's nineteenth-century history:

> Gateway cities were a peculiar feature of North American frontier settlement. To return to the argument of the Canadian geographer A. F. Burghart, they were not central places and did not conform to the expectations of the central place theory that a metropolis should sit like von Thünen's isolated city at the center of a symmetrical network of medium- and low-ranked cities, towns, and farms. Instead, the gateway served as the entrance and exit linking some large region with the rest of the world, and it therefore stood at one end—usually the eastern end—of a large tributary hinterland that had no other means of communication with the outside."[27]

There is, then, a history of Chicago in terms of what Cronon calls "capitalistic geography." Chicago was a "temporary" gateway, and the Middle West was "not a very Western place at all."[28] And in the culmination of the plot in Cronon's conclusion we return to a discredited Turner: "Our ending of this story, then, is about the rise and fall of the greatest gateway City of the Great West. Viewed from Chicago, the process which the historian Frederick Jackson Turner described as the reenactment of social evolution in isolated frontier places has a very different meaning."[29]

Enmeshed in the ecological stories that Cronon tells are the accounts of ecosystems. We witness the killing of Indians and wildlife and the destruction of the pre-Columbian pine forests of Michigan and Wisconsin. There was prosaic truth in stories of cutover woodlands and the killing of wild creatures; second nature was the remaking of woodland and prairie wilderness.[30] Near the grand climax of his narrative, Cronon takes up a haunting and dramatic topic that is not found anywhere in Turner's massive accumulation of notes, letters, or publications: the violent treatment of animals throughout the history of the West. Here Cronon finds a kinship with Patricia Limerick, Richard White, and Don Worster, who have written eloquently on the abysmal slaughter of American wildlife.[31]

Cronon, however, takes on a third dimension in telling of western violence toward the creatures we eat: the wanton cruelty in the killing of food animals. In a dramatic minor episode in his history of Chicago, he writes expressively about the "unremembered deaths" of thousands upon thousands of cattle, hogs, and sheep that formed a "great tide of animal flesh" staggering through the Union Stockyards of the nineteenth and early twentieth centuries.[32] The Chicago slaughterhouses, where animal flesh is turned into neatly packaged steaks and chops, were and continue to be sites of extraordinary brutality.

Cronon suggests a unique response to this largely ignored phenomenon in our western past. Is there, he muses, a kind of conspiracy among farmers, slaughterhouses, and consumers to set up a method of producing flesh and eating it while avoiding responsibility for killing animals so biologically close to us?[33] As Americans prospered, the lot of the food animals declined until, even today, the parade of killing has become a kind of horror story. This kind of interpretive thrust about the powerful Chicago meatpacking dynasties led by Philip Armour has brought enthusiastic comment even from Cronon's most able critics.[34] Turner would probably have turned away from this kind of western history; he loved his wine, steaks, and cigars. We cannot be surprised to know that Bill Cronon is a vegetarian, a compassionate environmentalist who has a feeling for his subject and the widest dimension it entails. As Aldo Leopold once argued, the main penalty of being exposed to an ecological education is that one then lives in a world of wounds.

There is still another fascinating aspect of Cronon's book. Somewhat unexpectedly, there are pleasant overtones of a lyrical spirit, an exuberance of feeling that harks back to the pastoral literature that Cronon seeks to refute. In his storylike chapters, he debunks the opposites between the innocence and simplicity of the countryside and the misery and corruption of the city, but if we read between the lines, distinctions between the country mouse and the city mouse remain, despite their sharing the same cheese.

A conclusion one can draw is that the new western historians are not always far adrift from the Turnerian mainstream. Cronon tends to agree with Patricia Limerick, who argues in *The Legacy of Conquest: The Unbroken Past of the American West:* "Just as Turner did, I take my clues from the present . . . a presentist view seems to me, as it did to Turner, worth the risk."[35] Her confession tells us that historians mediate among themselves. As Arnold Toynbee once said, there is such a thing as historical transference, when opponents imitate each other and go so far as to adopt each other's behaviors and arguments. Even so, there are backlashes, especially among western historians, and they reactivate controversies about Turner and his legacy. The next chapter focuses on a new explosion of Turnerian fireworks.

CHAPTER SEVENTEEN

AFTER A CENTURY
Minefields along the Turnerian Trail

The academic uproar of the early 1990s among western historians mixing uncollegial charges and countercharges seems at first to be more of an academic dustup about old versus new rather than a debate about the Turnerian legacy. Yet the course of the controversy indicates that individuals have taken certain positions on treatment of this legacy. Moreover, the most vocal of the spokespersons reveal that there continues to be a certain commonality in interpreting the old master, even after the contestants have taunted each other. Prescient observers of the esteemed students of western history Patricia Limerick, Richard White, and Donald Worster (plus a reluctant Cronon) charge that despite these scholars' claims to have found new truths, they have yet to unscramble the Turnerian egg even though the egg is often pictured as decayed and rotten. David Kennedy contends that the new westerners have been "harmful" to the degree that they have "fragmented the picture of the past" and "deflected" attention "from questions of power." Novelist Larry McMurtry concludes that negative sides of the western story have already been told "by abler historians than most of the revisionists," and Martin Ridge, Turnerian scholar, asserts that "it is a history where ideology is too often substituted for evidence."[1]

Among the new western historians (excepting Cronon), there is the perception that traditional Turnerism should be cast aside because it is not relevant in the modern history of the West. Supporters of the new western historians have argued that the field of western history has been invigorated by their work, stressing, as we have seen, a disheartening story of avarice and rapacious conquest. Accused of debunking and grandstanding and taking on other historians' ideas, these revisionists have incensed many scholars in the field of western history.

The important point, however, is to recognize that this controversy tends to settle down to another quarrel about the Turnerian legacy. Janny Scott, gifted journalist for the *Los Angeles Times*, reached this conclusion after having had interviews with a number of contending scholars. With extraordinary perception she pinpoints the main issue: "At the heart of the matter is the traditional view that the westward movement of the frontier uniquely shaped American democracy and character."[2] This is it. The debate really revolves around the Turnerian view of American western history as set forth in Turner's 1893 essay arguing that the frontier experience had a unique role in forming the American character and democracy. The new western historians may disown the frontier idea, but they have not succeeded in discrediting its defining role.

It is interesting to observe that two of those scholars who have debunked Turner are at times still undecided about what to do with him. For instance, while they have built a new anti-Turnerian vocabulary that substitutes the words "conquest" or "place" to replace the "F" word ("frontier"), both Richard White and Patricia Limerick have seemingly modified their views of Turner. During a question period at a recent western history conference at the Huntington Library, White stunned his audience when he declared that Turner was a "genius" and, in comparison, Buffalo Bill was "brilliant."[3] And at the 1993 Organization of American Historians (OAH) meeting in Anaheim, California, Patricia Limerick confessed that when she lectured in the first half of a U.S. survey course in American history (she usually taught the second half), she was obliged to use the "F" word for want of a suitable alternative.[4] These comments may be a good indication that a commonality underlies the quarreling; Turner may still be the intellectual bridge between the old westerners and the new.

A stylistic element in Turner's writings makes it easier to build such bridges. As Sarah Deutsch argued at the OAH meeting in a session devoted to Turner, the old master is often so vague in his generalizations that he can be quoted to justify a myriad of interpretations.[5] At this same meeting, in a descriptive analysis of Turnerian literature, Allan Bogue stressed that Turnerian writers from Fulmer Mood to Merle Curti and from Curti to the new western historians have followed the Turnerian preference for connection and consensus.[6] Fredrika J. Teute, in her current study of four stages of Turnerian frontier advance, agrees. At a Huntington Library seminar on April 28, 1993, she argued that Turner's four "stages" (sometimes Turner evoked five or six stages of frontier advance), reverberate with the romantic myths dominating the writings of seventeenth- and eighteenth-century authors in Europe and America. The stages, she argues, are embedded in our past as a blending of myth and historic truth.[7]

The book *Trails: Toward the "New" Western History* makes it possible to summarize some of the main arguments of new western historians. Limerick's precepts, formulated some four years after the appearance of her probing volume, *Legacy of Conquest: The Unbroken Past of the American West*, are in a sense models of interpretation.[8] Limerick's main argument, a potent one, is that the old western history and its successor, which she aptly names the restored old western history, "totters" in "embracing the complexity." Her example is New Mexico's history. She makes the very good case that in an examination of vast West, the lands west of the 90th meridian, Turner and his work are simply not relevant; it is better in her view to look to the new western historians who follow her conquest-legacy theme and the geographical boundary lines depicted by Richard White. In his essay "Trashing the Trails," White concludes, as he also argues in his textbook, that the West is nothing less than a "region."[9] My particular hero among the new westerners is the wise and articulate Don Worster, who argues that the new westerners should "discover a new regional identity and set loyalties more inclusive and open to diversity than we have known and more compatible with a planetwide sense of ecological responsibility."[10] William G. Robbins perhaps best summarizes Worster's position on Turner with the observation that Worster's book, *Rivers of Empire*, argues that Turner's West "has no water, no aridity, no technical dominance in it, that indeed has very little of the West as geographically defined today."[11] Above all, Worster tells us we must listen to Patricia Limerick, who "challenges us to transcend the details of our research."[12]

How can we respond to such eloquent statements? Is this, as William Cronon once suggested, Turner's last stand? We can only reply that for every generalization that excludes Turner from western history, there is a counterargument because the old master and his writings—antiquarian, outdated, racist, paternalistic, and antiintellectual as they have been portrayed—will not go away. Turner is, as I have found in reading his papers, lectures, and books, a canny character who, if resurrected, could quickly jump on the newest of the new western history bandwagons without batting an eye. How could he do it? He would just say, "Of course, that is what I've been saying!"

Ironically, Limerick, in a *Trails* essay, characterizes Turner as a "newer" western historian and as an advocate of "updating our thinking about the past in response to current events."[13] One can argue that there is a further irony in that this "updating" is key to the Limerick methodology. In *Legacy* she has relied upon her skills as a historian and writer to fuse new western history presentist interpretations with notable blocks of history in such topics as mining, Indians, the slaughter of wild animals, and ranching and agricultural happenings. In her *Trails* essay she pinpoints overarching new western guidelines: the West is a place and a region that has a historical "process at work"; western historians avoid "progress" and "improvement" models; and even more noteworthy, "New Western historians surrender the conventional, never-very-convincing claim of omniscient, neutral objectivity."[14] Few observers will deny that Patty Limerick stands for her principles; as an old westerner who felt a sense of isolation in our profession, I welcome her to the old and new western history campgrounds.

Martin Ridge strikes the aged Turnerian drum to alert the old guard in the noteworthy *Atlas of American Frontiers*,[15] which now serves notice on all western historians that there are more trails than Patricia Limerick anticipated. For Ridge, "frontiers" are marked by trails and routes, and there are maps with learned commentary to prove it. Moreover, those new westerners who persist in describing the West as a "place" will be obliged to explain away the geographical landmarks discussed in chapters on "the frontier's dawning," the "early frontiers," the "frontier across the Mississippi," and the "legacy of the frontiers" documented by maps, breathtaking photographs, historical illustrations, and precise introductions. The legacy section tells of the frontier's "long shadow," the "restless, aggressive march of pioneers," who "carried the flag of the United States through the Cumberland Gap, and then through the South Pass of the Rocky Mountains, and on to the Pacific Ocean." Although the frontier people "were described as individualistic, self-sufficient, mobile, aggressive, practical, democratic," Ridge points out that "the frontier spirit has also been perceived as racist, wasteful, and violent." He concludes that "confronted with the problems of their society and the challenge of living within the limited resources of the earth, Americans are reinterpreting this legacy."[16] In this sense, Ridge echoes environmentalist-presentist concerns accepted by the new western historians.

Students of modern western American history must acknowledge their indebtedness to two senior scholars besides Ridge who have overseen much of the infighting about who said what and about who best knows the Turner legacy, the now retired deans of our profession, Allan G. Bogue and Howard Lamar. They preside over what has been perceived increasingly as a generational gap— a point of view presented by baby-boom scholars on the Turnerian trail who do not always agree with each other—that has opened a minefield of Turnerian and non-Turnerian issues.

Bogue, who wrote the learned and comprehensive "Significance of the History of the American West: Postscripts and Prospects," knows Turner well and has worked with his papers at the Huntington Library.[17] A number of other historians have written at length on Turner and our best journals have published their writings, but Bogue has had the advantage of probing this formidable collection of Turner's papers. We can argue that he appreciates and understands the ramifications of the full-blown frontier-sectional theory with its social-science orientation and thus the essence of

Martin Ridge, one of Billington's students. After serving as editor of the Journal of American History, *Ridge succeeded Billington as senior research associate at the Huntington Library. Following the fourth edition of* Westward Expansion, *Ridge became a coauthor and made major revisions in the book.* (From the author's collection)

Turner's message. In his essay he orients his readers with a kindly, constructive overview of contending positions. He emphasizes, for instance, the actuality that Turner fleshed out his early career as a faculty member of the "School of Political Science, Economics, and History" at the University of Wisconsin.[18] It is important to Bogue that Turner appreciated that the social-science aspect of history might well be incorporated into the modern curriculum.

As for Howard Lamar, the accolades accorded to him as a living "father of the field" at the 1992 New Haven meeting of the Western Historical Association were all deserved. He had close ties with Ray A. Billington in formulating and editing the American Frontier Series, and the number of able scholars he has trained, including such luminaries as Patricia Limerick and William Cronon, demonstrates that his "sons and daughters" have made an enormous impact upon the teaching and writing of American western history. Moreover, Lamar has been a leading interpreter of Turner's thought, having never lost respect for the innovative role that Turner had in the writing of frontier-western history. He has, moreover, been a persistent advocate for comparative frontier history and for new views about the twentieth-century West. Additionally, he has given us a sense of appreciation for writers of the past and expressed those sentiments in a recent lecture, "Keeping the Faith: Forgotten Generations of Turnerian Writers and Historians, 1920–1945."[19]

Both Lamar and Bogue view western history in a way that our best senior scholars have a right to do. They have been in the saddle long enough to see that western history profits from a harnessing of the old and the new interpretations. The new western historians have left a powerful imprint on our ways of thinking, but their contributions refine and enlighten rather than replace. The frontier-sectional concepts live on with Al Bogue and Howard Lamar despite the controversies that Turner's legacy has engendered.

We are fortunate as well to have the wisdom of historian John Mack Faragher, who in a learned essay in the February 1993 issue of the *American Historical Review* appraises the controversy engulfing modern western history.[20] There was, as Faragher reminds us, a time when the wide arena of western America was metamorphosed into a financial juggernaut by means of prodigious federal expenditures of capital. Historians coming of age in the wake of World War II were, Faragher reminds us, historians of a western America that was in an era of boom, when the region jet-propelled itself into a cultural and economic "pacesetter" for

America as a whole. Seeing history from such a perspective makes it difficult to accept a version of western history in an altogether "negative light." Faragher recalls that although Bernard DeVoto, in his *Harper's* Easy Chair essays, long ago complained about the West being a "plundered province" looted by eastern financiers, World War II turned western economies upside down. Westerners nowadays tend to pay tribute to each other rather than to eastern bankers. There can be little doubt about Don Worster's assertion that the modern West "best exemplifies the modern capitalistic state at work."[21] Faragher, in surveying the claims and counter-claims in his conclusions, tends to support Worster's views and those of David J. Weber, historian of the Southwest. Faragher cautions us that "mean-spirited rhetoric . . . debases and trivializes the debate" and points out that there are "charges impugning the scholarship of unnamed people."[22]

We cannot leave the siege on Frederick Jackson Turner's frontier-fort without acknowledging a fundamental axiom of physics, namely, that for every blow there is a response. In the chain of recriminations the issue of presentism rears its head, particularly as it relates to ideological commitments. This concern, to be sure, has bedeviled writers long before rival western historians tried to put their own brand on the frontier. As Peter Novick maintains in his provocative book, *That Noble Dream*,[23] there is wide disagreement among historians over present-minded issues. Yet Richard Hofstadter argues that "the urgency of our national problems seems to demand, more than ever, that the historian have something to say that will help us, and the publisher's puff on the jacket of almost every historical work of any consequence tries to suggest its relevance to the present." Hofstadter, in wading through issues of historical relativism in the course of writing *The Progressive Historians, Turner, Parrington, and Beard*, concludes that "history may remain the most humanizing of the arts."[24]

Certainly, the new western historians have already found seats on this presentist bandwagon, but the question is how loudly do they wish to play the hard rock that will wake up the traditional historians. A favorable test for tolerance of present-mindedness can be seen in the ready acceptance of Richard White's pathbreaking non-Turnerian textbook, *It's Your Misfortune and None of My Own*. Differences are nevertheless evident in a political and generational struggle for leadership in western history. The old westerners can retire gracefully, but the new westerners have the most to lose. Already there is a younger generation to confront the revisionists on Turnerian issues. We can conclude that the bole and root of western history is the sturdy Turnerian tree.

EPILOGUE

Whatever the larger legacy of the "realwestern" history, it left behind extraordinary benefits for its practitioners. The Turnerians fulfilled grand expectations. Turner himself, Merk, Billington, and a host of allies, disciples, and admiring students were advocates for the frontier school, even though some followers moved in and out of western history. They formed networks to promote one another. They elected one another to high office in learned societies and placed one another in professorships in the best universities. As a "school," they earned bigger salaries and accumulated as many academic laurels as any group in modern times. Turner himself enjoyed an income from lecturing, from the sale of his popular essays, and from plums provided by such friends as J. Franklin Jameson. This pleasant, middle-sized, blondish, small-town Wisconsin professor was manifestly a genius worth emulating.

In a quiet but persistent way, Turner moved the entire historical profession. Younger scholars throughout the western world were eager to hear him lecture or to attend his classes. Time and again he lectured on the "realwestern" history, telling his audiences about the marvelous complexities of his frontier-sectional theory. They were amazed to hear it applied to almost any phase or aspect of American history. No one else had ever proposed such an inclusive concept that could be applied to many historical phenomena, from the colonial controversy of Tidewater versus Piedmont or the North-South rivalry dominating the Civil War era. His theory could be relied upon to generate an interpretation of an

237

Turner in an idealized modern portrait, ca. 1960, by Robert Fabe. The painting was commissioned by Billington's students and presented to him; in 1980, a year before his death, Billington gave the painting to the Huntington Library. (Courtesy, Henry E. Huntington Library and Art Gallery)

American federation of sections or, as we have seen, a federation of nation states based upon international political parties. Edward Channing, one of Turner's Harvard colleagues, used to show his students a small locked box. Here, he would say, "is the place where Turner keeps his ideas."

There is much debate over the origin of Turner's ideas, but we can be sure he never locked them in Channing's box. We can, however, examine the evolution of his theorizing. In surveying Turner's commitment to his theory, the year 1890–1891 stands out as a threshold; at this time he formulated seminal "problems" in American history. His critique of Hermann Von Holst's multi-volume history reveals the direction of Turner's thinking. He contended that Von Holst failed to understand historical realities. The history of the United States, its politics, economics, and social life, "should deal," he said, "with at least these great historical processes":

1. the evolution of a composite non-English nationality
2. the movement away from the European state system and the rise of an American system
3. the movement westward
4. the democratic movement
5. industrial transformations
6. the slavery struggle
7. the struggle of particularism, and sectionalism with nationalism
8. the growth of the Constitution by evolution of political institutions[1]

Turner reasoned that each of the eight processes was "related to all the others, and the list might properly be extended."

When he compiled his list of processes Turner, barely thirty, was decidedly aiming for a major revision in American history. Subsequently, in his address of 1893, which linked his provocative frontier essay and the issue of sectionalism, he recounted his "processes." They were especially useful in clarifying mysteries of the westward-moving frontier of settlement flowing into geographic or "physiographic provinces." These "provinces" were emerging sections, and the history of their interaction was Turner's indicator demonstrating the complexity of our historic past.

By 1895 Turner had reduced his list of eight processes to five, which he called "aspects." They would be of special concern to the sociologist. First was the "evolution" of society on the East Coast with three "well marked sections." Second, he said, "We have the expansion of these sections West," the blending and transformation of "institutions" as society flowed westward. Third, the successive waves of "social development," the hunter, rancher, farmer, manufacturer, brought about "continual change." "Fourth, each area reached by the successive waves changed its social and political ideals as it underwent economic changes." And fifth, he wrote, "The Continent was crossed by settlement. American character has been formed by this expansion of the American social organism. Moving westward the European became more and more Americanized. . . . That dominant individualism, working for good or evil, and withal that buoyancy and exuberance which comes with freedom—these are the traits of the West." Or as he put it in a "physiographical" context, "As successive shore lines mark a receding lake, so each frontier of American expansion left behind it traces which persisted in the American people."[2]

We have here an early, condensed version of the frontier-sectional theory. Turner saw the frontier and the section as "mutually interpretative" concepts. As Michael Steiner has argued, Turner in his later years concluded that his ideas on "space history" gave special importance to the interaction between regional geography and history.[3] In his most meaningful essay Turner contended that "there is and always has been a sectional geography in America . . . a geography of political habit, a geography of opinion, of material interests, of racial stocks, of physical fitness, of social traits, of literature, of the distribution of men of ability, even of religious denominations." Turner quoted Josiah Royce on a "province" as being a part of the national domain that was "unified" and that had a "sense of its distinction from other parts of the country."[4]

Making distinctions among Turner's "processes," "provinces," "waves," "aspects," "problems," "multiple hypotheses," and "frontiers and sections" can be a challenge of no small dimensions. As a consequence, my foregoing seventeen perspectives on Turner and the West deal with a score of Turnerian propositions. Some of these locked themselves into individual chapters, but others escaped to resonate throughout the book.

One of these perspectives is Turner's optimism about his work and about America. He was describing a society on the ascent.

Magnificent opportunities were out there: "Free land" was for the taking (Turner was no more concerned about Indian land rights than his pioneers were). Without knowing it, Americans were part of a process of momentous social change. Westward-moving settlers, even in hard times, believed they were headed for a better life than that enjoyed by those who had come before. Although the rate of improvement varied with economic change, there was, as Turner sensed, a feeling that things would get better still.

Such an outlook creates confidence that in turn produces optimism capable of exploding into a nationalistic spirit of social strength. For Turner, the expanding frontier both generated and harnessed this social power. In his analysis of the data stockpiled in his huge collection of note cards to buttress his frontier-sectional theory, Turner found clues of evolving social betterment in an expanding agrarian democracy. Class lines were increasingly blurred, particularly in the West. As the frontier moved westward and left in its wake a terminal moraine of sections, old resentments about class lines tended to be muted, particularly after the Civil War. "Work hard and get ahead"; Turner found this creed in his sources. Pioneers had a work ethic, a sense of appreciation for self-made men, and pride in their accomplishments.

Another aspect of Turner's life and work is illuminated in his teachings and in his theorizing. He had superb teachers, some of whom were experts in rhetoric. He was at heart an orator and used the appropriate rhetoric. The students who heard his lectures were aware of the pleasure he took in making more intelligible a portion of his country's past by telling it in "realwestern" history form. His letters to his students reveal that love of country was a driving force in motivating his studies. In a letter to Carl Becker, June 5, 1899, he demonstrated that history was no abstract entity but was rooted in the countryside of America. "The sharp contrast between New England's interior and the tidewater James is a delight to my historical feelings. . . . We came to New England via the Lehigh Valley (& Wyoming valley) route—a former channel of frontier migration. That too, was immensely stimulating. 'Laurel crowned heights' mean more to me now than they once did, for I came over them. Good heights to take a breath upon—glorious deep breath—and then to leave."[5]

Turner's papers, particularly his letters and research materials, reveal his unquestioned devotion to his subject. Despite the intractability of his sources, he never stopped trying to put down on paper the fruits of his investigations. It cannot be an exaggeration to say that his entire life was devoted to a single effort—to throw light on the past. Everything else took second place. Why did he turn down a prestigious position at Princeton tendered by Woodrow Wilson? The library was lacking in midwestern materials such as Turner found in profusion at Wisconsin. Whatever other offers Turner had from leading universities of his time, his first concern seemed always to be the library. Could he carry on his research? That this was his primary concern in the face of his constantly precarious financial situation is a measure of his commitment to his profession. Turner had no private income and had little hope of extra income through his books. He was largely dependent upon the modest salary of a university faculty member. If Turner was a "nonwriting writer," producing a thin stream of essays, he was nevertheless protective of them and the need to buttress his arguments with a database of hard evidence. For this he had to have adequate library resources.

Still another quality that can be observed in the record that Turner left behind, especially in his relations with students who propagated the "realwestern" history, is that of genuine kindness and sincerity.[6] Turner might use his pen to knock down scholars in error with harsh book reviews, but with his brood of admiring students and disciples he was fair, just, and considerate. Nowhere in preserved correspondence is there a malicious note or a tone of cynicism or sarcasm. He wrote hundreds of letters discussing the personal qualities of students and associates. Whatever could be said in a person's favor Turner said. His letters are full of praise, encouragement, and good advice, and his tactful criticisms were designed to spare the feelings of the recipient as much as possible. Just as Turner helped former students along their professional paths (long after they had left his seminar), so he encouraged projected studies (especially those with a frontier-sectional interpretation) with praise and expressions of confidence in the ability of various authors to complete their undertakings. Qualities such as these are rare, and in a teacher they are invaluable. It was this side of Turner's personality that drew the affection and gratitude of his students and disciples. And it was also this aspect that commanded the fierce loyalty of his followers and the aggressive stance they assumed to defend their master. The recollections of former students (see Appendix B) reflect the unique relationship they had with Turner. Moreover, Turner was as fiercely loyal to his students as they were to him.

Another significant observation offered in this book is that Turner was worried about the fate or possibly the slow death of his frontier-sectional theory. We sense his anxiety in his constant repetition of the concept, which, as a ruling theory, was in trouble. How could it be applied to socioeconomic and political issues after 1890 and the disappearance of the frontier? Yet, for Turner, it had to be reaffirmed. He found himself in a quandary. What happened to the pioneers whose great design had been to complete their coast-to-coast westward march? Americans were suddenly without a visible purpose. Like the hound who chased rabbits and caught one, the hunt suddenly came to a halt. The national race for new territories ended with a cold bath in the Pacific Ocean.

As Turner pondered the results of this phenomenon, he engrossed himself in probing our national purpose. What would Americans do with their new-found wealth? He was aware of the threat of urbanization, the growing sense of economic disenfranchisement, and social bitterness in the cities. Could this threaten the frontier values emerging from over a century of pioneering? Should we expand to new frontiers in the islands and territories of the Pacific?

These matters deserved thorough investigation. Thus, in the rainbow years of his life Turner moved both forward and backward: forward to consider modern problems; backward to reach for the sectional part of his frontier theory in order to apply old ruling concepts in the attempt to solve a range of complex international problems. He plunged into research on the intricacies of such issues as war and peace, population control, and the governance of nations. He proposed a scheme of international political parties based upon a classification of European nations as "sections," bargaining through the League of Nations. His plan pitted one country against the other, much as American sections debated and argued in an effort to achieve national consensus. But there

Turner, ca. 1924, about the time of his retirement. (From the author's collection)

was one flaw in the setup: the Bolsheviks. How could any international political party system endure the threat of Marxist revolutionaries? Turner floundered on this issue.

Nor could he master the pressing issues arising from the exploding populations of Third World countries. They threatened to flood the United States. Was there any way to control accelerated birthrates among peoples of color? In any kind of family planning, Americans and Northern Europeans would be the first to limit the number of children, but other peoples might produce millions of offspring. Turner was never able to come to terms with this issue. Yet we cannot help but admire his ingenious manipulation of data, trends, and theorizing as he found applications for his frontier-sectionalism concept, and it is in his efforts that we find the mature Turner's mind at work. The more he researched subjects, the more frustrating the problems became. The closing of the American frontier brought an explosion of new issues, social, political, and economic; then there were the alarming international threats. If international sectional conflicts could not be avoided, the turmoil might result in the use of a terrifying "Chemist's Bomb."[7]

Undaunted by challenges, Turner tried to solve the insolvable. He even tried to remake the League of Nations. In ferreting out new solutions to old national and international predicaments, he was soon almost overwhelmed with the magnitude of the problems. But he fought back by first identifying the issues and forces involved and then by writing down plausible courses of action. He made somber forecasts. His analyses, tinged by a progressive yet conservative bias, are described in the last chapters.

We should point out that Turner was not alone among his contemporaries in harboring gloomy thoughts about the future. Yet he was bent on doing something that could improve his world. We can picture him, as Huntington staff members remember, greyhaired, slightly stooped, and increasingly delicate in health. In those years he continued to exhibit concern about his wife's health. Photographs show her as more vigorous and robust; in contrast he appears fragile, with increasing lines on his face.

There is something foreboding about Turner's sense of humor as he described in one of his last letters a kind of St. Vitus's dance he performed: slightly dizzy, he staggered about the Huntington Library parking area clinging to a no-parking sign that wobbled with him until he regained his balance. The old ruling theories that he had protected and projected for so long were likewise somewhat wobbly. Yet they would regain their health in Turner's books, published posthumously, and take on new life through generations of new admirers. Frederick Merk and Ray A. Billington would lead the way to a renaissance of Turner studies. But then the attacks would begin all over again with the new western historians. Who knows how the debate will end? My bet is on Turner and the frontier-sectional theory. It offers a dexterity of movement that will, I think, give it immortality.

A current surviving aspect of Turner's thinking is the proposition that the modern regional West is the repository for and the memory bank of the old frontier past. Thus the history of the bygone frontier days becomes a memory, a myth that helps us to comprehend the legacy of the West. Significantly, this argument about the West as a region and its relationship to the old Turnerian themes of frontier history comes from the editors of a splendid book, *Under an Open Sky, Rethinking America's Western Past.*[8]

Seeking to distance themselves from Turner by stating that the regional West is a repository "for a national frontier past," the editors contend that their introductory essay and those that follow offer "non-Turnerian foundations for a new frontier and regional history."[9] Ironically, in seeking a non-Turnerian identification, the authors have given us a pro-Turnerian picture of the West as a section that emerges in the wake of the frontier advance.

Turner is tricky to attack or to defend, especially when one pursues him on the complicated trails of frontiers and sections. He is like mercury: Squeeze him to pin him down and he pops up in another place with new propositions, novel claims for multiple hypotheses, and fresh data. His collected research materials, voluminous correspondence, and mass of unpublished writings reveal how complex a man Turner really was; thus the old master can be as easily misunderstood as understood. Coincidentally, Ray Billington seems to have contributed to the confusion by pleading for a contradictory multiple-hypotheses–frontier hypothesis and by virtually ignoring Turner's complex socioeconomic and political-sectional studies. Nonetheless we must credit Billington for his longstanding advocacy. He preserved for modern generations the singular import of Turner as the father figure of western history. Billington was no instant authority on Turner who had read an essay or two. He engaged in an exhaustive study of the man and his work in order to define his legacy, however debatable that might be.[10] And undoubtedly this book of seventeen perspectives on Turner will add further to the discussion. The inescapable conclusion persists that after one hundred years Turner remains the most influential of American historians, among the brightest and the best we have produced.

APPENDIX A
Turner's Lecture on Washington and Lincoln in 1896

There are few better examples of Turner's application of his frontier-sectional theory than his lecture on Washington and Lincoln given at the University of Wisconsin in 1896. The lecture shows that only three years after his frontier essay of 1893, Turner had already fused his ideas on the frontier and the section into one ruling theory. In the modulated tone of a Wisconsin orator, he dwelt on the stature of the two "heroes" who were true nationalists in transcending sectional interests. Washington "understood the West" and demonstrated his "freedom from sectionalism." Lincoln likewise comprehended that "the Great West could have no sectional dividing line. It must be a unit."

Two of the men of whom I am to speak tonight have been recognized by the voice of history as among the great figures of the world. No one would dispute Washington's place in the pantheon of the world's heroes, and Lowell rightly said of Lincoln, "Here was a type of the true elder race / And one of Plutarch's men talked with us, face to face." Andrew Jackson possessed less of this supreme quality of greatness, and has not been so broadly recognized in the catalog of the world's worthies; but in our American world he holds a lofty place, and as the type of the national hero proper he was at least as definitely selected by the voice of the common people as was either Washington or Lincoln. Washington and Lincoln then were great in themselves, cosmopolitan heroes; Jackson was great in his representative elements, a national hero. But all three were clearly recognized by America as genuine sons of America, as personifications of some of her highest aspirations and achievement.

Now when we turn to ask what have been the fundamental ideals, the most abiding interests in American life—ideals and interests which her heroes must represent,—we cannot fail to see how profound a formative influence in our life has been the steady march of our civilization into the West. Year after year since the earliest settlements the American wilderness has opened before the people. A wilderness to be won from stubborn nature, from the savages, from the French who seized and held it while the English colonists were fringing the Atlantic coast.[1] Into the West, as into a crucible, have been poured European men, ideas, and institutions, and the West has transmuted them into American life, and given individuality to the nation.

It is the tremendous import of this movement that gives significance to the topic, "Washington and the West." We wish to know how Washington was related to the West, not only from the natural desire to find in a great man some bond of connection with the locality in which we live, some relationship with the interests that have shaped the lives of our fathers. The enquiry goes deeper than this. It even raises the question of Washington's greatness. Did he represent in any way these expansive forces in American life?[2] Or was he, as some have said, merely the last and greatest of the colonials?[3]

George Washington was born in 1732, not long after the beginning of the march of American democracy toward the mountains. In the period of his life this democracy surmounted the Alleghenies.[4]

He understood the West, he foresaw this mission, he believed in it. He knew its inevitable expansion over the Mississippi Valley, and he neither feared nor sneered. He trusted in these larger lines of American growth. He was not a colonial planter, he was no narrow provincial, he was an American,—perhaps the first of our public men who by his freedom from sectionalism, by his independence of European influence and by the continental sweep of his vision, is entitled to bear that name.[5]

I have now tried to show how Washington is rightly a Western hero in that he stood for the acquisition and retention of the Mississippi Valley. I have tried to show next how a distinct American life arose in the West beyond the Allegheny Mountains, which wove the sections together in the West, which gave the tone to American society and whose forces of democracy and nationalism finally ruled the nation in the person of that other Western hero, Andrew Jackson. I pass, in conclusion, to consider the place of the West in the great slavery struggle. Along the coast in colonial days three sections had arisen, Puritan New England; the Middle region, materialistic, democratic, and mixed, typical of the present United States; and the slave holding South. Each section was on the march toward the West. The Middle States and New England mingled into a northern current which followed the line of the Mohawk and the Great Lakes. The southern current was really a part of the northern current. The southern current was made up of hardy pioneers, small farmers without slaves, coming chiefly from Pennsylvania to the interior of the South and thence west, and so the West of the War of 1812 had a unity, a solidarity and an individualism of its own. In the earlier years of the government when Kentucky and Tennessee were being settled even in the South slavery had been declining and the western parts of the South were turning to the cultivation of corn and wheat. But the invention[6] of the cotton gin, and the English devices for spinning and weaving cotton occurred together. The industrial revolution, the age of machinery and the factory system followed. A prodigious demand for cotton arose, and the South turned to cotton culture and slavery.[7] In 1791 the total yield of cotton was only 2 million pounds—limited to the tidewater areas of South Carolina and Georgia.[8]

These states were uneasy as they saw settlement from the South sweeping past them into Missouri. Nevertheless, on this side of the Mississippi there was a historical and physical boundary between freedom and bondage. The Ohio was a plain dividing line. But beyond the Mississippi appeared Missouri in 1820, demanding admission with slavery. The dividing line was lost. The Free and the Slave sections were irresistibly drawn into a struggle for power. On the waters of the Mississippi, North and South met and mingled. The Great West could have no sectional dividing line. It must be a unit.

The Missouri Compromise made a truce, but the Kansas-Nebraska [struggle][9] showed how hollow a truce it was. The great apostle of the Kansas-Nebraska legislation whereby the West was reopened to slavery, and the principle of squatter sovereignty, was Stephen A. Douglas of Illinois. But Illinois now found a backwoods champion for freedom to pit against Douglas in the historic debates that preceded the secession of the South. This backwoodsman's ancestors had passed along the great valley road into the back country of the South, with[10] other pioneer families of the type of the Boones, and the Jacksons. His father had joined the stream of immigrants that flowed from Kentucky into Indiana, and from Indiana into Illinois. He was raised in the log hut and grew with the West. He was the very fruitage of western life. Tall, gaunt, awkward, and massive, his very bearing revealed the pioneer stock. And this rail splitter, this flatboatman, this politician and stump speaker, this backwoods' lawyer, this son of the Illinois prairies, this frontiersman was Abraham Lincoln. With the vision before him of the Mississippi flowing in uninterrupted course from the wheatfields of Minnesota to the port of New Orleans, he spoke these fateful words: "A house divided against itself cannot stand. I believe this government cannot endure permanently half slave and half free. It will become all of one thing or all of the other." This was the final word of western Democracy. In the great Mississippi valley a boundary line between two antagonistic civilizations was impossible. The nation took this great souled, patient, tender hearted Lincoln from the fields of Illinois to the White House. For four years with weary eyes, he saw the storms of war beat on the devoted land. He saw the silent Grant hew a way down the Mississippi past Vicksburg for the products of the North. He saw him stand sphinx like in the gloom of the Battle of the Wilderness.[11] What a culmination of the mission of the West. When the Constitution was framed thirteen states had created the Union. In 1861 the majority of the states were the western creations of the general government. The very map speaks for the changed conditions. These western states marked off in squares and parallelograms like a checkerboard, were artificial creations of congress. They regarded a nation with filial affection. More than this, western migration had fused all sections in the West—Steam and telegraphs and railroads had interpenetrated the West, like the veins and arteries of a body. Amputation of a member meant death. And so "Physics prevailed over metaphysics," and the nation was saved.

Lincoln like the true frontiersman believed in the dignity of labor, and abhorred slavery. He is known as the Great Emancipator. But a higher title to fame is found in one of his letters to Greeley and is carved on his statue in Lincoln Park, Chicago. There are the words:

> If there be those who would not save the Union less they could at the same time save slavery, I do not agree with them. If there be those who would not save the union unless at the same time they could destroy slavery, I do not agree with them. My paramount object in this struggle is to save the Union, and is not either to save or to destroy slavery. If I could save the Union without freeing any slave I would do it; if I could save it by freeing all the slaves, I would do it. And if I could save it by freeing some and leaving others alone I would also do that. What I do about slavery and the colored race, I do because I believe it helps to save the Union. And what I forbear, I forbear, because I do not believe it would help to save the Union.

Slavery was bound to perish in this country. The fates were against it. And the peaceful mission of the federative union meant untold blessings for humanity. Lincoln spoke for the West when he uttered those words of Union. The East was accustomed to smile at this frontiersman at first. The South heaped him with insult. But the West understood and loved him. Today he stands the best product of the West, the best type of the American statesman.

In his noble Commemoration Ode, James Russell Lowell sang:

> Nature, they say, doth dote,
> And cannot make a man
> Save on some worn-out plan,
> Repeating us by rote.

For him her Old-World moulds aside she threw,
  And, choosing sweet clay from the breast
    Of the unexhausted West,
With stuff untainted shaped a hero new,

His was no lonely mountain-peak of mind,
Thrusting to thin air o'er our cloudy bars,
A sea-mark now, now lost in vapors blind;
Broad prairie rather, genial, level-lined,
Fruitful and friendly for all human kind,
Yet also nigh to heaven and loved of loftiest stars.
Nothing of Europe here,

Great captains, with their guns and drums,
Disturb our judgment for the hour,
But at least silence comes;
These all are gone, and, standing like a tower,
Our children shall behold his fame.

The kindly—earnest, brave, foreseeing man,
Sagacious, patient, dreading praise, not blame,
New birth of our new soil, the first American.

Lincoln

He is the true history of the American people in his time. Step by step he walked before them; slow with their slowness, quickening his march by theirs, the true representative of this continent.

Emerson

APPENDIX B

Turner as a Teacher—Testimonials from His Former Students

In preparation for a paper, "Frederick Jackson Turner—Master Teacher," read at the 1952 meeting of the Mississippi Valley Historical Association in Chicago, I sent a number of questionnaires to Turner's surviving students. Not all of the people who responded had actually completed their doctoral work under Turner, but they nevertheless had been in his classes and seminars and were generous in responding to me, a Turner enthusiast, just beginning my career as an assistant professor of history at the new campus of the University of California in Santa Barbara (UCSB).[1]

I confined my questionnaire to one page and asked for replies on six topics. I received elaborate commentaries from several former students, and all his former students were enthusiastic. Turner, in fact, was seen as a kind of a demigod teacher because of his personal qualities and his intellect.

My topics for the questionnaire that brought forth such favorable responses are as follows: (1) Turner's personality as a teacher; (2) Turner's method of lecturing and teaching undergraduate classes; (3) classroom techniques used by Turner to stimulate interest in subject matter; (4) points of emphasis included in lectures that were not in Turner's writings; (5) methods used by Turner in conducting his graduate seminars; and (6) Turner's methods in counseling individual graduate students who worked closely with him. Looking back on those topics, I'm sure they reflected the recent experience I had had in obtaining general secondary teaching credentials and putting teacher-education concepts into practice at Montebello High School and at Pasadena City College before beginning university teaching at Stanford and then at UCSB.

I had had the pleasure of knowing some of the former Turner students personally. At Stanford I had known Edgar Eugene Robinson when I was a Western Civilization instructor and he was executive head of the history department. Robinson and I talked frequently about his memories of Turner. His reply is brief because he had already read portions of his diary to me describing his associations with Turner. Merle Curti's reply is also brief, but he too had talked with me about his views. What surprised me was Herbert Eugene Bolton's elaborate commentary, certainly an auto-biographical statement that tells us as much about Bolton himself as about Turner. I had met Bolton during visits to the Bancroft Library when I was searching for Turner letters. Homer C. Hockett in his reply enlarged on a number of topics he had brought up during our many conversations in Santa Barbara where he retired in the 1950s. I had met Avery Craven at historical association meetings; he had told me that he was pleased to know about my project and was "delighted" to respond to my questions. I never met James A. James, Turner's former friend and colleague at Northwestern, but I had a passing acquaintance with Guy Stanton Ford, editor of *American Historical Review.* I had not known Thomas Martin, then visiting professor at Indiana University, or Colin B. Goodykoontz, legendary teacher and scholar at the University of Colorado. In later years I found that Goodykoontz had asked his mentor's advice about accepting an appointment at the Colorado campus in Boulder. In one of his letters Turner was cautious, suggesting that it might be difficult to concentrate and carry on research at such a high altitude! At the moment I cannot put my hand on the letter, but I do remember searching for Goodykoontz's reply. I don't recall that Goodykoontz complained about lofty thinking on the Boulder campus.

Here, then, are the testimonials, nine of them, testifying that Turner was indeed a master teacher.

EDGAR EUGENE ROBINSON, NOVEMBER 6, 1951

1. Turner's personality as a teacher
   Vivid appearance. Clear eyes. Rich voice of unusual rhythm.
   Deep interest in every item. No form; no preparation.
2. Turner's method of lecturing and teaching in undergraduate
   classes
   From the sources. No outline. Summaries.
3. Classroom techniques used by Turner to stimulate interest in
   subject matter
   Nothing except slides and maps.
4. Points of emphasis included in lectures that are not found in
   Turner's writings
   Humor. Brilliant summaries. Personalities.
5. Methods used by Turner in conducting his graduate seminars
   Brought his own notes and plans. Assigned topics. Reports.
   Participation. Took notes on reports. Problems.
6. Turner's method in counseling individual graduate students
   who worked closely with him
   Reading reports. Criticism at length. Brought out more materials of his own. Urged students to *write*! Hearty commenda-
   tion.

MERLE CURTI, 1951

1. Turner's personality as a teacher
   Warmth. Interest in his students, especially in their locale, parental background, whether NE stock, old immigration, new
   immigration, whatnot. As I have said so often, he made us feel
   he expected a great deal of us, and we didn't want to disappoint
   him. And after we left Harvard, he continued to be interested
   in us and to be as helpful as he could be.
2. Turner's method of lecturing and teaching in undergraduate
   classes
   As you know, Turner, at least in his Harvard period, used a
   great many slides—maps of the westward migration of ethnic
   stocks, grains, cattle—maps of land use and public land policy,
   of illiteracy. He was not in the ordinary undergraduate course

Merle Curti at the Huntington Library, ca. 1972. Curti, a former student of Turner and a lifelong friend of Billington, also incorporated Turnerian themes in his books. (Ray Billington Snapshot Photo Album, Huntington Library Archives; courtesy, Henry E. Huntington Library and Art Gallery)

an exciting or brilliant lecturer, though he seems to have had such a reputation at Wisconsin.

3. Classroom techniques used by Turner to stimulate interest in subject matter
Term papers, which were much emphasized. Constant reference to interdisciplinary approaches and materials—geography, economics, sociology, literature.

4. Points of emphasis included in lectures that are not found in Turner's writing
The lectures were what might be called substantive American history—as in the book US 1830–1850—this general pattern was worked out chronologically for the whole span of American history.

5. Methods used by Turner in conducting his graduate seminars
The year I took it we worked on 1830–1840, each man taking one state, and being regarded as the "authority" on it. Reports were given orally. Turner tried to get the group to criticize reports, and he himself gave a critical evaluation at the end. He was always appreciative, if he could be, as well as critical and suggestive.

6. Turner's method in counseling individual graduate students who worked closely with him
Very generous conferences. When I took a research individual

course with him on my thesis, I saw him for the best part of an hour every other week. He was immensely stimulating and informing. Here he was really at his very best—better certainly than in the lectures, better even than in the seminars.

HERBERT EUGENE BOLTON, NOVEMBER 19, 1951

Herbert Eugene Bolton's reply, scarcely a year before his death, contained an analysis of many of Turner's leading ideas.

My Dear Professor Jacobs:

Herewith I am sending a few comments regarding Turner, some of which I fear may not fit into the theme of your paper. You may use them if and whenever they may apply. Turner was a great thinker and inspirer, but I fancy he could not have described himself or his methods categorically according to a topical outline, and I fear I have not succeeded in doing so, but I hope that some of the things I have written may be useful to you. I shall look forward with great interest in your paper when it is finished.

All good wishes,
Herbert E. Bolton

Then followed an excellent word-picture of Turner as a professor at the University of Wisconsin in the 1890s. Bolton's comments were, however, even more revealing of himself and of Turner's impact upon him.

Students of the "Bolton School" are familiar with the many parallels their master drew between the westward development of the United States and the expansion of other parts of the Americas. "The significance of the frontier" was "an intriguing phrase" that Bolton never forgot. "It epitomized," he continued in his comments, "the historical beginnings of every American area." In his presidential address before members of the American Historical Association in 1933 Bolton set forth his whole "synthesis" with the question, "Who has tried to state the significance of the frontier in terms of the Americas?"[2]

That Turner had a profound influence upon Bolton in the formulation of the ideas in the "Epic of Greater America" there can be little doubt. The frontiers of the Americas, the borderlands of the Western Hemisphere, were key in the struggle for nationality and the emergence of national characteristics. Bolton, however, "is to be credited with effective discovery of the Spanish borderlands as a field for historical research. The name is his. It refers to what was the northern fringe of the Spanish empire in America, from Florida and Georgia on the Atlantic to California on the Pacific."[3]

Turnerian patterns of thought are found in most of Bolton's books, especially in the prefaces.[4] Perhaps the most pointed acknowledgement of Turner's influence that Bolton ever made is in the comments and "supplements" concerning his former teacher written in the fall of 1951.

Turner As I Remember Him

I knew Turner quite intimately at the University of Wisconsin, where I took courses with him as [a] Junior, Senior, and Graduate Student, and this acquaintance was never broken so long as he lived.[5] For two years I was a member of his famous seminar, and I conducted a correspondence course for him, which led to closer contacts. After I went from Wisconsin to Pennsylvania[6] and he to Harvard, I saw him periodically at meetings of the American Historical Association, including the session when he delivered his Presidential Address in Richmond. [Bolton is in error here. Turner's address was delivered in Indianapolis on December 28, 1910.] Later I saw him occasionally when he was working in the Huntington Library at San Marino, California; and I visited him at his home in Los Angeles a short time before he passed away.

Turner began his historical research in the area where he had spent his early life.[7] He was born at the old "Portage" between the Fox and Wisconsin Rivers, famous in the days of the French fur trade; and he studied and wrote about the influence of that commerce on the life and institutions of the area. This interest was partly due to the fact that he was an outdoor man, especially addicted to fishing. He used to tell us that he captured his father's rod, while his . . . brother Jack inherited the parental shot gun.

A personal reason for my interest in Turner's work was the fact that I frequently passed through his home town of Portage on my way to and from Milwaukee or Madison, and that after graduation

Herbert Eugene Bolton, one of Turner's students, on the trail. (From the author's collection)

from the University of Wisconsin I lived a year or more in [the] Fox River Valley, the scene of Turner's early writings. In that period, at my invitation, he gave a public lecture at Kaukauna, where I was then living.

Turner had a most charming personality. He was of middle stature, blond, handsome, graceful, and endowed with a marvelous voice (not a boisterous one), which contributed toward his winning of oratorical contests in his undergraduate days, and made him a pleasing and effective lecturer in class and in public, always without ostentation or bombast.[8] In the years when I first knew him he generally wore a close-clipped brown mustache, which in later years he sacrificed to the razor.

On the platform, as elsewhere, Turner was graceful and at ease. He was modest, never dogmatic or sarcastic, and he had a fine sense of humor which he quickly displayed. His classroom lectures told us more of what he was trying to learn than of what he knew, a trait that won the confidence of his students, and encouraged them to independent thinking and inquiry. If he was still trying to learn why shouldn't we? He usually brought to his seminars a stack of notes, and sometimes had difficulty in sorting them out, a fact which in itself was an insurance against oratory. He paid little attention to text books, or to "authorities" as distinguished from "evidence."

He had no formal method that one could label, except reliance on evidence and an honest effort to interpret it. And he had a lively imagination and choice diction that made his lectures vivid and his observations penetrating. "Freddie" as among ourselves we students affectionately and egotistically called him (never to his face), was friendly, helpful, and encouraging. He had an inquiring and philosophic mind, and he was seldom sarcastic in commenting on the work of a student or on the ideas of writers with whom he disagreed. His work being constructive, he spent little time in destructive criticism.

Turner was interested in geographic, economic, and cultural factors, especially those of the frontier, and in their influence on regionalism and sectionalism, as well as on national affairs. In his thinking and interpretation, physiography always loomed large. Many of his generalizations were evolved from the history of Wisconsin and the Old Northwest, where he spent more than half of his life. Turner and Haskins were cronies in Madison;[9] Haskins, a man with a prodigious mind, was called to Harvard, and Turner soon followed. Perhaps after living a number of years in New England some of Turner's earlier ideas were modified, a matter on which you may throw some interesting light in your paper.[10]

My closest associates in Turner's seminar were Guy Stanton Ford and Carl Becker, both of whom became distinguished. Becker died young [Becker was actually seventy-two when he died on April 15, 1945], greatly to the disadvantage of historical scholarship, for he was an original thinker. Ford is still doing a full time job as secretary of the American Historical Association and as a writer of important books and articles. I also was well acquainted with O. G. Libby who is now at North Dakota.[11] You will of course consult him in regard to Turner.

Brilliant Paxson,[12] a classmate of mine in the University of Pennsylvania and later a colleague here at the University of California, although he never studied with Turner, made the most comprehensive synthesis of Turner's views on the "American Frontier," and contributed important additions to Turner's thesis. I have not kept track of the younger men among Turner's disciples and critics, and therefore cannot speak of them with authority. You will doubtless list them and consult some of them, and thereby learn something of Turner's later development of his ideas.[13]

Turner's influence on historical thinking was perhaps greater than that of any of his contemporaries in the United States field. "The significance of the frontier" was a phrase with basic meaning. It was "catchy" and resonant, and at one time or another it has been applied to almost every area within the continent of America. It captivated Turner's disciples, often with embarrassment to the prophet. At Harvard, outside of his early environment, Turner modified some of his early generalizations, which is another evidence of the integrity of his mind and of his willingness to learn. It would be very helpful if you could follow these changes in his thought and emphasis.

Among all our historians of American development Turner was unquestionably one of the "great," not because of voluminous writings, but for the freshness of his ideas and for his influence as a teacher and a writer in two of our most important universities. "The frontier" was an intriguing phrase, and it epitomized the historical beginnings of every American area. It gave significance to the history of every township, country, territory or state. It appealed to local patriotism everywhere across the Continent, from Plymouth to San Francisco, from Florida to Los Angeles, and now, outside of our own borders, the history of the frontier illuminates the history of all the other Americas—British, Spanish, Portuguese, French and Dutch. No wonder Turner is worshipped as a prophet.

It is difficult to say much about Turner's seminar technique, in-so-far as he made us conscious of any but the most obvious procedure, which was to seek widely for evidence, check its validity, consider its significance, and use it where it applied. Turner was not interested in method in a pedagogical sense, and in-so-far as I know he never gave a formal course under that heading.[14] By checking the Wisconsin and Harvard catalogues you can answer that question. To him, method was the employment of all the available means of learning, what had happened and why, including economic, social, political, religious, psychological and personal factors, and interpreting them with reference to their influence. Alluding to Turner's early work in the development of the Fox-Wisconsin Valley and adjacent areas, vital factors were the river systems, the short and easy portage from one stream to another, the friendly Indians who sold furs to the traders, and the hostile tribes who impeded the trade, reduced profits, and hindered access to the Great Lakes, the St. Lawrence River, and the markets of Europe.

If these notes have any value for you I shall be very glad—and agreeably surprised.

Supplement 1

Dear Professor Jacobs:

Having just now read a copy of what I wrote to you the other day, I see that I did not give you what you requested. What I wrote was chiefly about Turner himself rather than about his seminar methods. I will try to add a few comments now.

In his seminar each student chose or was assigned to a topic within the general theme of the course, and after work got under way he presented his paper before the class, after which there was a discussion, supplemented by comments by Turner. The procedure was informal and was determined largely by circumstances. A good paper got attention; a bad one was its own condemnation and merited little comment.

If you get in touch with a considerable number of Turner's disciples it will be interesting to discover how well they remember the Master's techniques. They will not fail to remember Turner, but in most cases their recollections will be hazy as to methods and procedures, or if your witnesses are teachers they are likely to base their answers on their own techniques and attribute them to Turner. Among them there may be some who have saved their class notes, term papers, but probably not many. As for myself, I have not a single page of my student notes. What I saved, if any, were burned in the great Berkeley Fire of about 1923. If you get testimony from a number of witnesses it may enable you to form some generalizations.

Supplement 2

1. Turner's personality as a teacher was just a part of Turner. He was handsome, had a marvelous voice, spoke easily and with fine diction. He was modest and never noisy or pretentious.

2. He made free use of maps, and humanized his story, both as to subject matter and as to environmental factors. He described French pirogues, and sang French boatman's songs. We seldom "recited our lessons," but he encouraged questions and student contributors. And we wrote term papers on subjects of our own choice.

3. He described costumes and apparatus, houses, crops, marketing facilities, religious and political ideas, "obsessions." He never had to resort to claptrap or devices to hold his audience. He had something interesting to say and students listened.

4. It is so long since I have read his writings extensively that I would now find it difficult to say which was which, lectures or published writings, and I wonder how many of his former students could now separate these two elements. Turner has been gone a good many years and I have covered vast regions since I was in his classes. And I doubt whether I now have a single note taken from his lectures or from his books. I'm sorry!

5. Turner always emphasized the *opportunity* of a witness to know, his trustworthiness (intellect, bias, self interest, or any other factor that would bear on the value of personal testimony).

He was indifferent to formal *method*, because every problem involves factors not duplicated in any other problem. Generally speaking, the student reported on his source materials, then told of his findings on the basis of the evidence.

6. Turner gave general talks on kinds of evidence, reputation of witnesses for intelligence, veracity, opportunity to know, bias, self interest, and questioned students on these matters, but he had few formulas. Students were made conscious of fundamental principles of evidence by the free for all discussions. And we soon learned that, except in an elementary degree, no two problems of evidence are the same.[15]

JAMES ALTON JAMES, FEBRUARY 10, 1952

Dear Dr. Jacobs:

I have two personal letters from Dr. Turner. They were loaned to the Huntington Library and I suspect copies were made of them in that collection, one of them dated Jan. 21, 1894 and the other Nov. 10, 1909.

The first related to his suggestion that I permit him to bring my name before the Regents of a new Normal School at Stevens Point, Wisconsin. He set forth in excellent fashion the possibility of relating the Normal Schools more closely with the University of Wisconsin. Before going to Johns Hopkins for graduate work, I had been graduated from the Platteville State Normal & also the University of Wisconsin. I was then in my first year as Professor at Cornell College, Iowa & decided *not* to make a change. Quoting from Professor Turner's letter:

> I said to them that the main thing was to get a man who possessed not only Normal School training and knowledge of pedagogic ideals but also a man who would add university breadth of culture & the inspiration of university ideals. They must in the future partake more & more of university spirit, by this infusion of University men & methods into them.

He enlarged on this thesis somewhat at length & I was in complete accord with his view.

The second letter deals with his acceptance of a professorship at Harvard. I was then carrying on research at Wisconsin in the George Rogers Clark material and had a number of conferences with him. At first, I urged him not to go but finally agreed with him.

I then sent personal letters to men in several universities who had done their *major* work for degrees under his direction. These letters were collected & bound in a volume which was presented to him. They deal with his influence at Wisconsin. This collection is probably in the possession of Mrs. Turner at Madison or is in the Huntington Library. They would give you some clue to your proposal.

"Harvard," he wrote on the date named, "seems to offer an opportunity to me to do some work which I haven't done here. It is an inspiration to know that you & other friends think I have been useful in the past. . . . I shall watch your work with the interest of a fellow laborer even though in other soil."

These letters demonstrate something of Turner's spirit.

In my own case, I may add that it was his influence which led me to do graduate work at Johns Hopkins and this friendly relationship extended through his life. In other words, his seminars which brought out his interpretations of American History were inspiring to students at all times, for his approach was then comparatively unknown. He was always ready to advise his students on studies which might be undertaken by individuals. He kept in touch with students even after they had gone out from the university & sought their advancement at all times. What more could be asked of any real teacher?

I shall be interested to hear your paper and to meet you personally.

Are you acquainted with Fay Cooper Cole one of my former students & friend who has done some lecturing at Santa Barbara? Please remember me also to Dr. [Philip W.] Powell.

THOMAS P. MARTIN, FEBRUARY 22, 1952

1. Turner's personality as a teacher
   He was congenial yet impersonal without appearing to be coldly or rigidly so. He lectured to the class, not to individual students. No one in the class felt that he was being addressed personally. Professor Turner's eyes and face lighted up with considerable animation at times. But he was always dignified and calm, speaking objectively and obviously enjoying the response of the class.
2. Turner's method of lecturing and teaching undergraduate classes
   Professor Turner's courses at Harvard, where I attended, were for upperclassmen and graduates. He usually entered the class-

room informally and with a stuffed brief case which contained, along with materials on which he was working, some illustrative material, chiefly maps and charts mounted on linen in connected sections, which he meant to use before the class. The maps ranged from those of glacial times in certain regions to the most recent charting of votes.

The lectures were in detail well-organized, interpretative, and sometimes liberally salted with "digs," as in the case of New England's neglect to expand her frontier to the northward. He used the fortnightly written quiz with excellent effect. His published *List of References on the History of the West* contained no detailed outlines such as are sometimes seen in the mimeographed syllabus. The student had to take notes and organize his materials. Professor Turner's prepared hour tests and final examinations were made out with care, and he gave equal attention to the marking of the papers.

3. Classroom techniques

Professor Turner usually lectured without stopping to engage in oral quizzing. Not unfrequently he provoked questions and lively but brief discussions by members of his class. He was never dogmatic; always showed an open mind. This is particularly important, because some of the questions were very like those raised now by Turner's critics.

4. Points of emphasis included in lectures that are not found in Turner's writings

Professor Turner did not much repeat what he had written. Rather he gave fuller developments from later studies and writing which he had not yet published. He was constantly emphasizing the continuity and the recurring patterns of history by recalling previous examples in sectors of the frontier or in developments within the sections.

The romantic elements in the history of the West Professor Turner usually presented as products of environment, spearheads impelled by natural forces. A favorite illustration was that of the pre-historic glacial influence in the settlement and political development of Uncle Joe Cannon's congressional district in Illinois.

5. Methods used by Turner in conducting his graduate seminars

I did not enroll in a seminar course with Professor Turner, but occasionally attended. Individual members of the seminar reported to him and to the group orally or by submitting a draft of written work, maps, statistics, and graphs. Sometimes Turner would take the material in hand and go over it in detail.

6. Turner's method in counseling individual graduate students

Professor Turner usually gave advice on request or when request was implied. He left it to the student to raise questions. That is to say he did not offer advice when to do so would have deprived a student of initiative. Nonetheless he was unusually good in picking up at just the right time and place.

HOMER C. HOCKETT, FEBRUARY 1952

1. The first year that I spent at the University of Wisconsin (1901–1902), Turner was gradually turning over the basic course in American History—for Juniors and Seniors—to Carl R. Fish. Fish was on his mettle to make the best possible impression, while Turner was devoting his interest to his advanced work. He gave me the impression of being full of his subject, but not inclined to prepare specially for each class meeting. He spoke readily and connectedly, as he thumbed through his notes, but occasionally seemed to have a hiatus in both memory and notes. At times he gave a spontaneous twist of brilliant character to an interpretation which the ordinary student missed. One felt his personality because of his earnestness. He was never dull. The foregoing refers to his teaching of the basic course. Students enjoyed Fish more, because of his careful organization and his clever phrasemaking.

2. The above partly answers the second question. I may add that in all of his lecture courses Turner preserved continuity by beginning each lecture with words equivalent to "at the last meeting of the class we were discussing . . ." followed by a brief summary of the preceding lecture. When beginning a new topic he always dictated a list of references to standard histories. How students' reading was checked I do not know, except that a list of reading was asked for at appropriate times and examinations included questions on the assigned readings. (The *List of Readings on the History of the West* which he later used at Harvard was not available during the days at Wisconsin.) This answer applies

chiefly to his advanced courses, mainly the History of the West, which was taken by some undergraduates. Here his style in lecturing approximated a soliloquy at times, as he stated facts and sought the answer to the problems they presented. He was not dogmatic, but full of suggestions of possible interpretations.

3. I think it fair to say that Turner showed little interest in conventional techniques designed to stimulate student interest in subject matter. History was for him so full of potential meaning, and he believed that it was so appealing to superior students, that I think his unspoken motto must have been "he that hath ears to hear let him hear." The idea has been abundantly justified by results.*

4. With the exception of the *Rise of the New West* which is by nature general, the Turner writings tend to be topical, and therefore lack the flexibility possible in lectures. I recall no place where in writing he states the theory of multiple hypotheses (not original with him, but important in his method). An illustration of his use of it is in his pointing out of the *persistence* in new settlements of habits of emigrants from older regions, while at other times he stresses the *modifying influences* of new environments. The latter is on the whole the more prominent in his thinking, and, of course, the two seem contradictory. Under the latter he deals with a great variety of factors and effects: climate, soil, topography, forest, mountain, stream, prairie, desert, mineral resources, native plants and animals, Indians. Among the effects are: changes in the cultural life of the people which vary with time and the development of natural resources; frontier freedom from old restraints, established customs, bringing new economic, educational, & political liberty, equality, and opportunity; international rivalries for

---

*One device which may have stimulated the interest of some students but was more often a means of checking their work was the assignment of data to be filled in on outline maps. This was done in connection with the study of the westward movement of population, and was, of course, a good means of visualizing the movement. On the whole Turner's procedures seem very simple when compared with the elaborate methods favored nowadays. Old timers may doubt whether present methods are much better.

control of the West; intersectional rivalries for political and institutional control of the unsettled regions, rivalries which supply the clues to much of the history of our political parties.

Much of this is nowhere more than hinted at by Turner either in his writings or his lectures. Much of it has been worked out by his students. Much of it remains to be done.

5. All students taking graduate seminars were supposed to have had advanced courses in which they had prepared topics involving some training in methods of research, criticism, and composition. Professors were supposed to have given guidance and criticism in the preparation of these. Each graduate in history at U.W. was also required to write a senior thesis displaying an acceptable degree of ability to deal with simple historical problems. Turner's seminars for graduates in the early years of the century contained from eight to a dozen graduate students with about the amount of previous training indicated. The topic was the same for the whole group, say Monroe's first term, and each student was assigned or chose a phase of it which could be studied from source material. What the appropriate material was, each student was supposed to know, or to know how to find out and how to handle. A minimum of instruction was given concerning critical method. Reports were read and criticized by the group— not very acutely. Sometimes they were written, sometimes given from notes. Turner's theory seemed to be that one learned to use the tools by cutting one's fingers with them rather than by formal instruction. Lack of training in critical method is what I am most conscious of as I look back.

6. In counseling with individual students Turner was generous of his time to the point of allowing himself to be imposed upon. More than once I have known him to stop in the midst of dictation on his writing to help Smith or Jones. Indeed, in his later years he realized that he had limited his own productivity by this practice, but I do not know that he regretted it. It was a tribute to the warmth of his nature, and few of the masters have commanded such affection from their students and followers. His concrete suggestions were often bibliographical, but his best aid was in planting some inspiring thought in a capable student's mind, or encouraging him to pursue a promising plan he had conceived for his own study.

GUY STANTON FORD, APRIL 1, 1952

Dear Professor Jacobs:

In looking at the program of the Mississippi Valley Historical Association meeting, I am reminded of my promise to write you about Professor Turner. It may be too late to be of any use to you, but, for what they are worth, here are my memories of a good many years ago.

Perhaps it would be well to recall that I entered the University of Wisconsin in the fall of 1892 as a transfer from a small Methodist college in Iowa. The miscellany of subjects I had taken there, including Butler's *Analogy of Natural and Revealed Religion* and Paley's *Natural Theology,* gave me a tentative sophomore standing at Wisconsin. In the Iowa institution, I had known only textbooks. They had no footnotes, there was no library, and the instructors knew no more, in general, than was in the textbooks. I roomed at one of the professors' houses and heard his wife reading a lesson in English history from Green as he and I on the next floor prepared to go to class. On the advice of Professor Charles Haskins, who became my class officer, I took Turner's "Social and Economic History of the United States." He had not yet developed it into a distinct history of the West. The class was not large, I should say between 30 and 40. We had as a text or textbooks the little series of volumes called *Epochs of American History,* I think, by Thwaites, Hart, and Woodrow Wilson. Turner totally disregarded them. I do not recall that he made specific assignments, but he did pour on us a generous assortment of bibliographical suggestions. It gave me the feeling that I had to read most of the University library and I struggled gallantly with this task. Turner's lectures did not do much to clarify my reading or help me organize it. As the term is usually applied, he could not be called a good undergraduate teacher. He came in briskly, alert, with [an] armful of material, and poured out on us stimulating suggestions and flashing insights while handling over the miscellany on his desk. His voice was pleasant, almost musical. His eye was bright and roved over the class but not with any disciplinary intent. He would occasionally stop to ask a question, because I think he thought that was necessary, and occasionally flash a comment on the answer. If said less gaily, it would have sounded rather sarcastic. He assigned papers that first semester. I do not recall my subject then, but he gave us no instructions about bibliographies, citations. To me at that time, I recall, the *Britannica* and Ridpath's *History of the United States* were important authorities. I received, so far as I recall, no comment on this immature effort. The next semester, I chose a subject of "sectionalism" in the Constitutional Convention. There were no books on this, therefore to me no authorities and I had to work from the sources. This paper Turner asked me to read to the class, then when I finished, he turned to me with that toss of his head that was so characteristic and said, "What are your authorities, Mr. Ford?" Not having read any of what I considered authorities, I said that I had none. With a smile that I have not yet been able to interpret, he said, "Then, Mr. Ford, you are the authority." That paper I still have. His examinations were unpredictable. He might here ask a question about the tariff of 1828 to which he had paid no attention but of which there was a slight account in the little book by Hart. Despite all of these irregularities from the standard pedagogical point of view, he would inspire those who wanted to work to read for themselves. I fear not too many appreciated him in that undergraduate class. A student (?) who was in that class is reported to have said two years later as he came out, "That is the third time I have heard that lecture." Needless to say, he never got a degree.

When I returned as a graduate student in 1898 after three years of teaching history in a Wisconsin high school, I entered Turner's seminar in American History. It was at that time, dealing with the late colonial period and each of us had a state or colony to account for, it seemed like a rather dry task, but the great compensation was that you felt you were participating in something in which the instructor was himself deeply interested. Turner had that faculty of giving you the feeling on the graduate level that you were a participant in making the history that he someday would write. He would take notes on what the students reported. Carl Becker asked him rather slyly once, "Are you just bluffing or do you really get anything out of what we do?" Turner almost indignantly said, "Why, of course I do get something." When, the next year, I registered in seminars at the University of Berlin, I learned nothing from the greatest of that staff, and there was a great one at that time, beyond what I had seen exemplified in Turner's seminar, namely the idea that you were participating with a scholar in a creative work. Earlier, I might have said about the undergraduate course that after my experience in a little college, it was a great thing to sit under a man who, to my early astonishment, disagreed with textbooks and even more ponderous historical works. It was an emancipating experience for a textbook-bound mind.

Nothing of what I have said quite conveys that stimulation that came from the mind and personality of Turner. I am sure these were the abiding values that all of his students who were serious minded carried away. I was too shy and retiring at that time to take advantage of all that I might have had in the way of personal contact with Professor Turner. I did feel somewhat nearer to him in my senior year when, though I had no other courses with him, I elected to write my senior thesis under him and took as my topic "The Economic Ideas of Thomas Jefferson". We had practically no conferences over the matter and he accepted my thesis which, with others, was bound and put in the library. Some years later I saw it on the shelves and discovered, on the same topic and in the same form, a thesis written by a clever and immoral student who had submitted it to an easy-going old professor of political science as his senior thesis. Turner evidently kept a kindly interest in me and when I was finishing my graduate work at Columbia, he and Haskins were both advisers to me as to which of several positions I might better take, reminding me that if nothing else better turned up they would have a place for me at Wisconsin. As some acknowledgment of my debt to Professor Turner, I initiated and carried through the volume of tributary essays at the time of his presidency of the American Historical Association. That was the first in a long line of similar volumes that have followed. I saw him while I was at Harvard on leave after he had gone there and I had the distinct impression that he would be happy when his term expired and that he did not feel certain that he had made a wise move in the transfer from Madison to Cambridge.

I think I will let these remarks stand as my memories of a great teacher who was not in any formal way a great pedagogue.

AVERY CRAVEN, 1952

1. Turner's personality as a teacher

   His voice had unusually fine quality and he lectured in a quiet way. The twinkle in his eye was about all that indicated humor or unusual interest. He was very effective by use of source material at given times, even with undergraduates.

2. Turner's method of lecturing and teaching in undergraduate classes

   Here he was always dignified and restrained giving the impression of strength and knowledge. Yet there always was a genuine modesty about the man before his classes.

3. Classroom techniques used by Turner to stimulate interest in subject matter

   I remember nothing except the use of source materials and the habit of piling up facts and then suddenly lifting you up so that you saw "the forest" and got a glimpse of profound insight.

4. Points of emphasis included in lectures that are not found in Turner's writings

   Turner was always suggestive and those who think of him only in connection with the Frontier or even the West are wrong. He gave an excellent course in U.S. History with the interplay of environment and imported cultures (Sections) often as the central theme.

5. Methods used by Turner in conducting his graduate seminars

   Heavy use of source materials and the ability to get you interested in problems. I can't explain it for it was a subtle way of assuming some interest and your love of exploration!

6. Turner's method in counseling individual graduate students who worked closely with him

   A friendly, kindly way that put you at ease and made you feel that he was really interested in you.

P.S.   I doubt whether it is possible to do justice to Turner by a questionnaire. Personality is an illusive thing and hard to fix.

COLIN B. GOODYKOONTZ, 1952

1. Turner's personality as a teacher
   I found Turner an inspiring teacher because of his command of his subject, his intellectual honesty and his simplicity in manner.
2. Turner's method of lecturing and teaching in undergraduate classes
   Although his lectures had been carefully prepared, there was a certain air of informality about them. He was controversial rather than oratorical in delivery. He almost always brought to class a large portfolio filled with books, maps, or notes. Sometimes he would stop the lecture to turn through this mass of material in search of a quotation or set of figures to illustrate a point.
3. Classroom techniques used by Turner to stimulate interest in subject matter
   I was most impressed by the maps he had made himself. Many of these were large outline maps of the U.S. on which the counties had been colored or shaded so as to show correlations of population, land values, place of nativity, literacy.
4. Points of emphasis included in lectures that are not found in Turner's writings
   There was a more systematic coverage of the History of the West in his lectures than in his writings. He followed closely the topics in his *List of References on the History of the West*.
5. Methods used by Turner in conducting his graduate seminars
   I recall attitudes more than specific methods. His seminar was a joint venture of students and teacher in a search for truth.
6. Turner's method in counseling individual graduate students who worked closely with him
   His questions and comments on work submitted to him for criticism usually had to do with possible new approaches and the interpretation of data. He was more concerned with the "Why" than the "What" in a series of historical facts—but he insisted that the facts be verified.

NOTES

Chapter One. Turner's Essay of 1893

1. Merrill H. Crissey, Turner's devoted secretary, collected boxes of biographical data including honors, prizes, and bibliography. These boxes, along with newspaper clippings on Turner's early published orations, are among his papers at the Huntington Library, San Marino, California. The abbreviation HEH TU and the assorted boxes, files, and drawers are identified in W. R. Jacobs, *The Historical World of Frederick Jackson Turner* (New Haven, Conn., 1968), pp. 256–63.

2. *The World's Columbian Exposition Illustrated*, no. 22 (Chicago, 1892), contains photographs and descriptions of the various congresses scheduled for the Art Institute building. In Turner's correspondence (HEH TU Box 1), there are letters to his parents and other data on the Chicago meeting. See also W. R. Jacobs, "Turner's Visit to Chicago in 1893," in Jacobs, *The Historical World of Frederick Jackson Turner*, pp. 1–7; Jacobs, foreword, F. J. Turner, *The Frontier in American History* (Tucson, Ariz., 1986); Martin Ridge, "The Life of an Idea, The Significance of Frederick Jackson Turner's Thesis," *Montana, the Magazine of Western History* 41:1 (Winter 1991):3–13; William Cronon, *Nature's Metropolis: Chicago and the Great West* (New York, 1991), pp. xvi, 30–31, 34, 39, 46–47; Cronon, "Revisiting the Vanishing Frontier: The Legacy of Frederick Jackson Turner," *Western Historical Quarterly* 18 (1987):157–76; and Cronon, "Turner's First Stand: The Significance of Significance in American History," in *Writing Western History: Essays on Major Western Historians*, ed. Richard Etulain (Albuquerque, N. Mex., 1991), pp. 73–102.

3. The *Report of the American Historical Association for the Year 1893* (Washington, D.C., 1894), pp. 3–9, contains an account of the proceedings of the meeting. F. J. Turner's *Reuben Gold Thwaites: A Memorial Address* (Madison, Wis., 1914), is a tribute to his longtime friend.

4. Woodrow Wilson, Albion Small (sociologist), and Charles M. Andrews, along with Turner, are recorded as being active members of Herbert Baxter

Adams's "seminary." Manuscript records of the seminary are preserved in the Department of History, Johns Hopkins University.

5. Turner to William Poole, May 10, 1893, copy in HEH TU Box 1.

6. The Turner papers in the Huntington Library include some correspondence and photographs that refer to summer fishing and camping trips. For his early correspondence, see HEH TU Boxes 1 and 2. Turner, according to the economist Allyn Young at Wisconsin, had an extremely pleasant manner of speaking. "My wife," Young wrote, "who is nearly blind and upon whom voice, therefore, makes a deep impression, has said that Turner has the most pleasantly modulated voice and the most winning manner of speech that she has ever heard" (Young to Carl Becker, October 9, 1928, Becker Papers, Cornell University). See also Ronald H. Carpenter, *The Eloquence of Frederick Jackson Turner* (San Marino, Calif., 1983), pp. 3–95, and Turner's scrapbook, HEH TU Box 62.

7. *Report*, pp. 3–9.

8. Quoted in Jacobs, *Historical World of Frederick Jackson Turner*, p. 11.

9. See, for example, Turner's comments on the European heritage in his friendly argument with Charles M. Andrews in "What Is Colonial History?" in W. R. Jacobs, ed., *Frederick Jackson Turner's Legacy* (Lincoln, Nebr., 1977), pp. 105–15.

10. These are published in Fulmer Mood, ed., *The Early Writings of Frederick Jackson Turner* (Madison, Wis., 1938), pp. 41–69.

11. Ibid.

12. Ibid.

13. Frederick Jackson Turner, "The Significance of the Frontier in American History," address to the American Historical Association, Chicago, July 12, 1893.

14. Ibid.

15. Beard to Turner, May 14, 1921, HEH TU Box 31. Beard's review appears in *New Republic* 25 (1921):349–50.

16. Turner wrote to Arthur M. Schlesinger, April 18, 1922 (HEH TU Box 33), "The truth is that I found it necessary to hammer pretty hard and pretty steadily on the frontier idea to 'get it in' as a corrective to the kind of thinking I found some thirty years ago."

17. See Merle Curti's exemplary study, *The Making of an American Community, A Case Study of Democracy in a Frontier County* (Stanford, Calif., 1959).

18. For a discussion of Turnerian revisionism in the 1990s, see Part Five and the Epilogue.

19. For a discussion of Turner's background reading, see chapters 2 and 3, Jacobs, ed., *Turner's Legacy* pp. 8–34, and Ray A. Billington, *Frederick Jackson Turner, Historian, Scholar, Teacher* (New York, 1973), 110–23. Billington's biography, though carefully researched and eloquently written, differs from my work in basic interpretations about formative influences on Turner, the concept of multiple hypotheses, and a range of other topics. Certain Turnerian

themes set forth in Billington's textbook writings also appear in his biography of Turner. See chapter 13 of this book.

Patricia Limerick discusses her view of Billington's shortcomings in her essay, "Persistent Traits and the Persistent Historian: The American Frontier and Ray Allen Billington," in *Writing Western History,* pp. 277–310.

20. Richard Hofstadter, *The Progressive Historians: Turner, Beard, Parrington* (New York, 1968), 111–17.

21. Michael C. Steiner, "Frederick Jackson Turner and Western Regionalism," in *Writing Western History,* pp. 103–35.

22. Ibid.

23. Hofstadter compared Turner unfavorably with Beard in luncheon conversations with me while he was working on the Turner papers at the Huntington Library in 1966–1967. See also his views in *Progressive Historians* (p. 293) where he points out that Beard was indebted to Turner's essay of 1911, "Social Forces in American History." Turner had written that "we may trace the contest between capitalist and democratic pioneer from the earliest colonial days." This quotation is reprinted in *Frontier in American History,* p. 325.

24. See chapters 7 and 8; Hofstadter, *Progressive Historians,* pp. 112–17. E. Digby Baltzell, *The Protestant Establishment, Aristocracy and Caste in America* (New Haven, Conn., 1987), pp. 13, 150n., 153, 162, 163, generally links Turner to the establishment of his day.

25. See my introductions to Turner's unpublished essays in *Turner's Legacy,* "Frontiers and Sections," pp. 45–47, and "American Social History," pp. 151–52. Here I argue, among other things, that sociological factors, the frontier and the section, were at the heart of Turner's work.

Chapter Two. Turner's Apprenticeship

1. John D. Hicks, *My Life with History* (Lincoln, Nebr. 1968), pp. 1ff.

2. Ibid., pp. 158–59.

3. John D. Hicks, *The Populist Revolt* (Minneapolis, 1941), pp. vii, 95.

4. Richard Hofstadter, *The Age of Reform, from Bryan to FDR* (New York, 1961), pp. 48–49.

5. Hicks, *My Life with History,* 145–46.

6. Turner to Arthur M. Schlesinger, May 5, 1925, HEH TU Box 34.

7. For example, there was "the Squire," the wealthy William Hooper, husband of Mrs. Alice Forbes Hooper, with whom Turner carried on a long correspondence. A large number of Turner's letters to her are reproduced in R. A. Billington, ed., *Dear Lady: The Letters of Frederick Jackson Turner and Alice Forbes Perkins Hooper, 1910–1932* (San Marino, Calif., 1970); see pp. 20–21, 75ff.

8. Turner to Mrs. Hooper, December 3, 1923, HEH TU-H uncataloged.

9. Turner to Mrs. Hooper, February 19, 1916, in Billington, *Dear Lady,* p. 203.

10. Ibid.

11. Turner to Mrs. Hooper, November 12, 1926, HEH TU-H uncataloged.

12. "Turner Genealogy, 1628–1919," HEH TU Box 62.

13. "Harvard History Club, 1923 or 4," HEH TU Box 56.

14. Turner to Carl Becker, December 16, 1925, HEH TU Box 34A.

15. "Material on Turner and Hanford Family Genealogies" includes notes in Turner's handwriting (HEH TU Box K).

16. Ibid.

17. Turner to Constance L. Skinner, March 15, 1922, HEH TU Box 31.

18. Turner to Max Farrand, August 8, 1908, HEH TU Box 11.

19. A. J. Turner to Frederick Jackson Turner, August 21, 1878, HEH TU Box A.

20. Turner to Carl Becker, December 16, 1925, HEH TU Box 34A.

21. Ibid.

22. Quoted from Turner's earliest writing, "History of the 'Grignon Tract' on the Portage of the Fox and Wisconsin Rivers," *Wisconsin State Register* (Portage, Wis., June 23, 1883, in Fulmer Mood, "The Development of Frederick Jackson Turner as a Historical Thinker," *Transactions of the Colonial Society of Massachusetts* 34 (Boston, 1943):284.

23. Turner to Carl Becker, December 16, 1925, HEH TU Box 34A.

24. Turner to Mrs. Hooper, February 13, 1921, HEH TU-H Box 5.

25. Turner to Constance L. Skinner, March 15, 1922, HEH TU Box 31.

26. HEH TU vol. 3. Turner's commonplace books have key references to Parkman. Turner also refers to having read Parkman as a youth in a number of his letters. On May 2, 1889, Parkman wrote Turner that he had "examined with much interest 'The Fur Trade in Wisconsin'" (HEH TU Box 1). Turner had kept this particular letter in a special container apart from his other correspondence.

27. See discussion and notes on Turner's essay, "The Hunter Type," in W. R. Jacobs, ed., *America's Great Frontiers and Sections* (Lincoln, Nebr., 1965), pp. 153–57.

28. See the excellent discussion on this point in Edward N. Saveth, *American Historians and European Immigrants, 1875–1925* (New York, 1948), pp. 122ff.

29. Joseph Dorfman, *Thorstein Veblen and His America* (New York, 1945), pp. 3–9, 13; Mood, "Turner as Historical Thinker," p. 285.

30. John Muir, *The Story of My Boyhood and Youth* (Boston, 1913), pp. 168–69, 199. This kind of war against the wild animals was carried on in a more extended manner by transplanted easterners, the Mormons of Utah in 1849. Considered "destroyers," Mormon leaders John D. Lee, Brigham Young, and others decided to "make war" on all "wolves, wildcats, polecats, minks, bears, panthers, catamounts, coyotes, eagles, hawks, crows, and ravens" (see Juanita Brooks, *John Doyle Lee: Zealot, Pioneer, Builder, Scapegoat* [Glendale, Calif., 1962], p. 141).

31. Muir, *The Story of My Boyhood*, pp. 218–19.

32. Carl F. Brand's lecture notes, "History of the West," September 17, 1917, HEH TU uncataloged.

33. The plundering of Wisconsin's great white pine forests is briefly detailed in Ernest F. Swift, *A Conservation Saga* (Washington, D.C., 1967), pp. 84, 90ff., and in Charles Van Hise, *The Conservation of Natural Resources in the United States* (New York, 1910), pp. 219ff. This last volume, inscribed to Turner by Van Hise (Huntington Library Rare Book no. 13950) contains Turner's marginalia and underlining and may have sparked his revisionist thinking on conservation in the later part of his life; see also pp. 208–10.

34. "Will" or William F. Turner was born in 1864 and later became a Portage businessman. There is correspondence about family finances, including a note to Will referring to his loan of $5,000 on life insurance (Turner to Will Turner, October 9, 1905, HEH TU Box G). Turner's pocket notebooks, 1908–1912, HEH TU Box 62, give Will's birth as 1864; the Turner genealogy in this box gives 1872 as the birthdate of Turner's younger sister, Ellen Breese Turner. In later years a number of letters passed between the two brothers on such subjects as politics (Will hoped the government in 1911 would not put every big *"Business"* out of business) and family finances. After a severe illness, Will Turner died in summer 1918. Turner to Mrs. Hooper, October 9, 1918, HEH TU-H Box 4.

35. Mood, "Turner as Historical Thinker," p. 285.

36. "The Power of the Press," June 20, 1878, clipping in Turner's scrapbook, HEH TU Box 6.

37. Israel Holmes to Mr. and Mrs. A. J. Turner, HEH TU Box 1.

38. Johann Gustav Droysen's *Grundriss der Historik* (Leipzig, 1882) and E. B. Andrews, trans., *Outline of the Principles of History* (Boston, 1893), Huntington Library Rare Books nos. 124357 and 124480, are among Turner's personal books. He quoted Droysen's dictum from *Historik* "that History was the self-consciousness of humanity—in other words, the effort of the present to understand itself by understanding the past." Turner to Merle Curti, August 8, 1928, HEH TU Box 38.

39. Turner's scrapbook, HEH TU Box 6.

40. Ibid.

41. Isaiah Thomas, *The History of Printing in America with a Biography of Printers and an Account of Newspapers*, 2d ed., 2 vols. (Albany, N.Y., 1874), 1:35ff.

42. Turner's complete college transcript, covering the years 1878–1884, shows him to have studied Greek, Latin, algebra, and geometry in his first two years; he revived his high school talent for oration when he began classes in rhetoric in 1881 (HEH TU uncataloged material). Turner's commonplace books are in HEH TU vol. 3.

43. Turner to Merle Curti, August 28, 1928, HEH TU Box 39.

44. Ibid.

45. Printed in the *University Press* (Madison, Wis.), May 26, 1883, and quoted more fully in Mood, "Turner as Historical Thinker," p. 291.

46. HEH TU vol. 3 (2).

47. Printed in the *University Press*, June 21, 1884, and awarded the Lewis

Prize. Additional quotations from the address are in Mood, "Turner as Historical Thinker," pp. 292–93.

48. Fragment of a letter signed by Turner, with letterhead, 7 Philips Place, Cambridge, Mass. (HEH TU Box 60).

49. For another point of view on Turner's early years and the significance of his oratory, see Ray A. Billington, *Frederick Jackson Turner: Historian, Scholar, Teacher* (New York, 1973), pp. 3–33. Ronald H. Carpenter, *The Eloquence of Frederick Jackson Turner* (San Marino, Calif., 1983), pp. 3–95, argues convincingly that Turner "is an examplar of the historian as persuader." William Cronon has also noted Turner's important skills in oratory. See "Revisiting the Vanishing Frontier: The Legacy of Frederick Jackson Turner," *Western Historical Quarterly* 17 (July 1986):157–76.

Chapter Three. The Making of a Historian

1. HEH TU vol. 3(1), labeled "F. J. Turner–1881."

2. Merle Curti and Vernon Carstenson, *The University of Wisconsin: A History, 1848–1925*, 2 vols. (Madison, Wis., 1949), 1:270.

3. Ibid., pp. 249ff; Fulmer Mood, "The Development of Frederick Jackson Turner as a Historical Thinker," *Transactions of the Colonial Society of Massachusetts* 34 (Boston, 1943):290.

4. Curti and Carstenson, *University of Wisconsin*, 1:342.

5. HEH TU vol. 3(1).

6. Ibid.

7. Curti and Carstenson, *University of Wisconsin*, 1:344, 400, 650.

8. Reminiscences of Edgar Eugene Robinson in conversations with author, Palo Alto, California, July 16, 1972; Turner's student record, 1878–1884, University Archives, University of Wisconsin, HEH TU uncataloged material.

9. "Address at funeral of Professor Frankenburger at Unitarian Church," February 8, 1906, Madison, Wis., HEH TU Box 55.

10. F. O. Matthiessen, *American Renaissance, Art and Expression in the Age of Emerson and Whitman* (New York, 1941), pp. 21ff., has a full discussion of Emerson's literary method of composition. See also Frederick Ives Carpenter, *Emerson Handbook* (New York, 1953), pp. 74ff., and William Cronon, *Nature's Metropolis: Chicago and the Great West* (New York, 1992), p. 392 n.13.

11. HEH TU vol. 3(3).

12. "Self Reliance" and "individualism" were character traits that Turner attributed to Americans in almost all his public lectures. See, for instance, a typical address, "Pioneer Ideals and the University," from "Notes for an address to the Phi Beta Kappa Society of Michigan," May 14, 1910, HEH TU Box 55.

13. William F. Allen, *Essays and Monographs*, ed. David B. Frankenburger et al. (Boston, 1890).

14. Turner to H. B. Adams, December 10, 1889, HEH TU Box 1.

15. Quotations on Allen's method and this tribute from Turner are from his letters to Carl Becker; see especially December 16, 1925, HEH TU Box 34A.

16. Ibid.

17. Ibid.

18. Ibid.

19. Allen to Turner, October 30, 1888, HEH TU Box 1.

20. Turner's American history notebooks, HEH TU vols. 13–18; William F. Allen's notebook on his History of American Civilization course, Wisconsin State Historical Society Film, Huntington Library Film no. 452.

21. Turner's American history notebook, HEH TU vol. 16.

22. Turner's American history notebooks, HEH TU vols. 13–18, contain notes from Allen's classes as well as brief summaries of lecture points and quotations and summaries from books he was reading.

23. Allen's notebook, History of Civilization Course, Huntington Library Film no. 452.

24. Turner, commonplace book no. 2, HEH TU vol. 3.

25. Turner to Carl Becker, December 16, 1925, HEH TU Box 34A. Turner's commonplace book of 1883, no. 2, HEH TU vol. 3, explains his method of research: "Investigate landholding peasantry about Madison . . . (Census— Ag. Reports—Talks)." Turner also wrote to Louis B. Porlier of Madison, a relative of the Grignon family, to obtain "the inside history" of the land transactions (Turner to Porlier, April 16, 1883, HEH TU Box 1).

26. Rough draft of a letter to William E. Dodd, October 7, 1919, HEH TU Box 29. A typed "copy" in the same folder differs slightly and probably was the version sent to Dodd. Turner repeated this criticism of Adams in a number of other letters.

27. Ibid.

28. H. B. Adams, "Mr. Freeman's Visit to Baltimore," *Johns Hopkins University Studies in Historical and Political Science*, vol. 1, *Local Institutions* (Baltimore, 1883), p. 8. See also Edward A. Freeman, "An Introduction to American Institutional History," *Local Institutions*, pp. 13ff.

29. H. B. Adams, "Saxon Tithing-Men in America," *Local Institutions*, 4:11, 10. Adams here portrays Indian serfdom in Plymouth as a rebirth of an institution established when the Normans subjugated the Saxons.

30. H. B. Adams "Germanic Origin of New England Towns," *Local Institutions* (1882), 2:5. Turner's later use of the term "process" may well be traced to Adams's use of the word here to describe the "process" of reproduction of institutions.

31. Charles H. Shinn, *Mining Camps: A Study of American Frontier Government*, ed. Rodman Paul (New York, 1965), pp. xii, xvi, 125, 176.

32. James Phalen, *History of Tennessee: The Making of a State* (Boston, 1888), pp. 190–91, 191n.

33. Quotations are from the doctoral dissertation version printed in the Johns Hopkins University Studies series, vol. 9 (Baltimore, 1891), and reprinted in *The Early Writings of Frederick Jackson Turner*, ed. Fulmer Mood and Everett E. Edwards (Madison, Wis., 1938); see pp. 9, 175–78 of *Early Writings*. Turner's M.A. thesis version of the fur-trade essay in *Wisconsin State Historical Society Proceedings* 36 (Madison, Wis., 1889):52–98, is in some respects a better

work since it lacks much of the racist Anglo-Saxonism of the later version and includes a more sympathetic treatment of the dilemma of the Indian. Turner's personal copy of the M.A. thesis (Huntington Library Rare Book no. 126675) contains his annotations for revision.

34. Mood and Edwards, *Early Writings of Turner*, pp. 64–65.

35. Adams to Turner, November 28, 1892, HEH TU Box 1.

36. Mood and Edwards, *Early Writings of Turner*, pp. 77, 76, 72–73.

37. HEH TU vol. 4; Huntington Library Rare Book no. 126761.

38. Ibid.

39. "Dr. Van Holst's History of the United States," dated by Turner "About 1889–1890?" in W. R. Jacobs, ed., *America's Great Frontier and Sections* (Lincoln, Nebr., 1967), p. 94. In this handwritten manuscript, Turner appears to have deleted the last two sentences of the quotations.

40. F. J. Turner, *The Frontier in American History*, ed. W. R. Jacobs (Tucson, 1986), p. 3.

41. Ibid., pp. 22–23.

42. Ibid., pp. 37–38.

43. Ibid., p. 36.

44. "The Hunter Type" is printed in Jacobs, ed., *America's Great Frontier*, pp. 153–55.

45. Turner, *Frontier in American History*, p. 39ff.

46. William Coleman, "Science and Symbol in the Turner Frontier Hypothesis," *American Historical Review* 72 (October 1966):22–49, 32.

47. Ibid., pp. 32, 34. Turner seems never to have reached the point of "reformed" Darwinists who concluded that a progressive society could make intelligent use of the environment.

48. Jacobs, ed., *America's Great Frontiers*, pp. 18–19.

49. Ibid., pp. 4–5.

50. Turner, *Frontier in American History*, p. 323.

51. See chapter 4.

52. Carl Becker, "Frederick Jackson Turner," in *Everyman His Own Historian* (New York., 1935), p. 213.

53. Turner, *Frontier in American History*, p. 3.

54. Turner's arrogant characterization of the Paiutes as "the most degraded and disgusting" Indians disqualified them from being identified with "a noble" canyon outlook to be called "Paiute Point" (Turner to Charles Van Hise, June 15, 1906, HEH TU Box 7).

55. See, for example, Turner to Caroline Mae Sherwood, April 19, 1888, HEH TU Box C.

56. Turner's "Studies of Immigration" written for the *Chicago Record Herald* in September and October 1901 are filled with racist remarks about the inferiority of Jews, Italians, Poles, and Slovacs. Turner preserved copies of these articles along with handwritten notes for possible expansion or revision. In his essay "Jewish Immigration," October 16, 1901, he argues against Jewish immigration, citing unfavorable Jewish traits: Jews "spread disease" in sweat-

shops; "the Jew is a typical wanderer"; Jews "live nearly twice as long as their neighbors"; they carry "fever germs"; Jews are "nimble-minded"; in New York City they form "pipelines that run to the misery pools of Europe"; Jews are "thrifty to disgracefulness"; "their ability to drive a bargain amounts to a genius."

57. Richard White, "Frederick Jackson Turner," in John R. Wonder, ed., *Historians of the Frontier* (New York, 1988), p. 665.

58. Richard Hofstadter, *The Progressive Historians: Turner, Beard, Parrington* (New York, 1968), p. 7. Hofstadter argues that most nineteenth-century American historians wrote for a conservative audience, but it seems to me that the argument applies particularly to Turner.

59. George C. Iggers, "The Idea of Progress, A Critical Reassessment," *American Historical Review* 80 (October 1965):16.

60. Ibid., pp. 15–16.

61. Richard Hofstadter's *Social Darwinism in American Thought, 1860–1915* (Philadelphia, 1944), includes an intriguing chapter, "The Vogue of Spencer" (pp. 18–36), and a valuable assessment of racism and imperialism. Among the writers he discusses are John Fiske, John R. Commons, and Franklin H. Giddings. Turner is mentioned only briefly. Certainly Theodore Roosevelt and Alfred Thayer Mahan as well as New England literary historians Bancroft, Prescott, Motley, and Parkman set forth basic evolutionary themes of Anglo-Saxonism.

62. Reginald Horsman, *Race and Manifest Destiny: Origins of American Racial Anglo-Saxonism* (Cambridge, Mass., 1981), p. 171.

Chapter Four. Developing a Ruling Theory

1. Homer C. Hockett to author, October 29, 1951; Frederick Jackson Turner to Merle Curti, August 8, 1928, HEH TU 39.

2. Emphasis on Turner's "profound" influence and on his use of the "multiple hypotheses in history" appears in a eulogy by Samuel Eliot Morison, Arthur M. Schlesinger, and Frederick Merk, "Minute on the Life and Services of Frederick Jackson Turner," July 14, 1932, Turner Papers, Huntington Library, San Marino, Calif. Turner's application of the multiple-hypotheses idea and the importance of his association with Thomas C. Chamberlin are noted in two perceptive chapters: Merle Curti, "The Section and the Frontier in American History: The Methodological Concepts of Frederick Jackson Turner," in *Methods in Social Science: A Case Book*, ed. Stuart A. Rice (Chicago, 1931), p. 357, and Curti, "Frederick Jackson Turner, 1861–1932," in *Probing Our Past* (New York, 1955), pp. 36, 39–40; see also, Ray Allen Billington, *Frederick Jackson Turner: Historian, Scholar, Teacher* (New York, 1973), pp. 141–50, 161–62, 179, 456, 468, 477. Turner's indebtedness to Chamberlin is also briefly discussed in Fulmer Mood, "The Development of Frederick Jackson Turner as a Historical Thinker," *Transactions of the Colonial Society of Massachusetts* 34 (Boston, 1943):286, 319; Ray Allen Billington, *America's Frontier Heritage* (New York, 1966), p. 19; Wilbur R.

Jacobs, ed., *Frederick Jackson Turner's Legacy: Unpublished Writings in American History* (San Marino, Calif., 1965), pp. 40–41; Maurice M. Vance, *Charles Richard Van Hise: Scientist Progressive* (Madison, Wis., 1960), p. 61; and William Coleman, "Science and Symbol in the Turner Frontier Hypothesis," *American Historical Review* 72 (October 1966):28n–29n.

3. Chamberlin to Turner, February 27, April 10, 1889, HEH TU Box 1.

4. Thomas C. Chamberlin, "The Method of Multiple Working Hypotheses," *Science* 15 (February 7, 1890):92–96; reprinted in *Science* 148 (May 7, 1965):754–59 (a revised version appeared in *Journal of Geology* 5 [November–December 1897]:837–48).

5. Chamberlin, "Method," *Journal of Geology*, p. 837n.

6. Marland P. Billings, *Structural Geology* (New York, 1954), p. 3. Commenting on Chamberlin's essay, a noted biophysicist wrote: "It should be required reading for every graduate student and for every professor" (see John Rader Platt, *Step to Man* [New York, 1966], p. 28).

7. *Encyclopaedia Britannica*, 25 vols. (Edinburgh, 1888), 24:616–19. The geology section of the article (pp. 616–17) has Chamberlin's initials: "T. C. C."

8. George L. Collie and Hiram D. Densmore, *Thomas C. Chamberlin . . . and Rollin D. Salisbury, A Beloit College Partnership* (Madison, Wis., 1932), pp. 1–47.

9. Chamberlin, "Method," *Journal of Geology*, p. 840.

10. Chamberlin, "Method," *Science*, p. 758.

11. Ibid., p. 759.

12. Ibid., p. 758.

13. Ibid., p. 759.

14. Chamberlin, "Method," *Journal of Geology*, p. 842 (slightly modified in *Science*, p. 754).

15. Chamberlin, "Method," *Journal of Geology*, p. 842, and *Science*, p. 755.

16. Chamberlin, "Method," *Science*, p. 756.

17. Bailey Willis, "Climate and Carbonic Acid," *Popular Science Monthly* (July 1901):242–56 (Turner's marked copy is Huntington Library Rare Book no. 246668).

18. Huntington Library Rare Book no. 246668.

19. Turner, "American Political Sectionalism," Pasadena lecture, February 28, 1928, HEH TU File Drawer 15.

20. Orin G. Libby, "The Geographical Distribution of the Vote of the Thirteen States on the Federal Constitution, 1787–8," *Bulletin of the University of Wisconsin*, Economics, Political Science, and History Series no. 1 (Madison, Wis., 1897), p. 116.

21. See Mood, "Turner as Historical Thinker," p. 331.

22. Turner Map Collection, Turner Papers.

23. Ibid.

24. "Turner's Notes on the Van Hise Lecture, 1898–Nov., Gulf Plains," HEH TU vol. 9. Turner's mutual interests and lifelong friendship with Charles Richard Van Hise are discussed in Vance, *Charles Richard Van Hise,*

pp. 61–62, 69–70, 72, 74, 118. See also Mrs. Turner's "Journal of a Camping Trip," August 10–September 10, 1908, HEH TU vol. 9.

25. Turner's annotated copies of Raymond Pearl's "The Population Problem" and Walter E. Wilcox's "On the Future Distribution of White Settlement" (both in the Huntington Library reference copy of *Geographical Review* 12 [October 1922]:636–45, 646–47) and his notes show his concern with this problem.

26. Turner to Curti, August 8, 1928, HEH TU Box 39.

27. Turner to Curti, August 27, 1928, HEH TU Box 39.

28. Turner, "Notes for a Talk on Political Maps, circa 1920," HEH TU File Drawer 10. See also Jacobs, ed., *Turner's Legacy*, pp. 70–73.

29. O. Lawrence Burnette, Jr., comp. *Wisconsin Witness to Frederick Jackson Turner: A Collection of Essays on the Historian and the Thesis* (Madison, Wis., 1961), pp. 100–16.

30. Ibid., p. 110.

31. Everett E. Edward, comp., *The Early Writings of Frederick Jackson Turner, with a List of All His Works* (Madison, Wis., 1938), p. 52 (the italics are Turner's).

32. Frederick Jackson Turner, "The Development of American Society," *Alumni Quarterly of the University of Illinois* 2 (July 1908):120–36.

33. Turner's three-by-five reference cards, some of which were compiled in the early 1890s, show his interdisciplinary approach to research. Even the early cards, dog-eared and written in lavender ink, are chronologically arranged under topics on the growth and expansion of American civilization in the eighteenth and nineteenth centuries.

34. Turner's commonplace book no. 2, vol. 3, HEH TU vol. 13.

35. In his draft of an oration, " 'Imaginativeness of Present' or its general worth as contrasted with past," Turner wrote: "New poets will read a lesson from Spencer & Darwin & sing Man and Nature. Evolution . . . is now in the intellect" (ibid.).

36. Jacobs, ed., *Turner's Legacy*, p. 166.

37. Ibid.; Curti, *Probing Our Past*, p. 36.

38. Jacobs, ed., *Turner's Legacy*, p. 82. In a brief but provocative essay, "Class and Sectional Struggles," Turner explored the economic and social conflicts that could result from a black revolution in the South and the triumph of "Bolshevistic labor ideas" (see pp. 77–78).

39. Frederick Jackson Turner, *The United States, 1830–1850: The Nation and Its Sections* (New York, 1938), was published after Turner's death by Max Farrand, Avery Craven, and Turner's secretary, Merrill H. Crissey. This book, which Turner had under preparation for some twenty years but left unfinished, analyzes each of the larger sections separately with special attention to cultural developments. For example, see Turner's discussion of culture in "South Atlantic States, " pp. 200–209. See Curti's astute appraisal of the book in *Probing Our Past*, p. 51. For a discussion of the culture concept or theory and Turner's contribution toward its development, see Caroline F. Ware, ed., *The Cultural Approach to History* (New York, 1940), pp. 10–14, 235–36, 279, 304–6.

40. Turner to Schlesinger, April 18, 1922, HEH TU Box 31.

41. Books and articles have appeared in the 1950s and 1960s that ostensibly suggest disagreement with Turner but are largely based upon an analysis and a restatement of his ideas. For example, the basic Turnerian themes of frontier mobility and abundant free land underlie David M. Potter's *People of Plenty: Economic Abundance and the American Character* (Chicago, 1954); Walter Prescott Webb's *The Great Frontier* (Boston, 1952); and George W. Pierson's articles, "The M-Factor in American History," *American Quarterly* 14 (Summer 1962):275–89, and "A Restless Temper," *American Historical Review* 69 (July 1964):969–89.

42. HEH TU File Drawer 15.

43. Turner, "Draft on League of Nations 1918,–November," HEH TU File Drawer 15.

44. Turner, "Turner, F. J. City, Frontier & Section: or, the Significance of the City in Amer. Hist.," HEH TU File Drawer 15.

45. For another view of Turner's theorizing, see Ray A. Billington, *Frederick Jackson Turner: Historian, Scholar, Teacher* (New York, 1973), pp. 447–655, 483–97. An excellent and sympathetic overview of Turner's frontier-sectional concepts is in Martin Ridge, "The American West: From Frontier to Region," *New Mexico Historical Review* (April 1989):125–41; see also William Cronon, George Miles, Jay Gitlin, "Becoming West, Toward a New Meaning in Western History," in *Under an Open Sky: Rethinking America's Western Past* (New York, 1992), pp. 3–27.

46. Billington, *Turner*, p. 154.

47. Richard Hofstadter, *The Progressive Historians: Turner, Beard, Parrington* (New York, 1968), p. 114.

48. My analysis of Turner's personality is based in large part on Cushing Strout's astute essay-review of Billington's biography of Turner in *History and Theory: Studies in the Philosophy of History* 13:3 (October 1974):315–25. Because Billington ignored the issue of psychoanalysis in his biography, Strout's appraisal is of key importance. My associate at the Huntington Library, Andrew Rolle, an able historian-psychoanalyst, states that Strout is correct in emphasizing Freud's point that biographers turn their subjects into "monsters of rectitude because of overidentification with them." Billington's identification with Turner, Strout argues, was such that Billington tended to cherish the shortcomings of his hero; that is, the faults in Turner's personality made him charmingly human. Billington thus traces Turner's problems in writing to his "perfectionism," emotion, and lack of discipline (see Strout, pp. 320–21). See also Strout, *The Veracious Imagination: Essays on American History, Literature, and Biography* (Middletown, Conn., 1981), pp. 268–69.

49. Strout, *History and Theory*, 13:323.

50. HEH TU Box 11. Allen Bogue, who has examined lists of doctoral candidates at the University of Wisconsin and at Harvard, has identified as many as eight women who appear to have been Turner's Ph.D. students (Allen Bogue to W. R. Jacobs, October 19, 1993).

51. See Martin Ridge, "A More Jealous Mistress: Frederick Jackson Turner as a Book Reviewer," *Pacific Historical Review* 55 (November 1987):49–63.

52. Allan Beckman, "Hidden Themes in the Frontier Thesis: An Application of Psychoanalysis to Historiography," *Comparative Studies in Society and History* 8 (April 1966):379ff. (cited by Strout in *History and Theory*, 13:321).

53. Strout, *History and Theory*, 13:320, cites Freud, *New Introductory Lectures on Psychoanalysis*, trans. J. Sprott (New York, 1933), p. 93.

54. As Turner recalled, "I do owe to Hart, and that is the steadfast way in which he has worked the reel and finally landed the MS. It's a poor sucker instead of a trout, but it fought like the devil against coming to landing net." Turner to Max Farrand, December 29, 1905, in Wilbur R. Jacobs, *The Historical World of Frederick Jackson Turner* (New Haven, Conn., 1988), pp. 184–85. See also Zachory Leader, *Writer's Block* (Baltimore, 1991), pp. 11, 15, 75, 78, 186–87, 252.

55. Peter Lowenberg, *Decoding the Past, the Psychohistorical Approach* (New York, 1983). See his analysis of narcissistic expressions of the creative person, pp. 112–33ff. See also Heinz Kohut, *Restoration of Self* (New York, 1977), pp. 13ff., 122ff., and 192ff., for a discussion of narcissistic personality disorders, and Karen Horney, *The Collected Works of Karen Horney*, 2 vols. (New York, 1945), for a description of the neurotic individual who embarks on a "search for glory" (1:186ff., and 2:13, 33, 65–88). Robert Smith of Eastern Montana College, a longtime student of C. G. Jung, has read papers at Western History Association meetings on the theme "Frederick Jackson Turner: Material Man in a Material World," suggesting that Turner's personality is best understood by concepts advanced by Jung.

Chapter Five. Explaining Colonial American History

1. See William Cronon, *Nature's Metropolis: Chicago and the Great West* (New York, 1991), pp. xvi, 53, 283, 378. Cronon's articles include "Revisiting the Vanishing Frontier, the Legacy of Frederick Jackson Turner," *Western Historical Quarterly* 28 (1987):157–76, and "Turner's First Stand: The Significance of Significance in American History," in *Writing Western History: Essays on Major Western Historians*, ed. Richard Etulain (Albuquerque, N. Mex., 1991), pp. 73–102. In this latter essay Cronon concludes, "Not all the Turner legacy is worth abandoning" (p. 95).

2. See Max Savelle, "The Imperial School of American Historians," *Indiana Magazine of History* 65 (1949):13–34. Writing some twenty years later, Savelle himself suggested that there was a "governor-to-governor diplomacy along the 'great frontier,'" which often differed from that of the home government. See Savelle, "The International Approach to Early American History, 1492–1763," in *The Reinterpretation of Early American History*, ed. R. A. Billington (San Marino, Calif., 1967), p. 268.

3. The organization of Turner's research materials is discussed in chapter 4.

4. See "The Generous Critic," in Wilbur R. Jacobs, *The Historical World of Frederick Jackson Turner with Selections from His Correspondence* (New Haven, Conn., 1968), pp. 193–228. Although Turner was a "generous critic" in assisting his advanced students, he was, as Martin Ridge has pointed out, often "unkind," even "ruthless" in book reviews. See Ridge, "A More Jealous Mistress: Frederick Jackson Turner as a Book Reviewer," *Pacific Historical Review* 55:1 (February 1987):49–63.

5. See, for example, *Essays in American History Dedicated to Frederick Jackson Turner* (New York, 1910), pp. 57–84, 113–36, 165–202. Carl L. Becker's popular but controversial Ph.D. dissertation, "The History of Political Parties in the Province of New York, 1760–1776" (University of Wisconsin, 1909), is given a critique in Bernard Friedman, "The Shaping of the Radical Consciousness in Provincial New York," *Journal of American History* 56 (1970):781–83.

6. See "The Case of Arthur H. Buffington," in Jacobs, *Historical World of Frederick Jackson Turner*, pp. 221–28.

7. Becker to Turner, May 16, 1910, quoted in ibid., p. 207.

8. Turner Map Collection, Turner Papers.

9. An address by Wertenbaker at the Mississippi Valley Historical Association meeting in 1931 is briefly summarized in Curtis Nettles, "Frederick Jackson Turner and the New Deal," *Wisconsin Magazine of History* 17 (1943):257–65. Nettles's article is reprinted in *Wisconsin Witness to Frederick Jackson Turner,* comp. O. Lawrence Burnett, Jr. (Madison, Wis., 1961), pp. 45–53.

10. See Burnett, *Wisconsin Witness,* p. 47.

11. The Parish-Turner friendship is documented in Turner's Correspondence, HEH TU Boxes 39–40.

12. See John Carl Parish, in *The Persistence of the Westward Movement and Other Essays,* ed. Louis Knott Koontz (Berkeley, Calif., 1943). John Walton Caughey, a younger colleague of Parish and Koontz at UCLA in this period, shared their enthusiasm for frontier history. Caughey had worked at Berkeley under Herbert Eugene Bolton, one of Turner's most admiring students.

13. Merle Curti, *The Growth of American Thought* (New York, 1943), pp. vi, vii. The importance of the environmentalist interpretation in the work of Curti and Becker is discussed in Robert A. Skotheim, "The Writing of American Histories of Ideas: Two Traditions in the XXth Century," *Journal of the History of Ideas* 25 (1964):266–70.

14. John Richard Alden, *The First South* (Baton Rouge, La., 1961), pp. 3–32. A Turnerian theme developed for seventeenth-century New York history is in Thomas Condon, "The Commercial Origins of New Netherland" (Ph.D. dissertation, Harvard University, 1962). Published in 1949, Ray A. Billington's influential textbook *Westward Expansion* (issued in various editions by Macmillan) made readily available a Turnerian view of early American frontier expansion.

15. See Clarence Ver Steeg, *The Formative Years, 1607–1763* (New York, 1964), pp. 152–53. Ver Steeg argues further that the southern "ruling class"

emerged from the area of Turner's "Old West." See also Billington, ed., *Reinterpretation of Early American History*, p. 94.

16. Turner to Henry Holt and Company, April 5, 1921, quoted in Jacobs, *Historical World of Frederick Jackson Turner*, p. 188.

17. Cecilia Kenyon, *William and Mary Quarterly* 16 (1959):588.

18. See Perry Miller's comments in *Errand into the Wilderness* (Cambridge, Mass., 1956). But Miller did recognize "all the drive, hope, and exuberance" of the frontier. See his introduction to Daniel Drake, *Discourse on the History, Character, and Prospects of the West* (Gainesville, Fla., 1955), p. xi.

19. Page Smith, *The Historian and History* (New York, 1964), p. 111. Elsewhere in this entertaining book Smith elaborates on his view of Turnerian history. He charges Arthur M. Schlesinger, Sr., with using a formula that "credited the [revolutionary] frontier with all that was progressive, and uniquely American" (p. 186).

20. For a discussion of the "frontier-West-mother-symbol complex" and its relevance to Turner's frontier theory, see Alan C. Beckman, "Hidden Themes in the Frontier Thesis: An Application of Psychoanalysis to Historiography," *Comparative Studies in Society and History* 8 (1966):10–34.

21. Maps of special value in studying colonial westward expansion include "A Map of the British and French Dominions in North America," by John Mitchell (London, 1755), William L. Clements Library, Ann Arbor, Michigan (the most accurate and complete of the maps made in the 1750s); Eman Bowen's "An Accurate Map of North America" (London 1763), John Carter Brown Library, Providence, R.I., which has less detailed information; "Map of the Southern Indian District of North America Compiled under the Direction of John Stuart," by Joseph Purcell (1773), Edward E. Ayer Collection, Newberry Library, Chicago, a large, cumbersome work in which the symbols for Indian towns and forts are not easily ascertained; and Henry Mouzon's "An Accurate Map of North and South Carolina with their Indian Frontiers" (London, 1776), Historical Commission of South Carolina, which is useful for the study of Carolina trading paths to the frontier.

22. Most of Turner's lecture notes are found in HEH TU File Drawers 1–22, especially Drawers 1, 2, 10, and 22. There are sets of student notes by George W. Bell (1910) and by T. C. Smith (1911) for his "History of the West" course in Drawer 14. I have also examined sets of notes taken for the same course by Thomas P. Martin, Everett E. Edwards, and Horace J. Smith; the best single set is that of Homer C. Hockett taken when he was acting as an assistant to Turner in 1902 (Special Collections, University of California, Santa Barbara Library). See also W. R. Jacobs, "Frederick Jackson Turner—Master Teacher," *Pacific Historical Review* 23 (1954):49–58.

23. H. Roy Merrens's article, "Historical Geography and Early American History," *William and Mary Quarterly* 22 (1965):529–48, includes an excellent summary of interpretations of historical geographers on early American history.

24. Ibid., p. 533. Turner's concept of a "frontier type" of settler is questioned by another geographer, James T. Lemon, in "The Agricultural Practices of National Groups in Eighteenth-Century Southeastern Pennsylvania," *Geographical Review* 56 (1966):467–96. Critiques of the Turnerian concept of the Indian as a kind of geographical obstacle to the colonial westward movement are in W. R. Jacobs, "British-Colonial Attitudes and Policies toward the Indian in the American Colonies," in *Attitudes of Colonial Powers toward the American Indian*, ed. Howard Peckam and Charles Gipson (Salt Lake City, 1969), pp. 81–100, 106.

25. See Wilbur R. Jacobs, ed., *America's Great Frontiers and Sections: Frederick Jackson Turner's Unpublished Essays* (Lincoln, Nebr., 1969), pp. 1, 40, 41, 72. Turner, however, seems to have confused the comparative and interdisciplinary approaches to research with scientific methodology (see chapter 4).

26. Printed in Jacobs, ed., *America's Great Frontiers and Sections*, pp. 105–8.

27. Charles M. Andrews, *The Colonial Period* (New York, 1912), pp. vi–vii. This viewpoint is expressed in a less dogmatic fashion in Andrews, *The Colonial Period in American History*, 4 vols. (New Haven, Conn., 1934), 1:xi–xiv. Lawrence H. Gipson, in *The British Empire before the American Revolution, The Triumphant Empire*, 15 vols. (New York, 1967), 13:381–82, maintains that Andrews viewed the colonies "as a projection of English civilization" and not as background for the history of the American nation.

28. Jacobs, ed., *America's Great Frontiers and Sections*, pp. 105–8.

29. Ibid., p. 107.

30. Turner to J. Franklin Jameson, June 9, 1895, HEH TU Box 2. Gilman M. Ostrander, in "Turner and the Germ Theory," *Agricultural History* 32 (1958):259, takes the view that Turner never completely rejected the idea of racial determinism in the germ theory, the idea that "those same Germanic racial germs, carried to America both directly and by way of England, had produced those same Germanic forms of free political life."

31. Turner to Merle Curti, August 27, 1928, HEH TU Box 38.

32. Ibid.

33. Turner, *The Frontier in American History*, ed. W. R. Jacobs (Tucson, Ariz., 1985), pp. 112, 116, 118–19, 121. See also W. R. Jacobs, ed., *The Paxton Riots and the Frontier Theory* (Chicago, 1967), pp. 1–4, 46–49.

34. HEH TU File Drawer 15, folder marked "Talk by F. J. Turner to the Pacific Coast Branch, 27, Decbr 1928."

35. Turner to Curti, August 8, 1928, HEH TU Box 38.

36. Turner, "The Development of American Society," *Alumni Quarterly of the University of Illinois* 2 (1908):120–36. (Turner's revised copy, Huntington Library Rare Book no. 126668, published in Jacobs, ed., *America's Great Frontiers and Sections*, pp. 168–70.)

37. Turner to Curti, August 8, 1928, HEH TU Box 38.

38. Ibid.

39. Turner to Becker, October 3, 1925, HEH TU Box 34.

40. See Turner's "Development of American Society," in Jacobs, ed., *America's Great Frontiers and Sections*, p. 170.

41. Clinton Rossiter, *Seedtime of the Republic* (New York, 1953), p. 9.

42. Ibid, p. 11.

43. Frederick B. Tolles, "New Approaches to Research in Colonial History," *William and Mary Quarterly* 12 (1955):456–61, 459.

44. Merle Curti, *The Making of an American Community* (Stanford, Calif., 1959); for a statement of the objectives and results of this case study of democracy in a frontier county, see pp. 1–11, 442ff.

45. Edmund S. Morgan, "The American Revolution: Revisions in Need of Revising," *William and Mary Quarterly* 14 (1957):3–15.

46. Ibid., pp. 13, 14. Despite these parallels Morgan clearly has little enthusiasm for either Turner or C. A. Beard, whose influence, Morgan wrote, "was and is stifling." See Edmund S. Morgan's thoughtful essay, "Historians of New England," in Billington, ed., *Reinterpretation of Early American History*, pp. 47ff.

47 Bernard Bailyn concludes that colonial political and social structures were "strangely shaped" in the New World; see his "Politics and Social Structure in Virginia," in *Seventeenth-Century America: Essays in Colonial History*, ed. James Morton Smith (Chapel Hill, N.C., 1959), pp. 90–115. Sigmund Diamond, in "An Experiment in Feudalism," *William and Mary Quarterly* 28 (1961):3–34, stresses free land and the resulting problems of shortage of labor in New France. Jackson Turner Main in an important study has concluded that "geographic mobility" in migrations to areas such as western Pennsylvania gave the colonial an opportunity to improve his social and economic position; see Main, *The Social Structure of Revolutionary America* (Princeton, N.J., 1965), p. 280.

48. HEH TU File Drawer 15, folder marked "Turner's queries for a Ph.D. exam ca. 1920."

49. Beginning in 1919 Turner participated in a Harvard history department course on the history of liberty. Turner's "scheme" for his lectures (HEH TU File Drawer 10, folder marked "History of Liberty Scheme [1919—Nov.]") includes notes to himself:

"Throughout I must organize these lectures more clearly around the central subject of liberty as conceived in America, (a) European inheritance of ideals of liberty and contradicting actual conditions brought over in institutions & prepossessions to America by colonists, (b) American modification of these ideals and institutions under wilderness conditions.

Not a brief history of U.S., but a survey of the idea of liberty, its embodiment in institutions, growth and transformation under changing conditions, American and European. . . . Relation between American frontier associational idea to European philosophical remedies."

50. HEH TU File Drawer 15, folder marked "Turner's queries for a Ph.D. exam. ca. 1920."

51. Beard to Merle Curti, August 9, [1928], HEH TU Box 40.

52. Discussion of early criticisms of the frontier theory appears in Ray A. Billington, *America's Frontier Heritage* (New York, 1966), pp. 16–22, and in Billington's bibliographical notes, pp. 242–45.

53. Turner's argument here is partly developed in Sumner Powell's Pulitzer Prize–winning volume, *The Formation of a New England Town* (Middletown, Conn., 1963), an examination of a seventeenth-century Puritan village and a superb study in local history. Powell offers convincing evidence that certain institutions of Sudbury differed widely from those the settlers had known in England and that a new kind of citizen, the "free Townsman," emerged as a significant figure in the pioneer community. Kenneth A. Lockridge, in his perceptive, readable volume, *A New England Town, The First Hundred Years, Dedham, Massachusetts, 1636–1736* (New York, 1970), maintains that Powell "repeated the myth that Americans wanted to hear" and suggests "a more cautious point of view" (p. 190). Yet Lockridge himself acknowledges that a basic theme in his book is a variation of the Turner frontier process, "though not quite in the way Turner envisioned" (p. 174n). In a somewhat similar study of another pioneer New England town, Philip J. Greven, Jr., argues that few changes took place in the traditional family life of settlers until after the passage of three and four generations; see Greven, *Four Generations, Population, Land, and Family in Colonial Andover, Massachusetts* (Ithaca, N.Y., 1970), pp. 272–74. Robert Middlekauff, in analyzing conflicting interpretations, points to the local character of early American history as well as to the "great idea" of the imperial historians and the need for toleration in both points of view in "The American Continental Colonies and the Empire," in *The Historiography of the British Empire Commonwealth* (Durham, N.C., 1966), pp. 44–45.

54. Turner to Merk, January 9, 1931, in Jacobs, *Historical World of Frederick Jackson Turner,* pp. 168–69.

55. One of the most recent books in the *Histories of the American Frontier,* formerly edited by Billington but now edited by Howard Lamar, Martin Ridge, and David J. Weber, is Elliot West's superb *Growing Up with the Country; Childhood on the Far Western Frontier* (Albuquerque, N. Mex., 1989). West's book concentrates on the history of childhood in the Great Plains and the Southwest in the middle decades of the nineteenth century. His is thus a "far western" frontier project that easily bridges the old and the new concepts of frontier history.

This particular book is also Turnerian in flavor in the sense that it deals with what Turner called "mass history." Years ago when I was more of a Turner enthusiast than I am now, I argued with the late Douglass Adair about Turner's virtues as a social historian. Although Adair had a genuine distaste for Turner, he did on one occasion write to me with this perceptive observation: "You quote Turner's commitment to mass history. Do you know Tocqueville's comment on the democratic vs. the aristocratic perspectives of historians—a chapter in his second volume. Democratic historians deal with social forces and social movements; aristocratic historians emphasize the actions of great men" (Adair to Jacobs, December 9, 1966). Alexis de Tocqueville's commentary on "aristocratic" and "democratic" historians is found in any of the various editions of *Democracy in America*.

West, in *Early Childhood*, has an appreciative comment on Turner's leadership as a social historian, quoting the 1893 address: "American social development has been continually beginning over again on the frontier" (see pp. 248–49).

56. Jack Greene himself, although he quietly protests, is a member of the imperial school that has apparently been victorious over the Turnerian nationalists. At a recent meeting of the colonial history seminar at the Huntington Library he presented an evocative paper, "The Concept of Virtue in Late British America," originally written for the sixteenth Lawrence Henry Gipson Symposium on "Political Virtue in the Eighteenth Century" held at Lehigh University on March 6, 1990. In footnotes peppered with references to Gordon S. Wood, J. G. A. Pocock, and Isaac Kramnick and with an armada of British sources, Greene easily demonstrates that concepts of virtue came from sources other than the colonial frontier backwoodsmen or their leaders.

57. See W. R. Jacobs, "Lo the Poor Indian," *AHA Newsletter* 9 (March 1971):38–40.

58. For an appreciative essay by an able historical geographer, see Robert H. Block, "Frederick Jackson Turner and American Geography," *Annals of the Association of American Geographers* 70:1 (March 1980):31–42. Block concludes that Turner was "geography-bound" with a "space-obsessed mind" (p. 42).

Chapter Six. Explaining Agricultural History

1. HEH TU File Drawer 15, folder marked "Address 'Agricultural History'–1922–Dec. 28." Ray A. Billington, in his biography *Frederick Jackson Turner: Historian, Scholar, Teacher* (New York, 1973), p. 365, concludes that Turner was a "pioneer" in the field.

2. See HEH TU File Drawer 15, folder marked "Address," for Turner's annotated copy of the *Programme of the Thirty-seventh Annual Meeting of the American Historical Association*, New Haven, 1922.

3. Nils A. Olsen to Turner, November 11, 1922, and December 4, 1922, HEH TU Box 31.

4. HEH TU File Drawer 15, folder marked "Address," p. 4, "final draft."

5. Olsen to Turner, December 4, 1922, HEH TU Box 31.

6. See "Introduction," in Wilbur R. Jacobs, ed., *Frederick Jackson Turner's Legacy: Unpublished Writings in American History* (San Marino, Calif.:1965), pp. 4–5ff.

7. Major writings by Joseph Schafer, Benjamin Horace Hibbard, and Henry Charles Taylor were listed by Turner in *Guide to the Study and Reading of American History*, which he edited with Edward Channing and Albert Bush-

nell Hart (Boston, 1912) (see index references in this revised edition). Schafer, author of a number of books and articles relating to the occupation of the Pacific Northwest, became one of the leading supporters of the Turnerian safety-valve theory. His most important article was probably "Was the West a Safety-Valve for Labor?" *Mississippi Valley Historical Review* 24 (December 1937):229–314. Turner in 1908 wrote about the accomplishments of students he had trained, a twenty-two-page "draft" of a letter to Pres. Charles Van Hise of the University of Wisconsin, June 19, HEH TU Box 11. Turner wrote that he had been under attack because of his light teaching load and therefore felt obliged to point out the accomplishments of his students, including those in agricultural history, Ulrich Phillips, W. A. Schaper, and Emory R. Johnson.

8. See Turner's collection of maps, Turner Papers. He included notes on them about the types of crops and livestock as well as elections, illiteracy, and population movements.

9. See chapters 7, 8, and 9 and HEH TU File Drawer 15 folders on "World Crisis" and "Notes for a Shop Club Lecture—1923, Winter."

10. During summer 1925 Turner delivered a lecture on "Changes in New England," at Logan, Utah (HEH TU Box File Drawer 15), in which he discussed economic changes and the impact of the Irish on "native population."

11. Arthur Schlesinger, Jr., "On the Writing of Contemporary History," *Atlantic Monthly* 19:3 (March 1967):69, 74.

12. Martin Ridge, "Frederick Jackson Turner and His Ghost: The Writing of Western History," *Proceedings* of the American Antiquarian Society, 101, Part 1 (Worcester, Mass., 1991), pp. 65–76.

13. Howard Lamar in a perceptive essay, "From Bondage to Contract, Ethnic Labor in the American West, 1600–1890," in *The Countryside in the Age of Capitalist Transformation, Essays on the Social History of Rural America,* ed. Stephen Hahn and Jonathan Prude (Chapel Hill, N.C., 1985), p. 317, concludes that Turner's idea of "free land meant a free people." Although economic expectations rather than racism accounted for slavery and bondage, the abundant land had its impact on the real West, sometimes very different from Turner's ideal West (ibid.).

Chapter Seven. The Twentieth Century

1. The essay of 1893 as well as other published essays discussed in this chapter are listed with place, publisher, and date of publication in *Frederick Jackson Turner, A Reference Guide,* ed. Vernon E. Mattson and William E. Marion (Boston, 1985), pp. xxix–xxxiii.

2. HEH TU File Drawer 15; Turner dated the manuscript "Oct. 1922."

3. Ibid.

4. Richard Hofstadter, *The Progressive Historians: Turner, Beard, Parrington* (New York, 1968), pp. 111–14. See also chapter 4 discussing the issue of writer's block.

5. Turner's brackets.

6. Joseph Schafer Papers [1931], Wisconsin Manuscripts, Illinois State Historical Society.

7. Turner, "Problems in American History," *Aegis* 7 (November 4, 1892): 48–52.

8. See Turner's review of Wilson's *History of the American People* in *American Historical Review* 8 (1903):762–65. For another interpretation of this hostile review, see Martin Ridge, "A More Jealous Mistress: Frederick Jackson Turner as Book Reviewer," *Pacific Historical Review* 55:1 (February 1987):59–60. For an example of another caustic review by Turner, see his critique of James K. Hosmer, *A Short History of the Mississippi Valley* (New York, 1901), which had "serious defects" (*American Historical Review* 7 [1893]:801–3).

9. See W. R. Jacobs, ed., *Frederick Jackson Turner's Legacy* (Lincoln, Nebr., 1977), pp. 79–80, 85–104.

10. Turner's drafts and essays on the League of Nations are preserved in HEH TU File Drawer 14.

11. All quotations are from Turner's "draft on the League of Nations, Nov. 1918," HEH TU File Drawer 14.

12. "American Sectionalism and World Organization by Frederick Jackson Turner," ed. William Diamond, *American Historical Review* 47, no. 3 (April 1952):545–51. Turner wrote this paper (found among the Woodrow Wilson Papers) for the National Board for Historical Service, of which Turner was a member and probably a founding father. The board was composed of a number of historians not serving in the armed forces of World War I who sought to contribute to the war effort with their knowledge and skills. Turner, for example, recruited Herbert Bolton and other scholars to write articles, some of which appear by their titles to have been overly patriotic in describing Germany as a historical aggressor. See Newton D. Mereness, ed., "American Historical Activities during the World War," in *Annual Report*, American Historical Association, 1919 (Washington, D.C., 1923), pp. 137–293.

13. HEH TU File Drawer 14, folder marked "Syllabus of Considerations on Proposed League of Nations, 1918 January 10."

14. From a typed carbon draft on the League of Nations, November 1918.

15. Ibid.

16. See "Syllabus," HEH TU File Drawer 14.

17. See Diamond, ed., "American Sectionalism," p. 550.

18. Turner to Mrs. William Hooper, October 9, 1919, HEH TU-H Box 4.

19. Turner to Mrs. William Hooper, November 23, 1919, HEH TU-H Box 4.

20. Ibid.

21. HEH TU File Drawer 16, folder marked "It would be a pity if the U.S. lost her isolation from Europe—1918."

22. HEH TU File Drawer 15, folder marked "Notes for a Shop Club Lecture, 1923—Winter."

23. Turner developed these ideas in a series of drafts of essays on the

League in 1918; one draft is marked as a copy sent to Woodrow Wilson (HEH TU uncataloged).

24. Turner, "Notes for a Shop Club Lecture, 1923—Winter," HEH TU File Drawer 15.

25. In 1923–1924, during his last year of teaching at Harvard, Turner began his wide-ranging investigations on problems of war, peace, and population pressures. Many of his notes are in uncataloged folders in the Turner Papers.

26. In a book of the 1960s, Walter LaFeber wrote in *The New Empire, An Interpretation of American Expansion, 1860–1898* (Ithaca, N.Y., 1963), pp. 62–65, that Turner's frontier theory became an argument justifying American overseas expansion. And more recently Patricia Limerick in her stimulating study, *The Legacy of Conquest, The Unbroken Past of the American West* (New York, 1987), pp. 25–26, argues in a similar fashion that the West was a place "undergoing conquest and never fully escaping its consequences."

27. Bernard Bailyn, *Boundaries of History: The Old World and the New* (Providence, R.I., 1992).

Chapter Eight. Turner and the Threats of the Twentieth Century

1. HEH TU File Drawer 10, "Strategy of a Saturated Earth," folder 10A2.

2. Ibid. In his notes, Turner often paraphrases writers he consulted.

3. Griffith Taylor, "The Distribution of Future White Settlement," *Geographical Review* 12 (July 1922):387, 402. The Huntington Library Reference Collection (call no. G1 G35) contains Turner's personal copy of issues of the *Geographical Review* with his marginalia.

4. Walter Wilcox, "On the Future Distribution of White Settlement," *Geographical Review* (October 1922):646–47. Turner's handwritten marginal note refers to "Taylor's Reply Geog. Rev. Jan. 1923." There, Wilcox in a one-page statement, "Future White Settlement: A Rejoinder," *Geographical Review* (January 1923):130, argues that the future of the "white race . . . will be much more controlled by climactic factors."

5. Raymond Pearl, "The Population Problem," *Geographical Review* (October 1922):636–45.

6. Raymond Pearl, *The Biology of Population Growth* (New York, 1925).

7. Huntington Library Reference Collection call no. HB 851 (see p. 42). This volume, along with others cited below, was part of Turner's personal library. Such volumes have his marginalia but are not housed in the library's Rare Book Collection.

8. Pearl, *Biology of Population Growth*, p. 212.

9. Louis Israel Dublin, "The Fallacious Propaganda for Birth Control," *Atlantic Monthly* (February 1926):186–94.

10. *Who's Who*, 1930–1931.

11. Clippings in an envelope and notes found in Pearl, *Biology of Population Growth*, Huntington Library Reference Collection call no. HB 85142.

12. HEH TU Drawer 10, "Strategy" folder.

13. Ibid.

14. Ibid.

15. Harold Wright, *Population* (Cambridge, Mass., 1923), Huntington Library Reference Collection call no. HB 851 W7.

16. Edward M. East, *Mankind at the Crossroads* (New York, 1923), Huntington Library Reference Collection call no. HB 871 E3.

17. Warren S. Thompson, *Population: A Study in Malthusianism* (New York, 1915), Huntington Library Reference Collection call no. HB 875 T4.

18. Ibid., p. 162.

19. East, *Mankind*, p. 167.

20. Wright, *Population*, pp. 163, 174.

21. *Who's Who*, 1930–1931.

22. See Turner, "Alarmist Arguments," HEH TU File Drawer 10, for quotations in this paragraph. See also Frank William Taussig, *Principles of Economics* (New York, 1911), Huntington Library Reference Collection call no. HB 171 T3, p. 10.

23. Turner cites articles by John M. Clark, "The Empire of Machines," *Yale Review* 12 (October 1922):132–43; see "Alarmist Arguments," HEH TU File Drawer 10. Turner's essay "Sections and the Nation" was the lead article in *Yale Review* 12:1–21.

24. Underlined section in a review of Wright's book from *New York Evening Post* or *Literary Review*, January 5, 1923.

25. See Wright, *Population*, p. vii.

26. Ibid., but not underlined by Turner.

27. John Maynard Keynes, "Is Britain Overpopulated?" *New Republic*, October 31, 1923, pp. 247–48.

28. Harry Elmer Barnes, *The New History and the Social Studies* (New York, 1925), and *The History and Prospects of the Social Sciences* (New York, 1925), Huntington Library Reference Collection call no. H 51 B3.

29. Barnes, *New History*, p. 66; underlined reference by Turner in index.

30. Ibid., p. 7.

31. HEH TU File Drawer 15, folder labeled "Talk at Thursday Club, 1921 March 17."

32. HEH TU File Drawer 15, folder labeled "Lecture (U. of Wis.): Puritanism, American Early 1890s Sub-Course VI."

33. HEH TU File Drawer 14, folder labeled "Comment on Piney People of New Jersey, March 1923."

34. See Henry F. May, *The End of American Innocence: A Study of the First Years of Our Own Time, 1912–1917* (New York, 1959), p. 42; with some accuracy, May referred to Turner as "a moralist and synthesizer." William McNeill, in a major address to members of the Organization of American Historians at their April 1992 meeting in Chicago, vigorously attacked supporters of the frontier theory for ignoring slavery on worldwide frontiers of European colonialism.

Walter Nugent in a valuable and thoughtful essay, "Frontiers and Empires in the late Nineteenth Century," analyzes differences between colonizing and establishing imperialist, exploitative world frontiers (see Historical Society of Israel and the Zalman Center for Jewish History, *Religion, Ideology, and Nationalism in Europe and America* (Tel Aviv, 1986), pp. 263–75. See also Michael P. Malone's thoughtful essay, "Beyond the Last Frontier: Toward a New Approach to Western History," *Western Historical Quarterly* 20 (November 1989): 409–27.

35. See David Wrobel's excellent new book, *The End of American Exceptionalism: Frontier Anxiety from the Old West to the New Deal* (Lawrence, Kans., 1993). He effectively argues that Turner, along with other intellectuals, was a symbol of the frontier anxiety that began to take place as early as the 1870s.

Chapter Nine. Turner's Shadow on World Frontiers

1. William McNeill, *The Great Frontier: Freedom and Hierarchy in Modern Times* (Princeton, N.J., 1983). McNeill has used the frontier concept in an earlier book, *Europe's Steppe Frontier* (Chicago, 1964).

2. McNeill, *Great Frontier*, pp. 3–8, 25. The 1964 edition of Walter Prescott Webb's *The Great Frontier* (Austin, Tex.) has a lucid introduction by Arnold Toynbee asserting that Webb combined mastery of a special area of history with "a vision of the total history of the world" (p. vii). Had Webb lived to see the population explosion in Third World countries, Toynbee believes he would have written another volume to explain such developments "in his own masterly way" (p. xi).

3. McNeill, *Great Frontier*, p. 11. McNeill also attacks the work of Louis Hartz, whose studies on new societies, he states, were as provincial (with their Marxist) hues as Turner's writings (pp. 3–8). McNeill's *The Rise of the West, A History of the Human Community* was published in Chicago in 1963.

4. McNeill, the *Great Frontier*, pp. 16ff.

5. Ibid., p. 18. Enslavement of Indians in colonial South Carolina has been investigated by a number of writers, including M. Eugene Sirmans, *Colonial South Carolina: A Political History, 1663–1783* (Chapel Hill, N.C., 1966), pp. 17, 40–43, 53–54, 60, and Verner W. Crane, *The Southern Frontier, 1670–1732* (Ann Arbor, Mich., 1964), pp. 31, 80, 112ff. Richard Haan, in a thoroughly researched investigation, "The 'Trade Do's Not Flourish As Formerly': The Ecological Origins of the Yamassee War of 1715," *Ethnohistory* 28:4 (1981):341–58, shows that some tribes enslaved others and participated in the Indian slave trade.

6. McNeill, The *Great Frontier*, p. 31.

7. Ibid., p. 25.

8. Ibid., p. 25, 60ff.

9. Ibid.

10. McNeill cites Margaret Walsh's booklet, *The American Frontier Revisited*

(Atlantic Highlands, N.J., 1981), which lists a number of publications but contains little analysis that "summarizes recent debate." He also cites Ray A. Billington's *The American Frontier Thesis* (Washington, D.C., 1971), a work now out of date that gives little emphasis to the frontier-sectionalism complexities. McNeill states that this work is nevertheless "the best survey of the subject, offering a magistral and judicious, though firmly pious treatment of Turnerian historiography." Henry Nash Smith's *The Virgin Land* (Cambridge, Mass., 1950) gives an excellent but now dated literary overview of American frontier literature. Frederick Jackson Turner's *Frontier in American History* (New York, 1920) is a volume of essays, the first of which was his 1893 paper, "The Significance of the Frontier in American History."

11. Walter Prescott Webb, *The Great Plains* (Boston, 1931), *Divided We Stand: The Crisis of Frontierless Democracy* (New York, 1937), and *More Water for Texas: The Problem and the Plan* (Austin, Tex., 1954).

12. Turner, *The Significance of Sections in American History*, with an introduction by Max Farrand, was first published in New York in 1932, shortly after Turner's death. Other volumes of Turner essays that reveal his thought on the development of the frontier-sectionalism concept are *The Early Writings of Frederick Jackson Turner*, ed. Fulmer Mood (Madison, Wis., 1938), and *Frederick Jackson Turner's Legacy: Unpublished Writings in American History*, ed. W. R. Jacobs (1965; reprint, Lincoln, Nebr., 1972).

13. William A. Williams, in "The Frontier Thesis and American Foreign Policy," *Pacific Historical Review* 24 (November 1965): 379–95, and in his book *The Roots of the Modern American Empire* (New York, 1970), discusses the imperialistic aspect of American frontier expansion. The theme is also found in Walter LaFeber, *The New Empire: An Interpretation of American Expansion, 1860–1898* (Ithaca, N.Y., 1963). An older work but still one of the most stimulating interpretations is William Christie MacLeod's *The American Indian Frontier* (New York, 1928), which in Part 5, "The Sweep of Empire," pp. 395–544, makes an eloquent statement about European frontiers of conquest in the New World. The earlier chapters "The Conquerers," Part 2, pp. 67–143, give an excellent analysis of Indian enslavement and forced-labor systems in both North and South America. Francis Jennings in 1976 offered an eloquent and well-documented assessment of European expansionism in North America in *The Invasion of America: Indians, Colonialism, and the Cant of Conquest* (Chapel Hill, N.C., 1975), pp. 10–11, 11n, 14, 32n, 84, 87, 129n. Jennings attacks Turner's frontier thesis on multiple fronts, finding evidence of Anglo-Saxonism and social Darwinism in several of his essays, including Turner's address, "Social Forces in American History."

14. See Norman Harper, "Frontier and Section, A Turner Myth?" *Historical Studies, Australia and New Zealand* 5 (1952):135–53, and Harper, "The Rural and Urban Frontiers," *Australian Journal of Science* 35 (1963):321–34, an article based upon a study of Turner's papers at the Huntington Library. Robert F. Berkhofer, Jr., "Space, Time, Culture and the New Frontier," *Agricultural His-*

tory 38 (1964):21–30, suggests that Turnerian themes of sectionalism and social evolution were used to propagate doctrines or social laws to explain a range of historical developments. The ideas of sectional rivalry and conciliation are explored in two articles by W. R. Jacobs, "Wider Frontiers—Questions of War and Conflict in American History: The Strange Solution of Frederick Jackson Turner," *California Historical Quarterly* 47 (September 1968):219–36, and "Frederick Jackson Turner's Views on International Politics, War and Peace," *Australian National University Historical Journal* 6 (November 1969):10–15. The most recent assessment of Turnerian sectionalism is Michael Steiner, "Frederick Jackson Turner and Western Regionalism," in Richard W. Etulain, ed., *Writing Western History* (Albuquerque, N. Mex., 1991), pp. 103–35.

15. See especially Sherburne F. Cook and Woodrow Borah, *Essays in Population History: Mexico and the Caribbean* (Berkeley, Calif., 1972), pp. 115ff.; Henry R. Dobyns, "Estimating Aboriginal Indian Population: An Appraisal of Techniques with a New Hemisphere Estimate," *Current Anthropology* 7 (1966):395–449; and Sherburne F. Cook, *The Extent and Significance of Disease among the Indians of Baja, California, 1967–1733, Ibero-Americana*, 2 vols. (Berkeley, Calif., 1948), 2:19–22. Acknowledgment is also due to Carl O. Sauer, who, in *The Early Spanish Main* (Berkeley, Calif., 1966), a work often cited by Cook and Borah, gives much of the basic demographic data in determining the extent of Indian agricultural skills (see especially pp. 58–59, 252ff., 286–88). Although harsh Spanish policy, particularly systems of forced labor, caused a severe decrease in the number of Indians, Cook and Borah regard disease as the most important cause of Indian depopulation (letter from Woodrow Borah to W. R. Jacobs, April 13, 1973). Cook's estimates of population density, patterns of health, and general demographic changes after the arrival of the Spaniards in the New World are among the truly important contributions covering a breadth of the sciences. See "Sherburne Friend Cook, 1896–1974," by Hardin Jones, Woodrow Borah, Robert F. Heizer, and Nellow Pace, *University of California, in Memorium* (Berkeley, Calif., 1977), pp. 52–54; Albert L. Hurtado, "California Indian Demography, Sherburne F. Cook, and the Revision of American History," *Pacific Historical Review* 58 (1989):323–43; and Wilbur R. Jacobs, "Sherburne Friend Cook, Rebel Revisionist," *Pacific Historical Review* 54 (1985):191–99. Interrelationships between dispossession and depopulation of native peoples are discussed in W. R. Jacobs, "The Fatal Confrontation: Early Native-White Relations on the Frontiers of Australia, New Guinea, and America—A Comparative Study," *Pacific Historical Review* 40 (August 1971):293–309, and in Douglas Oliver's History of Oceana, *The Pacific Islands*, 3d ed. (New York, 1971), pp. 1–80.

16. Turner, "Shop Club Lecture, 1923," HEH TU File Drawer 16.

17. See, for example, George Perkins Marsh, *Man and Nature*, ed. David Lowenthal (Cambridge, Mass., 1965); John Muir, *The Story of My Boyhood* (Boston 1913); Bill McKibben, *The End of Nature* (New York, 1989); John Robbins, *Diet for a New America* (Walpole, N. H., 1987); Aldo Leopold, *A Sand*

County Almanac with Essays on Conservation from Round River (San Francisco, 1974); Fairfield Osborn, *Our Plundered Planet* (Boston, 1948); Rachel Carson, *Silent Spring* (Boston, 1962); Barry Commoner, *The Closing Circle: Nature, Man, and Technology* (New York, 1971); Rene Dubois and Barbara Ward, *Only One Earth: The Care and Maintenance of a Small Planet* (New York, 1972); Lewis Mumford, *Interpretations and Forecasts, 1922–1972* (New York, 1979); Roderick Nash, *Wilderness and the American Mind* (1973; reprint, New Haven, Conn., 1982).

18. D. W. Meadows et al., *Limits of Growth* (New York, 1972); Robert L. Heilbronner, *An Inquiry into the Human Prospect*, 2 vols. (New York, 1974–1975); and Arthur F. McEvoy, *The Fisherman's Problem: Ecology and Law in the California Fisheries, 1850–1980* (New York, 1990), a prize-winning environmental history.

19. Donella Meadows, John Richardson, and Gerhart Bruckmann, *Groping in the Dark* (New York, 1982), pp. 8–9.

20. See especially Turner, *Frontier in American History* and W. P. Webb, *The Great Plains*.

21. Ronald Carpenter, *The Eloquence of Frederick Jackson Turner* (San Marino, Calif., 1983), pp. 48–49.

22. Ibid., 49–50.

23. Howard Lamar and Leonard Thompson, eds., *The Frontier in History* (New Haven, Conn., 1981), pp. 314–15.

24. Ibid., pp. 309–10. See also Walter Nugent, "Frontiers and Empires in the Late Nineteenth Century," in Historical Society of Israel and the Zalman Center for Jewish History, *Religion, Ideology, and Nationalism in Europe and America* (Tel Aviv, 1986).

25. McNeill, *Great Frontier*, pp. 3–8.

26. This theme, the closing of the frontier, is set forth in a new volume by David M. Wrobel, *The End of American Exceptionalism: Frontier Anxiety from the Old West to the New Deal* (Lawrence, Kans., 1993).

Chapter Ten. The "Realwestern" History

1. Ferry Carpenter Reminiscences, March 31, 1968, sent to M. D. Williams, a former student of Edgar Eugene Robinson, who had been a student of Turner's; Robinson gave me a copy of Carpenter's recollections in a letter of April 24, 1968. Carpenter had been a student of Turner's when he attended Harvard Law School, 1909–1912. See also Turner's correspondence with Henry M. Stevens in 1910 in HEH TU Boxes 15 and 16.

2. See Howard Lamar's foreword in Sandra L. Myres, *Westering Women and the Frontier Experience, 1800–1915* (Albuquerque, N. Mex., 1982), p. xi; the arguments dealing with Turner, Merk, and Billington on the propagation of the "realwestern" history both agree and disagree with previous writers. For instance, my portrait of Turner and his work has been influenced by studies in ethno- and environmental history and thus exhibits some of the underbelly

of Turnerian thought arguing that Turner was far from being a dedicated multiple-hypothesis scholar as maintained by Ray A. Billington, *Frederick Jackson Turner: Historian, Scholar, Teacher* (New York, 1973), pp. 149–50, 161–62, 179, 456, 468, 477. I also give space to Turner's racism and his psychological problems as reflected in his work, topics that were not emphasized by Billington. As for Merk, my portrait tends to be more critical than that of Rod Paul's excellent and appreciative "Tribute" that appeared in *Western Historical Quarterly* 9 (January 1978): 141–48. My appraisal of Turner and Billington and their work and personalities also differs from the essays written by Billington's former student and coauthor, Martin Ridge: "Ray A. Billington (1903–1981)," *Western Historical Quarterly* 12:3 (July 1981):245–60; "Frederick Jackson Turner, Ray Allen Billington and American Frontier History," *Western Historical Quarterly* 19:1 (January 1988):5–20; and "The Life of an Idea," *Montana, the Magazine of Western History* 41:1 (Winter 1991):3–13. I cannot disagree with Ridge's eloquent positivism, but my thrust on Turner and Billington explores negative issues and misconceptions and their bonding with the positive traditions of the "realwestern" history. Moreover, I attempt to show the impact of the "realwestern" history on the new western history revisionists, including William Cronon, Richard White, and Patricia Limerick. Limerick's razorlike analysis of Billington's historical work in her essay, "Persistent Traits and the Persistent Historian: The American Frontier and Ray Allen Billington," in *Writing Western History: Essays on Major Western Historians,* ed. Richard W. Etulain (Albuquerque, N. Mex., 1991), pp. 277–310, supports much of what I have said about the "realwestern" history.

3. Turner to Henry Holt and Company, October 2, 1897, HEH TU Box 2.

4. Turner, *The Frontier in American History,* ed. W. R. Jacobs (Tucson, Ariz., 1986), p. 38.

5. Turner, "What Is Colonial History?" in W. R. Jacobs, ed., *Frederick Jackson Turner's Legacy* (Lincoln, Nebr., 1976), pp. 1, 5, 7.

6. An excellent commentary on the literary and historical importance of "Ancients vs. Moderns" in viewing the American past is in David Lowenthal, *The Past Is a Foreign Country* (Cambridge, Eng., 1985), pp. 118–21.

7. Turner, *The Character and Influence of the Indian Trade of Wisconsin,* edited and with an introduction by David H. Miller and William W. Savage, Jr. (Norman, Okla., 1977), pp. xiii, xvi, xvii, 3–6. In the first pages of his dissertation Turner makes the point that the trading post was a stage in the "development of society" that helped to break "the cake of custom." The "genesis" was the Phoenician trading post (p. 4). Turner's skills of professional self-preservation included building a genial relationship with departmental colleagues and those individuals who belonged to his Johns Hopkins ring of "seminarians," associates of Adams's seminar. Prominent among this group were Woodrow Wilson, Charles H. Haskins, and J. Franklin Jameson, who for years were key members of Turner's inner circle as indicated in his correspondence. In later years Turner formed a new inner circle with his students. He

gave special assistance to his favorite students, such as Carl Becker and Frederick Merk, who were both vulnerable in their first years of teaching. Becker, in particular, had problems in convincing his employers and colleagues that he was as well qualified as Turner said he was. This point is brought out in Turner's many letters seeking fellowships and job placement for Becker.

8. Although Turner is not named, C. Van Woodward in *Thinking Back, The Perils in Writing History* (Baton Rouge, La., 1986), discusses the southern historical orthodoxy presented in the writings of Ulrich Phillips (see especially pp. 29, 62–63). Turner's impact upon Phillips is set forth in the Phillips-Turner correspondence in the Turner Papers. What particularly impressed Phillips, when he heard Turner lecture at the University of Chicago, was the concept of frontier environmentalism, the idea of the emergence of the sections, and southern traits among the planter class. Turner, according to Phillips, had "made a school and created a tradition" in American historical writing (Phillips to Carl Becker, October 13, 1925, HEH TU Box 34A).

9. Turner to Constance Skinner, March 15, 1922, HEH TU Box 31. See also Turner's hostile assessment of Hermann Von Holst's *History of the United States*, accusing Von Holst of his ignorance of the eight "processes" in concentrating on the "slavery struggle." The essay remained unpublished in Turner's papers but appears in Jacobs, ed., *Turner's Legacy*, pp. 85–104. See HEH TU File Drawer 15, with a note in Turner's handwriting, "About 1889–90."

10. Turner to Constance Skinner, March 15, 1922, HEH TU 31.

11. Ibid.

12. *Bulletin* of the American Geographical Society 46 (1914):591–95, an address discussed in a Turner obituary, *Geographical Review* 22 (1932):449.

13. Turner to Merle Curti, August 8, 1928, HEH TU Box 39.

14. Turner, *The Frontier in American History* (Tucson, 1986), p. 37.

15. See Robert V. Hine's penetrating assessment of the frontier "in retrospect," in *The American West, An Interpretive History*, 2d ed. (Boston, 1984), pp. 320–21.

16. Turner map collection, HEH TU. Also see Hine, *American West*, pp. 320ff. for an early, new western history approach to Turnerian tradition.

17. Turner, *Frontier in American History*, p. 27.

18. Ibid., p. 31.

19. HEH TU Box 56, folder marked "1924, Feb., Notes for opening remarks . . . History of the U.S. 1800–1920 . . . final year of teaching at Harvard." Complete edited manuscript appears in Jacobs, ed., *Turner's Legacy*, pp. 81–84.

20. HEH TU File Drawer 15, folder marked "Turner, on opening a new course, 1924." Published in Jacobs, ed., *Turner's Legacy*, pp. 80–81.

21. "The Western Course of Empire," an unidentified review essay on R. G. Thwaites, ed., *Early Western Travels*, *The Dial* (July 1, 1906):6–9. Turner's annotated copy of this review is among his papers, Huntington Library Rare Book no. 222530.

22. HEH TU File Drawer 15, "Turner, on opening a new course, 1924."

23. See one of Turner's most important essays, "The Development of American Society," with all revisions and additions, Huntington Library Rare Book no. 126668. This piece, with subheadings on "space expansion" and "colonization of sections," embodies much of the theorizing set forth from time to time in Turner's classroom lectures. See also Jacobs, ed., *Turner's Legacy*, pp. 169–91, for the published version of this essay, with commentary on how it symbolized Turner's views on American social history.

24. Turner, "American Political Sectionalism," February 20, 1928, p. 20, in folder marked "Pasadena Lecture Feb. 28, 1928, First Draft?" HEH TU File Drawer 14.

25. Turner, "Lecture on Political Maps," in folder marked "Notes for a Talk on Political Maps, circa 1920," HEH TU File Drawer 10. The edited manuscript appears in Jacobs, ed., *Turner's Legacy*, pp. 70–73. On Turner's misuse of the multiple working hypotheses, the idea set forth by the geologist Thomas C. Chamberlin, see chapter 4.

Chapter Eleven. The Emergence of Frederick Merk

1. Frederic L. Paxson to Turner, May 31, 1911, HEH TU Box 16; Earl Pomeroy, "Frederic L. Paxson and His Approach to History," *Mississippi Valley Historical Review* 39 (March 1953):673–92; Richard W. Etulain's "After Turner: The Western Historiography of Frederic Logan Paxson," in Richard W. Etulain, ed., *Writing Western History: Essays on Major Western Historians* (Albuquerque, N. Mex., 1991), pp. 137–55, stresses Paxson's legacy as the most significant teacher-writer in Western history "after Turner" (p. 160). Paxson saw himself as heir to western history when he took over Turner's chair at the University of Wisconsin, bought Turner's house, and sent Turner a list of ninety lecture topics for his course on the history of the West. Paxson's lecture topics were, however, quite different from Turner's, stressing western urban history. For instance, Lecture no. 16 was entitled "The Rise of Chicago" (Paxson to Turner, January 16, 1911; HEH TU Box 16).

2. See, for instance, Homer C. Hockett's notes taken in Turner's course at Madison and Rodman Paul's notes taken in Merk's History of the West class in 1936 (borrowed by W. R. Jacobs, Huntington Library, July, 1986), and notes taken in Merk's classes in 1948-1949 by Francis Paul Prucha, S. J. Both Paul and Prucha later finished their doctoral work in western history under Merk.

3. Conversations with F. P. Prucha, July 18, 1986, Huntington Library.

4. See Frederick Merk, *History of the Westward Movement* (New York, 1978), 485–615, 636.

5. H. Roy Merrens, "Historical Geography and Early American History," *William and Mary Quarterly* 22 (October 1965):529–38.

6. See Merrens's comment on Brown's scholarship and use of historical sources in ibid., p. 544, and Ralph H. Brown, *Historical Geography of the United*

States (New York, 1948), pp. 96–98. Turner is mentioned twice by Brown but only in connection with the settlement of southern states and in reference to the aggressive attitude of frontiersmen, which "was to better" themselves (pp. 173, 183).

7. Turner, "Report on the Conference on the Relation of Geography to History," *American Historical Association Annual Report, 1907* (Washington, D.C., 1908), 1:57–91.

8. Merk, *History of the Westward Movement*, pp. 48, 51, 73, 74.

9. Ray A. Billington, *Westward Expansion*, 1st ed. (New York, 1949), pp. 80–81. This environmental theme is repeated and reemphasized by Billington in his fourth (and last) edition of *Westward Expansion* (New York, 1974), pp. 16, 90–91.

10. Conversations with Paul Prucha, July 17, 1986, Huntington Library.

11. Prucha lecture notes, Merk's History 162, History of the Westward Movement, Thursday, September 30, 1948.

12. Ibid., Saturday, October 16, 1948.

13. Frank J. Klingberg's notes, Turner's History of the West, University of Wisconsin, August 1909. An almost identical emphasis is found in Homer C. Hockett's notes from Turner's class in 1901. In the 1950s Hockett gave me a copy of his 1901 notes, probably the most complete record of Turner's lectures because, as Hockett told me, "I was an expert stenographer in those days." Klingberg's notes were recently made available to me through one of his former students at UCLA, Howard Kimball.

14. Turner, "The Development of American Society," *Alumni Quarterly of the University of Illinois* 2:3 (July 1908):120–36. Turner's revised version is published in W. R. Jacobs, ed., *Frederick Jackson Turner's Legacy* (Lincoln, Nebr., 1977), 168–92.

15. In Turner's correspondence at the Huntington Library, there are clear statements that reveal his anti-Semitism, his neglect of blacks and women, and his basic hostility toward the idea of giving Indians a place in history. David A. Nichols in his important essay "Civilization over Savage: Frederick Jackson Turner and the Indian," *South Dakota History* 2:1 (Winter 1971): 383–405, effectively analyzes Turner's racist ideas and his easy acceptance of Theodore Roosevelt's myopic portrayal of Indians.

16. For a sophisticated appraisal of this concept, see Robert Berkhofer, *The White Man's Indian: Images of the American Indian from Columbus to the Present* (New York, 1978). Berkhofer argues that historian Francis Parkman saw the Indian as an inferior "savage" (p. 108). It was not improbable that Turner's view of Indians as savages was distilled from Parkman, whose works he read as a student and later as a mature historian. See also Wilbur R. Jacobs, *Francis Parkman: Historian as Hero, the Formative Years* (Austin, Tex., 1991), pp. 45–89.

17. Turner, *The Frontier in American History* (New York, 1920), p. 13.

18. HEH TU File Drawer 15, copy of Turner's review of Elliot Coues, *History of the Expedition under the Command of Lewis and Clark*, in *Dial* (February 1,

1894):80–84. See also Turner to Van Hise, June 15, 1906, HEH TU uncataloged. Some of these letters are being added to the Huntington's Turner collection of boxed letters, arranged chronologically.

19. Conversations with Francis Paul Prucha, July 17, 1986, Huntington Library.

20. Otey M. Scruggs to Wilbur Jacobs, July 23, 1990. Merk, *History of the Westward Movement*, pp. 1–14, 69, 139, 154–155, 419, 423, 427.

21. In modern times the technique of revising stereotypes is called "up-streaming," that is, analyzing traditional historical sources on Indians in light of ethnological perspectives. It has often been discussed at meetings of the American Society for Ethnohistory, particularly in connection with the eth-nohistorical work of William H. Fenton. See, for instance, Michael K. Fosted et al., eds., *Extending the Rafters: Interdisciplinary Approaches to Iroquois Studies* (New York, 1984), pp. 11–12, 14. The method of attempting to understand Indian people and their culture in a historical context, especially in connec-tion with Indian-white contacts, was appreciated by writers as early as Francis Parkman. This point is emphasized in Jacobs, *Francis Parkman*, pp. 63ff. It is notable that in his lifelong interest in Parkman, Turner never said that Par-kman had a unique way of portraying Indian societies. See, for instance, Turner's long review of Parkman's work in *Dial* (December 16, 1898): 451–53, in which he eulogizes Parkman as a narrator who was born too soon to compre-hend the need for "institutional history."

22. Merk, *History of the Westward Movement*, pp. 184, 186ff. The proposition that Indians were to be relegated to the "Great American Desert" was created by Frederic L. Paxson and later repeated by Billington in *Westward Expansion* and in other American history textbooks, including those written by John Hicks. See Paul Prucha's comments in *Indian Policy in the United States, Histor-ical Essays* (Lincoln, Nebr., 1981), pp. 93, 94, 101, 110.

23. These recollections come from Henry May's gracefully written auto-biography, *Coming to Terms: A Study in Memory and History* (Berkeley, Calif., 1987), pp. 226–27.

24. Thomas C. McClintock's excellent essay, "Frederick Merk," in *Histo-rians of the American Frontier: A Bio-Bibliographical Source Book*, ed. John R. Wunder (New York, 1988), pp. 426–39, points to Merk's high standards of scholarship in books other than his *History of the Westward Movement*. This volume, the compilation of his lectures, showed a "lack of balance" and "unfortunately did not do him justice" (p. 435).

Chapter Twelve. Reverse Environmentalism and Other Teaching Themes

1. See William Cronon, Howard Lamar, Katherine G. Morrisey, and Jay Gitlin, "Women and the West: Rethinking the Western History Survey Course," *Western Historical Quarterly* 12:3 (July 1986):269–90, especially pp. 272–73.

2. Turner wrote and rewrote passages that improved his portrayal of the frontiersmen in such a way that the sterling qualities of the pioneer were accentuated. He went to great lengths to obtain rhetorical eloquence by imitating Robert Ingersoll, Robert La Follette, and other orators of his time who had an emotional impact on their audiences. Turner's essays were in fact orations designed to persuade by eloquence and by repetition of key phrases. See Ronald Carpenter, *The Eloquence of Frederick Jackson Turner* (San Marino, Calif., 1983). On the "cult of masculinity," see Robert V. Hine, *The American West, An Interpretive History*, 2d ed. (Boston, 1984), "Cattle and the Cult of Masculinity," pp. 321–22, and "the inherent violence in the profession: castrating a steer," illustration on p. 146. Billington, in his last book (which he considered his best), *Land of Savagery—Land of Promise: The European Image of the Frontier in the Nineteenth Century* (New York, 1981), fused the images of promise and savagery under the mantle of fiction. In a previous book, *The Far Western Frontier, 1830–1860* (New York, 1956), he had written about the mountain men as "a reckless new breed of men . . . aristocrats of the wilderness . . . calling no man their master" (p. 44). Here Billington echoed to a remarkable degree an earlier book by Robert Glass Cleland, *This Reckless Breed of Men, The Trappers and Fur Traders of the Southwest* (New York, 1950). See especially Cleland's treatment of this "bold drama" and his portrayal of "an adventurer to whom danger became a daily commonplace. . . . The course of empire followed his solitary pathways" (pp. 5, 10–54, 86–21, 344–46); "They were a tough, reckless, none too gentle a breed" (p. 346). John Mack Faragher, in his thought-provoking volume, *Women and Men on the Overland Trail* (New Haven, Conn., 1979), p. 14, points out that the diaries left by men dwell on violence, aggressiveness, fights, and competition; those written by women stress family relations, concern for the happiness and health of children, and friendships. Certainly this analysis shows that the sources used by Turner, Merk, and Billington as well as many other historians were those left by men (generally Yankee men), so it is no accident that there is a certain tendency in the "realwestern" history to accept violence, even to give it a respectability or, as in the case of Billington and Cleland, to give the "reckless" violence of the mountain men a romantic flavor.

3. Leopold is quoted in Curt Meine's excellent biography, *Aldo Leopold, His Life and Work* (Madison, Wis., 1988), pp. 233–44. See also W. R. Jacobs, ed., *Frederick Jackson Turner's Legacy* (Lincoln, Nebr., 1970), pp. 193–207, for Turner's comments on the need to avoid air and water pollution. Bill McKibben comments on themes discussed by Leopold in the 1920s and 1930s in *The End of Nature* (New York, 1989), pp. 5, 6, 37–38, 44–46, 63–64.

4. Joseph G. Jorgenson, *Western Indians: Comparative Environments, Languages, and Cultures of 172 Western American Indian Tribes* (San Francisco, 1980); see especially pp. 17–18, 119–47. Jorgenson's analysis and data on Indian environments and subsistence economies are particularly valuable because they represent what I believe to be the best description of the West before the

Anglo-American frontier advance. In a forthcoming study, "Footprints on the Land, Environmental Themes in American History," I take up some of the themes advance by Jorgenson, but I am indebted to him for his research in gathering data. See also William Cronon and Richard White, "Ecological Change and Indian-White Relations," in *Handbook of the American Indians,* ed. Wilcomb Washburn, vol. 4, *History of Indian-White Relations* (Washington, D.C., 1988) pp. 417–29.

5. Frederick Merk, *History of the Westward Movement* (New York, 1978), p. 593. R. A. Billington's fourth edition (*Westward Expansion* [New York, 1978]) does mention Negroes in connection with slavery and with the fur trade, as California pioneers, and with other topics (see pp. 32ff., 368, 578, 627, 643).

6. Francis Paul Prucha's comments on deleting "treacherous Indians" were prepared in confidence for the Macmillan Company; some of them were accepted by Billington. Prucha later gave copies of his critique to me, which included advice to avoid "Jacobsisms" about "conquistador" motives of expansionists.

7. HEH TU Box 20, vols. 1, 2, 3, well-worn copies of Turner and Merk, *List of References on the History of the West* (Cambridge, Mass., 1922), with Turner's annotations. Merk appears to have first taken up the second part of the course in 1922–1923, beginning with the "Development of Society in the Mississippi Valley, 1830–1850."

8. Ibid.

9. Turner's three-by-five reference file was augmented with other conventional file drawers holding newspaper clippings, student papers, lecture notes, and handwritten essays, many of which were drafts and unfinished papers. A brief description of these file drawers and Turner's annotated books is in Ray A. Billington and Wilbur R. Jacobs, "The Frederick Jackson Turner Papers at the Huntington Library," *Arizona and the West* 2 (1960):73–77.

10. See Turner's lecture notes in HEH TU File Drawer 22B and HEH TU Box 56.

11. Board of Regents to F. J. Turner, April 30, 1900, HEH TU Box 3. Another provision was the title of "Professor of European History" for his friend and colleague Charles Homer Haskins. See also President Charles K. Adams to Turner, March 22, 1900, HEH TU Box 3. Turner was in need of rest after the death of two of his children and his wife's illness. At Chicago he would have had an assistant as well as the salary of $3,500.

12. Turner to Max Farrand, January 31, 1907, HEH TU Box 8.

13. Benjamin Wheeler to Turner, January 20, 1906; Turner to Wheeler, February 2, 1906, HEH TU Box 1906.

14. See Turner's annotated copy of Turner and Merk, *List of References,* Table of Contents, pp. i–ii. HEH TU vol. 20, 1920–1924; W. R. Jacobs, ed., "Frederick Jackson Turner's Notes on the Westward Movement, California, and the Far West," *Southern California Quarterly* 46 (1964):161–68.

15. Turner to Constance L. Skinner, March 15, 1922, HEH TU Box 31.

16. Turner to Carl Becker, December 16, 1925, HEH TU Box 34a.

17. Preserved among his papers are notes demonstrating this synthesis by Horace Smith and scattered notes by Homer Hockett; W. R. Jacobs has a complete copy of notes taken by Homer C. Hockett and by Frank J. Klingberg.

18. Hockett often commented on this point in conversations with me in the 1950s at his home in Santa Barbara where he spent his final years revising his studies on constitutional history.

19. See their correspondence in W. R. Jacobs, *The Historical World of Frederick Jackson Turner* (New Haven, Conn., 1968), pp. 10, 16, 53, 148, 160, 199–200, 209, 211, 220, 226.

20. Haskins to James A. James, November 19, 1909, HEH TU Box 13.

21. Ibid.

22. Turner to Jameson, May 11, 1915, HEH TU Box 24. For Turner and politics in the AHA, see Peter Novick, *That Noble Dream* (New York, 1988), pp. 93, 98, 99; see also Ray A. Billington, *Frederick Jackson Turner: Historian, Scholar, Teacher* (New York, 1973), pp. 338–43.

23. Martin Ridge, "A More Jealous Mistress: Frederick Jackson Turner as a Book Reviewer," *Pacific Historical Review* 55:1 (February 1986):46–63. See also Ridge's penetrating essay on Turner's disciples of the era 1920–1940, "Frederick Jackson Turner and His Ghost," *Proceedings* of the American Antiquarian Society, vol. 10, part 1 (Worcester, Mass., 1991), pp. 65–76.

24. Charles A. Beard to Turner, May 14, 1921, HEH TU Box 31. See also Charles A. Beard, in *New Republic* 25 (1920):349–50.

25. HEH TU File Drawer 14. Turner dated the manuscript October 1922.

26. Turner to Dorothy Turner Main, February 18, 1921, HEH TU Box 31.

27. Jacobs, ed., *Historical World of Frederick Jackson Turner*, p. 126.

28. HEH TU File Drawer 15, folder marked "Draft on Sectionalism," published in Jacobs, ed., *Turner's Legacy*, pp. 48–51.

29. Ray A. Billington readily adopts and repeats Turner's view of himself as an advocate of multiple hypotheses; see, for instance, Billington, *Frederick Jackson Turner: Historian, Scholar, Teacher*, pp. 149–50, 161–62, 456, 458.

Chapter Thirteen. Merk Takes the Flag

1. Frederick Merk, *History of the Westward Movement* (New York, 1978), p. xvii. Here Merk modifies Turner's course name from "History of the West" to "History of the Westward Movement."

2. *Who Was Who in America with World Notables, 1977–1981* (Chicago, 1981), p. 400; Turner-Merk correspondence, 1925–1930, HEH TU Boxes 34–44; Rodman W. Paul, "Frederick Merk, Teacher and Scholar: A Tribute," *Western Historical Quarterly* 9 (January 1978):141–48; Richard W. Leopold, "Frederick Merk," *American Historical Review* 83:4 (October 1978):1152–53; Thomas McClintock, "Frederick Merk," in John Wunder, ed., *Historians of the Frontier* (New York, 1988), pp. 426–39, includes a list of Merk's writings.

3. Turner's seven-year-old son, Jackson Allen Turner, died in 1899; Turner to Carl Becker, November 17, 1899, HEH TU Box 2.

4. Turner-Merk correspondence, HEH TU, 1920s and 1930s; see especially Merk to Turner, July 4 [1927], HEH TU Box 37.

5. Turner to Max Farrand, March 8, 1927, HEH TU Box 57.

6. Merk to Turner, March 1, 1930; Turner to Merk, March 17, 1930 (HEH TU Box 44), and Paul, "Frederick Merk, Teacher and Scholar," pp. 145–46.

7. Turner to Merk, March 17, 1930, HEH TU Box 44.

8. Confidential interview with former Merk student.

9. Merk to Turner, January 11, 1931, HEH TU Box 45. The letter is also quoted in Paul, "Frederick Merk, Teacher and Scholar," p. 146.

10. Undated letter to Rodman Paul, in "Frederick Merk, Teacher and Scholar," pp. 146–47.

11. Frederick Merk, "A Safety-Valve Thesis and Texas Annexation," *Mississippi Valley Historical Review* 49 (December 1962):413–36.

12. Turner to Merk, May 6, 1925, HEH TU Box 34.

13. See "Comments on the work of FJT," 1919–1938, HEH TU Box 56.

14. Henry Holt and Company royalty statements, 1921–1930, HEH TU Box 36.

15. Benjamin Wright, "American Democracy and The Frontier," *Yale Review* 21 (December 1930):349–65.

16. Isaiah Bowman, "The Jordan Country," *American Geographical Review* 21 (January 1931):25–55.

17. Turner to Merk, January 31, 1931, HEH TU Box 45.

18. Frederic L. Paxson, in *American Historical Review* 38 (July 1933):773–74.

19. John D. Hicks, in *American Historical Review* 41 (January 1936):354–57.

20. Ibid., pp. 356–57.

21. Conversations with John Hicks on Turner and his work at meetings of the Pacific Coast Branch of the American Historical Association in the 1950s and at Berkeley at faculty club lunches in the 1960s. Hicks's popular textbook, *Federal Union* (Boston, 1937), and its sequel, *The American Nation* (Boston, 1941), incorporate much of the frontier-sectional interpretation. These texts, brought up to date with revisions and published by Houghton Mifflin, lost their popularity in the 1960s.

22. Ronald Carpenter, *The Eloquence of Frederick Jackson Turner* (San Marino, Calif., 1984). See also Ray A. Billington, "Popularizing the Frontier Thesis," in *Frederick Jackson Turner: Historian, Scholar, Teacher* (New York, 1973), pp. 184–208. Turner, the popularizer, wrote so much about the frontier-sectional theory that at times he felt, as he wrote to Arthur M. Schlesinger, May 5, 1925, "that I seemed to be plagiarizing myself" (see Wilbur R. Jacobs, *Historical World of Frederick Jackson Turner* [New Haven, Conn., 1968], p. 164).

23. See *Who's Who in America, 1948–1949* (Chicago, 1948), p. 1918; *Who Was Who in America* (Chicago, 1950), p. 416.

24. Tully Hunter, "Frederic Logan Paxson," in *Historians of the Frontier*, ed.

John Wunder (New York, 1988), p. 463, argues that despite Paxson's "generalist" work in U.S. history, he was "first and foremost a historian of the frontier." Herbert Bolton's papers at the Berkeley, California, Bancroft Library (B.P. 1931–32, outgoing letters) contain correspondence with Paxson showing how carefully Bolton arranged to provide Paxson with an open field to teach American frontier history in 1931–1932 at the time Paxson moved from Wisconsin to California.

25. There are a number of copies of notes taken by Turner's students, HEH TU File Drawer 15. Copies of notes taken by Frank J. Klingberg and Homer C. Hockett are in the possession of W. R. Jacobs; the best of these, the most detailed, are Hockett's. All of these collections have long, descriptive, chronological accounts of the westward migration from colonial times through the fall-line barrier to the Piedmont and then to the occupation of the Middle West. The accounts also contain detailed commentaries on political maps that were used to explain the behavior of westward settlers and their increasingly sectional characteristics.

26. Merk, *History of the Westward Movement*, pp. 495–96.

27. Interviews, June 22 and 27, 1986, Huntington Library, with Rodman Paul and Paul Prucha, S.J. Both men recall clearly their days as students in Merk's History of the West class. Though Paul had been in Merk's class in 1936 and Prucha a decade later, their memories of Merk and his lectures are quite similar.

28. See W. R. Jacobs, "Frederick Jackson Turner, Master Teacher," *Pacific Historical Review* 23 (1954):54–61.

29. Klingberg notes, and Merk, *History of the Westward Movement*, p. 50. The whole story of the Scotch Irish and the German settlers is basically the same in Turner's lectures, in Merk's lectures, and in R. A. Billington's *Westward Expansion*, 4th ed. (New York, 1978). Here is Turner, for instance, on the Scotch Irish: "All of them were noted for their individualism and fiery tempers" (Klingberg 1909 notes). Merk told his students the Scotch Irish "were a militant people, a fine physical stock, quick to learn from the Indians, and easily superior to them in the arts of border warfare" (*History of the Westward Movement*, p. 50).

30. Merk, *History of the Westward Movement*, p. 55 and preface.

31. Interview with Frederick Merk, December 1959, Cambridge, Mass.; interview with Prof. Daniel Howe of UCLA, January 1992, and examination of his classroom notes taken in Merk's classes in 1956–1957.

Chapter Fourteen. The Billington Era

1. See Martin Ridge's three essays, "Frederick Jackson Turner, Ray A. Billington, and American Frontier History," *Western Historical Quarterly* 19 (January 1988):5–20; "Ray A. Billington (1903–1981)," *Western Historical Quarterly* 12:3 (July 1981):245–50; and "Ray Allen Billington, Western History, and

American Exceptionalism," *Pacific Historical Review* 56:4 (November 1987):495–511. Richard E. Oglesby has written an appreciative essay, "Ray Allen Billington," in *Historians of the American Frontier: A Bio-Bibliographical Source Book*, John R. Wunder, ed. (New York, 1988), pp. 98–121 which lists Billington's publications. See also Oglesby's "Dedication to Ray Allen Billington," *Arizona and the West* 18 (1986):103–6. Billington's work has come under minor and major criticisms in two essays, Masaharu Watanabe, "Ray Billington's Work in Review" (1982, unpublished, new acquisitions, Huntington Library), and Patricia Limerick, "Persistent Traits and the Persistent Historian: The American Frontier and Ray Allen Billington," in Richard W. Etulain, ed., *Writing Western History: Essays on Major Western Historians* (Albuquerque, N.Mex., 1991), pp. 277–310. Autobiographical data on Billington is in *Who's Who in America* (Chicago, 1977) and in his short autobiography, "The Frontier and I," *Western Historical Quarterly* 1 (January 1970):2ff. An analysis of Billington's humor is in an unpublished essay by Paul Zall, "Ray Billington Laughing" (copy in possession of W. R. Jacobs). Zall writes, "We can say of Ray Billington what he said of Abraham Lincoln, 'He was a warm, compassionate, witty and earthy human being—a man who possessed that greatest of all virtues: the ability to laugh at himself.'" See also Billington's remarkable collection of limericks, *Limericks Historical and Hysterical, Plagiarized, Arranged, Annotated and Some Written by Ray Allen Billington* (New York, 1982).

2. R. A. Billington, *Westward Expansion* (New York, 1949).

3. This account is based upon dozens of letters from Billington to Curti in the Merle Curti Papers, State Historical Society of Wisconsin; see especially Billington to Curti, March 23, 1949. The two historians were drawn together by their devotion to Turner and his teachings. Billington read and reread Curti's essays on the master and assured his friend that he was indeed a "loyal Turnerian" who wanted nothing more than the opportunity to publish Turner's autobiographical letters as a tribute and to do a service to the profession (to Curti, February 24, 1960). Billington worked closely with Curti and other good friends on memberships for Mississippi Valley Historical Association nominating committees, and at the same time he wrote cordial letters to various noninsiders telling them that their suggestions for the association's presidency would be considered. In fact, however, on at least one occasion the decision had already been made, apparently in the case of Walter Prescott Webb (see Billington to W. E. Hollon, acknowledging Hollon's support for Webb, October 17, 1951, W. E. Hollon Papers, Ward M. Canady Center, University of Toledo).

4. See Billington's letters to Curti already cited and other letters in the 1949–1950 era, Curti Papers. I am indebted to Richard Leopold of Northwestern University, who in letters of July 2 and July 27, 1990, recalled his memories of Billington in the 1940s and 1950s.

5. See Billington-Curti correspondence, Curti Papers; part of this account of Billington comes from Richard Leopold's recollections in his letters of July 2 and 27, 1990.

6. See Homer C. Hockett's review in *Mississippi Valley Historical Review* 38 (December 1949):551–52.

7. See Billington, "The Frontier and I," pp. 5–20, especially pp. 9 and 10.

8. Ridge, "Ray Allen Billington (1903–1981)." Billington dedicated *Land of Savagery—Land of Promise: The European Image of the American Frontier* (New York, 1981) to his twenty-four Ph.D.'s and lists their names (p. vi). This volume is devoted to a lengthy discussion of exaggerated images of "promise" and "savagery" portrayed by European writers who wrote about such things as ostriches in the Blackfoot country (p. 96). Karl May, a German novelist writing about the West and one of the image-makers, has become a cult figure in Europe (see pp. 321, 326).

9. See R. A. Billington, *American Historical Review* 54:2 (January 1949):138, 55:3 (April 1950):705, and 56:3 (October 1950):223.

10. R. A. Billington, *American Historical Review* 56:2 (1951):360 and 56:4 (July 1951):907.

11. See Jack Abramowitz's review praising Billington's painstaking editorial work, *American Historical Review* 59:3 (April 1954):726.

12. In writing to Curti, Billington refers to Huntington Library Director John Pomfret's additional correspondence with Curti. There can be little doubt that Curti supported Billington's appointment as a senior research associate.

13. Billington, "The Frontier and I," p. 13.

14. Huntington Library coffee-hour banter, summer 1992, and interview with Paul Zall, July 2, 1992.

15. Robert Berkhofer, *Agricultural History*, vol. 41, pp. 313–15.

16. Billington, "The Frontier and I," p. 17.

17. Ridge, "Ray Allen Billington, Western History, and American Exceptionalism," p. 511 n.39.

18. See, for example, R. A. Billington, *America's Frontier Heritage* (New York, 1963), especially chapter 11, "The Persistence of Frontier Traits," pp. 219–35. Much of this book is restated in other publications, for instance, in Billington's *America's Frontier Culture: Three Essays* (College Station, Tex., 1977).

19. Sketches on Billington in various volumes of *Who's Who* in the 1970s and Ridge's essays (cited in note 1) list Billington's presidencies and awards.

20. Conversations with Rodman Paul, Huntington Library, in the 1970s and 1980s.

21. Homer Hockett, Rodman Paul, and Paul Prucha permitted me to make copies of their lecture notes. Howard Kimball, a former student of Frank J. Klingberg, presented me with a copy of Klingberg's classroom notes. See also chapter 11, note 13.

22. Prucha, who has given me duplicates of his critique, was asked by Macmillan Company to make suggestions for revisions; at the same time Ray Billington asked me to do much of the same work. On that occasion I had also suggested inclusion of such terms as "conquistador" and "imperialism." As a result Prucha found himself having to recommend deletions of these "Jacobs-

isms" and of references to savage Indians. My old friend Prucha and I now look back on this amiable rivalry with a good deal of heart. Billington, of course, never knew how much he was indebted to Prucha and did not acknowledge him in the preface to the fourth edition of *Westward Expansion*.

23. Billington, 4th ed., *Westward Expansion*, preface.

24. Ibid.

25. R. A. Billington edited and published the Hooper letters in *"Dear Lady," The Letters of Frederick Jackson Turner and Alice Forbes Hooper* (San Marino, Calif., 1970). He also published Turner's manuscript autobiographical letters in *The Genesis of the Frontier Thesis, A Study in Historical Creativity* (San Marino, Calif., 1971), pp. 181–298. Billington, as senior research associate at the Huntington Library, stipulated that these Turner materials could not be quoted until his work appeared in print. According to Huntington Library librarian, William Moffett, this stipulation was a violation of library policy.

Chapter Fifteen. The Challenge of Richard White to the Turnerian Legacy

1. William Cronon, *Nature's Metropolis: Chicago and the Great West* (New York, 1991).

2. See Michael Steiner's skillfully crafted and reasoned essay, "Frederick Jackson Turner and Western Regionalism," in Richard W. Etulain, ed., *Writing Western History: Essays on Major Western Historians* (Albuquerque, N.Mex., 1991), pp. 103–35.

3. See Cecil M. Roebeck, Jr., "William J. Seymour and the Bible Evidence," in Gary B. McGee, ed., *Initial Evidence: Historical and Biblical Perspectives on the Pentecostal Doctrine of Spirit Baptism* (Peabody, Mass., 1991), pp. 72–95. Although White mentions McPherson, he overlooks Seymour, the seed of the Pentecostal movement. A discussion of religious fundamentalism might also include the other end of the spectrum, illustrated by the emergence of the Unitarian Church of Pasadena in the late 1880s. Under the leadership of the Reverend Theodore Soares, this church became an intellectual center of Southern California in the 1920s and had among its members Robert A. Millikan, nobel laureate and founding father of the California Institute of Technology; the renowned historian, Frederick Jackson Turner, senior research associate at the newly established Henry E. Huntington Library and Art Gallery; and the philosopher Walter R. Jacobs. Allan Nevins, who took over a similar post at the Huntington in the 1960s, was also a member of the Pasadena Unitarian community.

4. One example I want to pinpoint shows how Richard Nixon's mendacious Indian policies poisoned Indian affairs. This case relates to acts of bribery and intimidation of Indians during Nixon's regime when the ninety-nine-year Four Corner leases were quietly signed by Indians and megapower oil corporations. In my judgment there is no scandal of greater importance in the 1960s that remains untold. This tangled mess involves billions of dollars,

environmental destruction of thousands of acres of desert topsoil, the seduction of Indian leaders by ruthless individuals who would not stop at murder, and unsavory connections with Los Angeles politicians.

One historian-journalist spent an afternoon telling me about Arizona investigative reporters he knew in the 1960s who were threatened with murder if they persisted in asking questions about Four Corners. Later, the nation's press reported that one of them was mysteriously killed. Those secretly negotiated ninety-nine-year leases, as we have since discovered, enabled speculators to borrow many millions of dollars because the leases were seen as a form of title not unlike fee-simple ownership. Roger L. Nichols, western historian at the University of Arizona, shares my interest in exposing the story behind Four Corners' scandals.

When I visited Four Corners' power center to follow up on a controversial Indian surface-mining article, I saw huge Navajo backhoe diggers, their cabs identified with Navajo names, ripping up virgin desert topsoil for subsurface layers of coal. I began taking pictures but soon discovered guards waving rifles at me. They wanted no photos, and it didn't take me long to beat a hasty retreat. Someone with more courage than I should investigate the story behind the power struggle at Four Corners.

5. See, for example, Terry Pristen, "'Taming' of the Wild West Is Rewritten by Scholars," in *Los Angeles Times*, November 14, 1990. Here Wilbur R. Jacobs, "considered a forerunner in the field of environmental history," is quoted: "Sometimes [revisionists] don't acknowledge the ancestors of the newer spirit, and it hurts our feelings a bit." The article continues: "White, 43, a soft-spoken man whose gray hair reaches his shoulders, said, 'The West instead of being a region that's the most individualistic is the region most dependent upon the federal government.'"

See also "How the West Was Really Won," *U.S. News and World Report*, May 21, 1990, pp. 56–70. Patricia Limerick is portrayed as arguing that the old western history was moonlight and magnolias tied to the domain of mass entertainment and lighthearted mass escapism (p. 56). Don Worster argues that the western problem has been "greed" and that the West is a "land of authority and restraint, of class and exploitation, and ultimately of imperial power" (p. 58). Limerick argues her case convincingly in "What on Earth Is the New Western History?" *Montana, Magazine of Western History* (Summer 1990):62–63.

6. There have been 1993 news releases showing cracks in the new western-ers' wall of interpretation on the West. William Cronon has renounced his affiliation on anti-Turner matters and has accepted the Frederick Jackson Turner Chair at the University of Wisconsin, Madison. And Richard White has set up an exhibit on Turner and his work at the Newberry Library in Chicago, celebrating the 100th anniversary of the publication of the famous essay of 1893. Surprisingly, White now argues that to understand Turner, one must compare his legacy to Buffalo Bill's (see "Frederick Jackson Turner and

Buffalo Bill, Commonalities between the Two," a paper White read at the Frontier and Region session, Conference on the American West, in honor of Martin Ridge, Huntington Library, April 12–14, 1993). Turner's message burns even more brightly in lamps tended by some of his most vocal critics of very recent times. Richard Slotkin's eloquent and persuasive *Gunfighter Nation: The Myth of the Frontier in the Twentieth Century* (New York, 1992), devotes more than a dozen pages to Turner, especially his "virilism" and identification with Theodore Roosevelt. Turner is portrayed as part of a frontier myth regenerating American imperialism (see pp. 51ff.).

7. See vol. 29, no. 1 (Santa Barbara, Calif., 1992).

Chapter Sixteen. Turnerian Echoes in William Cronon's Nature's Metropolis

1. W. R. Jacobs, ed., *Frederick Jackson Turner's Legacy: Unpublished Writings in American History* (Lincoln, Nebr., 1977), and Jacobs, *The Historical World of Frederick Jackson Turner* (New Haven, Conn., 1968).

2. William Cronon, *Nature's Metropolis* (New York, 1991), pp. xvi, xviii, xxiii, 7, 31–32, 47–48, 150ff.

3. William Cronon, *Changes in the Land* (New York, 1983).

4. Comment by William Cronon in conversations with Will Jacobs.

5. Cronon, *Nature's Metropolis*, pp. xviii–xxii.

6. William Cronon, "A Place for Stories: Nature, History, and Narrative," *Journal of American History* 79 (March 1992):1347–76; see especially pp. 1347–52. Using the story imagery, Cronon writes about Turner's concept of the transformation of the American landscape from woodlands to trading posts to farms to boomtowns as a saga of America (ibid.).

7. Ibid.

8. Turner's problems in completing his textbook are outlined in his letters to Henry Holt and Company in Jacobs, *Historical World of Frederick Jackson Turner,* pp. 37, 183, 186–90.

9. In a revealing footnote attached to his fascinating essay, "Revisiting the Vanishing Frontier, The Legacy of Frederick Jackson Turner," *Western Historical Quarterly* 18 (April 1987):157–76, Cronon confesses that it is great sport in lectures "to use him [Turner] as a foil" (p. 160).

10. Cronon, *Nature's Metropolis*, p. 150.

11. Ibid.

12. The subject of population dynamics, a term used by biologists, or population history, the historian's phrase, has been largely left to biologists. As Paul Erlich and Garrett Hardin have demonstrated, biologists have the facts. Historians are at a disadvantage in interpreting the data and have had charges of racism and social discrimination leveled at them, which may be why the subject has been neglected. See, for example, Russell R. Menard's probing essay, "Whatever Happened to Early American Population History?"

William and Mary Quarterly 50, 3d ser. (April 1993):356–93. In contrast, see Garrett Hardin, *Living within Limits: Ecology, Economics, and Population Taboos* (New York, 1993), especially pp. 3–134, and pp. 83ff. on the exponential growth of populations; and Hardin, "From Shortage to Longage: Forty Years in the Population Vineyards," *Population and Environment, a Journal of Interdisciplinary Studies* 12 (Spring 1991):339–49. For an astute analysis of labor in early twentieth-century Chicago, see Lizabeth Cohen, *Making a New Deal: Industrial Workers in Chicago, 1919–1939* (New York, 1993). Cohen records thousands of southern Europeans and blacks working in packing houses and other industries in the early 1900s; see pp. 17–19.

13. Hardin, in "From Shortage to Longage," gives two alternatives in determining population policies: (1) laissez-faire birth control plus no social welfare equals equilibrium, and (2) laissez-faire birth control plus welfare state equals runaway growth (p. 348). He argues that the state assumes responsibility for the survival of all children, no matter how imprudently conceived, and thus the self-correcting capability of what he calls the "Malthusian demostat" is negated: "If welfare functions are held to be too precious to be abandoned, then laissez faire in birth control must be abandoned. This is the bullet we hesitate to bite." For an overall assessment of Hardin's and Paul Erlich's work, see Charles C. Mann, "How Many Is Too Many?" *Atlantic* (February 1993), pp. 47–53, 56–67.

14. See discussions on "the Section," in Jacobs, ed., *Frederick Jackson Turner's Legacy*, pp. 45–79; Turner, *The Significance of Sections in American History* (New York, 1932), pp. 22–51, and references to Chicago and the Midwest, pp. 43, 336. Turner's pointed concern with the University of Chicago as a rival for his own department at Madison is revealed in his correspondence of about 1900. He eventually used an offer from the University of Chicago to gain support for his "School of History" at the University of Wisconsin. See Jacobs, *Historical World of Turner*, pp. 86–87, 90, 196, 205. Michael Steiner's excellent article, "Frederick Jackson Turner and Western Regionalism," in Richard W. Etulain, ed., *Writing Western History: Essays on Major Historians* (Albuquerque, N. Mex., 1991), pp. 103–35, includes an extensive bibliography on Turner and his interpretations of sectionalism; and Allan Bogue, Thomas Philips, and James Wright, eds., *The West of the American People* (Itasca, Ill., 1970), contains a number of penetrating essays on Turner and the West as well as a discussion of population increases; see pp. 21–25, 442–47, 518.

15. Turner's preoccupation with his frontier-sectional ruling theory is discussed in chapter 4.

16. Ray A. Billington, *Westward Expansion* (New York, 1949); for the sectionalism chapters, see pp. 329–405.

17. Cronon's argument is discussed in Patricia Limerick, Clyde Milner, and Charles Rankin, eds., *Trails: Toward a New Western History* (Lawrence, Kans., 1991), p. 101.

18. Billington, *Westward Expansion*, pp. 306, 393, 596, 675; Turner, *Sections*

in American History, pp. 22–53, 287, 315ff.; Jacobs, ed., *Turner's Legacy*, pp. 63–69. For Turner's comments on population increases and the consequent dangers to American and world societies, see pp. 59–62, 66, 83–84, 99, 163, 183–84, 186, ibid. Turner's engrossing studies of alarmist literature, held in Drawers 14 and 15 of his papers at the Huntington Library, led him to generalize that "the American population is gaining upon that of Europe and it will not be long before we have reached the limit of population on our present standard of living, our present birth rate, and our present self-sufficing economic life" ("Lecture on Sectionalism, temp. Pres. Coolidge," HEH TU File Drawer 15, printed in *Turner's Legacy*, pp. 52–73; see especially p. 62). Walter Prescott Webb, *The Great Frontier* (Boston 1952), enlarged on the Turnerian concept of frontier booms in a superb analysis, "The Boom Hypothesis in Modern History," pp. 13–28. Webb contended that in population growth and the consequent exploitation of the land "there is a limit beyond which we cannot go" (p. 27).

19. Bessie Louise Pierce, *A History of Chicago*, 3 vols. (New York, 1937–1957). It should be noted that although Pierce deserves credit for her pioneering study, there are now professors who, as needy graduate students, were paid to research and write pilot chapters; their work has not been acknowledged (confidential interview, Huntington Library, May 1993).

20. Cronon, *Nature's Metropolis*, pp. 54, 59–60, 65, 92, 93, 219, 222, 236ff.; compared to Turner, pp. 51–52. An English edition of Johann Heinrich von Thünen, *Der isolierte Staat*, is *The Isolated State*, translated by Carla M. Warternberg and edited with an introduction by Peter Hall (Oxford, 1966). See also Arthur H. Leigh's analytical essay on von Thünen in David Sills, ed., *International Encyclopedia of the Social Sciences*, vol. 16 (New York, 1968), pp. 17–20.

21. *Nature's Metropolis*, pp. 54, 59–60ff.

22. Ibid., pp. 51ff.

23. Ibid., pp. 282, 283.

24. Ibid., p. 282. Not all urban historians agree with this viewpoint. See, for instance, Martin V. Melosi, "The Place of the City," in *Environmental History Review* 17 (Spring 1993):1–23. Melosi argues that the central-place theory "does offer guidance for understanding urban growth" and that von Thünen's work complements "the theory of industry location found in the work of Alfred Weber" (p. 22). Although Melosi is especially enthusiastic about the environmental component of Cronon's book, he nevertheless does not speak of the gateway concept as a viable theory of urban development.

25. See endpaper railroad map of 1861 in Cronon, *Nature's Metropolis*, especially lines connecting Chicago to St. Louis, Cincinnati, Indianapolis, and Louisville.

26. Ibid., p. 307.

27. Ibid.

28. Ibid., p. 379.

29. Ibid., p. 378.

30. Ibid., pp. 266–67.

31. See, for example, Donald Worster's essay, "Alaska: The Underworld Erupts," in *Under Western Skies: Nature and History in the American West* (New York, 1992), pp. 154–224.

32. Cronon, *Nature's Metropolis*, pp. 247ff. See also John Robbins, *Diet for a New America* (Walpole, N.H., 1987), pp. 97ff., for a stirring indictment of the cattle industry and its threatening ecological impacts. Robbins, scion of a large ice-cream corporation family, has devoted his life to the study of nutrition and to an analysis of alternative diets and their ecological consequences.

33. This topic and others are discussed in "Perspectives on *Nature's Metropolis*, A Book Forum," by Malcolm J. Rohrbough, Timothy R. Mahoney, David B. Danbom, Philip V. Scarpino, and William Cronon, in *Annals of Iowa* 15 (Summer 1992):480–527.

34. Ibid.

35. Patricia Limerick, *Legacy of Conquest* (New York, 1987), p. 31. For an astute analysis of the significance of America's frontier heritage, see David M. Wrobel's *The End of American Exceptionalism: Frontier Anxiety from the Old West to the New Deal* (Lawrence, Kans., 1993), p. 146.

Chapter Seventeen. After a Century

1. Patricia Limerick, Clyde A. Milner, and Charles Rankin, eds., *Trails: Toward a New Western History* (Lawrence, Kans., 1991), p. 187.

2. Janny Scott, "Rival Old Western Historians Try to Put Own Brand on Frontier," *Los Angeles Times*, May 18, 1993; also printed in *Arizona Republic*, May 19, 1993. See also Gerald D. Nash, "Point of View: One Hundred Years of Western History," *Journal of the West* 32:1 (January 1993):3–4, and "Showdown in the New West," *Denver Post Magazine*, March 21, 1993, pp. 6–8 (no author given), which has quoted statements from Richard White, Patricia Limerick, Donald Worster, Gerald Nash, and William Savage. A historian of the West at the University of Oklahoma, Savage is quoted in his support of Nash: "I agree with him 100 percent." *Montana, Magazine of Western History* 43:1, (Spring 1993):69–72, has essay-reviews by Richard White, Martin Ridge, and others discussing disputed issues in new western history.

3. White's comments after presenting his paper "Frederick Jackson Turner and Buffalo Bill, Commonalities between the Two," April 13, Frontier and Region session, Conference on American West, in honor of Martin Ridge, Huntington Library, April 12–14, 1993.

4. Session on "Region and the United States," April 18, 1993, Meeting of the Organization of American Historians (OAH), Anaheim, California.

5. Session on "Frederick Jackson Turner Reconsidered," April 17, 1993, OAH meeting, Anaheim.

6. Ibid. Allan Bogue's paper is entitled "Frederick Jackson Turner Reconsidered."

7. Fredrika J. Teute, "Myth-Making and the Making: Frederick Jackson

Turner and the Historical Sources," HEH seminar, April 28, 1993. Roy Ritchie, Huntington Library director of research who presided at the seminar, stated that after reading Turner's description of the Greek frontiers of antiquity, he now feels at home in writing about Caribbean "frontiers" in early American history.

8. Patricia Limerick, *Legacy of Conquest* (New York, 1987).

9. Limerick et al., eds., *Trails*, pp. 26–39.

10. Ibid., p. 25. See also Donald Worster's penetrating essay, "New West, True West: Interpreting the Region's History," *Western Historical Quarterly* 18 (April 1987):141–56. Worster credits Turner with early recognition of the "hydraulic-irrigation-water-scarcity west" as early as 1903 (see p. 153).

11. Limerick et al., eds., *Trails*, p. 191.

12. Donald Worster, *Under Western Skies: Nature and History in the American West* (Oxford and New York, 1992), pp. 231–32.

13. Limerick et al., eds., *Trails* p. 62.

14. Ibid., p. 86.

15. Martin Ridge, in *Atlas of American Frontiers* (Chicago, 1993).

16. Ibid. See commentaries and conclusions in parts and chapters for the quotations.

17. Allan G. Bogue, "The Significance of the American West: Postscripts and Prospects," *Western Historical Quarterly* 24 (February 1993):45–68.

18. Ibid.

19. Paper read at the Frontier and Region session, Conference on American West, in honor of Martin Ridge, Huntington Library, April 14, 1993.

20. John Mack Faragher, "The Frontier Trail: Rethinking Turner and Reimagining the West," *American Historical Review* 98 (February 1993):109–17.

21. Ibid.

22. Ibid.

23. Peter Novick, *That Noble Dream: The "Objectivity Question" and the American Historical Profession* (New York, 1988), pp. 98–100, 261ff., 407.

24. Novick quotes Hofstadter, ibid., p. 407.

Epilogue

1. Turner, "Dr. Von Holst's History of the United States," [1889–1890], HEH TU File Drawer 15. Published W. R. Jacobs, ed., in *Frederick Jackson Turner's Legacy* (Lincoln, Nebr., 1970), pp. 85–104.

2. Turner, "Some Sociological Aspects of American History," lecture, April 13, 1895, HEH TU File Drawer 15. Published in Jacobs, ed., *Turner's Legacy,* pp. 155–68.

3. See ibid., pp. 47–48.

4. Turner, *The Significance of Sections in American History* (New York, 1932), p. 45. On sectionalism and politics, Turner maintained, "Throughout our history, then, there has been this sectionalism of East and West and this Eastern conception of the West as recruiting ground merely for the rival

Atlantic Coast sections. Nation-wide parties had their Eastern and Western wings" (p. 33). At the same time, Turner, like North Carolina's Howard Odum who wrote about regional determinants for behavior in the 1920s, denied the idea of state power and loyalty. For Turner, state sovereignty was an issue only when a whole section was behind the challenging state. There could be both good and bad sections because of extreme rivalry in discrediting opposing views. Daniel H. Boris comments on this point in his probing edition of *These United States, Portraits of America from the 1920s* (Ithaca, N.Y., 1992), p. 21.

5. Turner to Becker, June 5, 1899, HEH TU Box 2.

6. Turner was an exceptionally kind and considerate man; not only did his students and his friends talk about his quiet laughter and lovable ways, but his family had even more to say. Turner's sister, Ellen Breese Turner, preserved much of the family's correspondence (Edinger-Turner Papers, now in possession of Babette DeMoe Edinger of Los Angeles). There are many affectionate letters between Turner and his sister and his brother Will, a hardware store owner who had no real understanding of the accomplishments of "Fritz," his beloved brother who was constantly low on cash. Will freely lent Fritz money and waived the interest. "I love you . . . even if I don't take your advice" Will wrote to Fritz, November 2, 1910. [You are] a thorobred thro everything. I certainly send you a heap of love" (Edinger-Turner Papers).

7. For Turner on international sectionalism, see his "Shop Club Lecture," 1923, HEH TU File Drawer 15. I found myself sympathizing with Turner because of a similar though miniaturized experience I had while going through Turner's large "sectionalism" file drawer documents. I was an academic assistant to the president of the University of California, Clerk Kerr, in the early 1960s, and he asked me to prepare a report pinpointing the most important University of California regional-sectional problems and their possible solutions. What an assignment! There was, in the many-campused university, an intense north (UC Berkeley)–south (UCLA) rivalry that was to be dealt with at an upcoming conference at UC Davis, a neutral, middleground site. After a period of six months of intensive study, I found that we could only cope with several monumental "problems"; there were no solutions. Despite the sniping from a hostile governor and intimidating student riots, we began a series of political "processes": bargaining, fixing and repairing, supporting, cooperating, and arguing. With such sectional compromises we staggered to new and better times. As one solution to the problem of bitter sectional competition for library resources, especially between UCLA and Berkeley, we designated Berkeley and UCLA as central depositories and then initiated an intercampus library bus system linking them with the newer burgeoning campuses such as those at Davis, Santa Barbara, and Riverside. The compromise worked, but I'm still being blamed for setting up a wearisome bus system as a substitute for decent libraries on the smaller campuses. I plead guilty but have the inner satisfaction of having applied Turner's frontier-sectional theory with some minor success.

8. William Cronon, George Miles, and Jay Gitlin, eds., *Under an Open Sky:*

Rethinking America's Past (New York, 1992). This volume, dedicated to Howard Lamar by his students and friends, is composed of a series of carefully documented and stimulating essays on western history.

9. Ibid., p. 11.

10. In one of his later public statements about his beliefs, Billington is quoted in John Garraty's edition of *Interpreting American History, Conversations with Historians*, 2 vols. (New York, 1970), 1:2174. Speaking on the topic, "Westward Expansion and the Frontier Thesis" in a dialogue with Garraty, he called for a testing of the "frontier hypothesis" to determine its value.

Appendix A: Turner's Lecture on Washington and Lincoln in 1896

MS: HEH TU File Drawer 15, folder marked "Materials for a Lecture on Washington and Lincoln, Feb. 22, 1896, University of Wisconsin"; a manila envelope holding the notes is marked in Turner's handwriting: "Materials for a Lecture on Washington and Lincoln." Page 10 of the manuscript, also numbered page 23 at one time, has a penciled notation by Turner dating at least this portion of the manuscript as "Feb. 22, 1896" and "University of Wis." The manuscript consists of 32 pages, 5½-by-8½ inches, in Turner's handwriting in ink with revisions and deletions in pencil and ink. There are several series of paginations so that it is possible for one page to have three numbers; for instance, page 12 is also numbered "3" in blue pencil and "53" in pencil. It is evident that Turner revised his notes a number of times. The lecture, as here published, was given on at least one occasion.

1. Deletion: "A wilderness the conquest of which was to contribute powerfully to the cause of nationality and democracy, and by its offering freedom of opportunity was to keep American society young and buoyant even to the present day."

2. Deletion: "Was he, as some have said, the last and greatest of the colonials? Had he any vital part in this expansion and transformation of America?" At the top of the next page begins another sentence fragment that is deleted: "stand preeminent in the elements most powerful in shaping the nation. He must sum up and express its most strenuous endeavor, its most abiding ideals."

Another fragment on page 7 is not crossed out but does not appear to belong to this portion of the lecture. This fragment, a continuation of page 7, reads: "For when we turn to ask what are these endeavors, these ideals in America, we cannot fail to see how profound a formative influence in our life has been the steady march of our civilization into the West."

3. Deletion: "The tide water region of the Atlantic Coast was the home of this old colonial society, mirroring in many ways the England from which it came."

4. Pagination has been changed in the manuscript on pages 8 and 9, and several sentence fragments follow that are not crossed out: "It gazed upon

the," and "lay the least resistance to common action. And Washington led the way."

5. At the bottom of this page, page 10 of the manuscript, also numbered at one time 23, Turner has written his name and "University of Wis. Feb 22, 1896," an indication that at least part of the lecture, perhaps the portion on Washington, was given at that time.

6. Manuscript is torn.

7. Turner's interlinear note, perhaps for a comment on the expansion of slavery: "Black wave—Observer in Mars."

8. A fragment at the top of the next page, page 16 of the manuscript, is not crossed out: "petitioned to be allowed to rescind the abrogation of slavery," an indication that a larger part of the lecture was probably deleted by Turner.

9. Word is partly illegible because of a torn manuscript.

10. Page 19 of the manuscript that begins at this point has Turner's note across the top margin, "*Lincoln* FJT," perhaps an indication that this portion on Lincoln had at one time been given as a separate lecture.

11. Deletion: "where men fell like withered beans in Autumn."

Appendix B. Turner as a Teacher

1. See W. R. Jacobs, "Frederick Jackson Turner—Master Teacher," *Pacific Historical Review* 23:1 (February 1954):49–59.

2. Herbert Bolton, "The Epic of Greater America," *American Historical Review* 38:3 (April 1933):474. Turner's name is mentioned twice in the address, both times near the conclusion.

3. John Walton Caughey, "Herbert Eugene Bolton," *Pacific Historical Review* 22:2 (May 1953):109–12. Caughey mentions Bolton's association with Turner, and references to their relationship appear in other eulogies. See also *Hispanic American Historical Review* 33:1 (February 1953):184–86; *American Historical Review* 58:3 (April 1953):791–92; *Bancroftiana*, no. 8 (May 1953):1–2; *Mid-America* 35 (April 1953):75–80. Albert Hurtado, Arizona State University, is now at work on a biographical study of Bolton that revises the older eulogies to Bolton published by John Francis Bannon. See Hurtado, "Herbert E. Bolton, Racism and American History," *Pacific Historical Review* 62:1 (May 1993):127–42.

4. See, for example, the prefaces in Bolton's *Outpost of the Empire: The Story of the Founding of San Francisco* (New York, 1931) and *Rim of Christendom: A Biography of Eusebio Francisco Kino, Pacific Coast Pioneer* (New York, 1936). Bolton even draws Coronado into the perspective of the California gold rush in his preface to *Coronado: Knight of Pueblos and Plains* (New York, 1949). Also see Bolton's acknowledgment of Turner in "The Mission as a Frontier Institution in the Spanish-American Colonies," *American Historical Review* 23 (October 1917):42–61.

5. Guy Stanton Ford, Bolton's fellow-undergraduate during this period,

has informed me by correspondence that Turner had not yet developed his "Economic and Social History of the United States" into a distinct history of the West. Fulmer Mood points out the emphasis upon the West as it appeared in early catalog descriptions of this course. See Mood, "Turner's Formative Period," in *The Early Writings of Frederick Jackson Turner* (Madison, Wis., 1938), p. 35.

6. Bolton graduated from the University of Wisconsin in 1895 and remained there as a graduate student until 1897 when he was awarded a fellowship in history at the University of Pennsylvania; he received a Ph.D. there in 1899, working under John Bach McMaster.

7. For additional data on Turner's early life in Portage, see "Turner's Autobiographical Letter" to Constance Lindsay Skinner, *Wisconsin Magazine of History* 19 (September 1935):90–108.

8. The fact that Turner was a pleasing and effective lecturer is affirmed by many of his former students.

9. The reference is to Charles Homer Haskins. Interestingly, Woodrow Wilson tried to bring both Turner and Haskins to Princeton during this period. See the Wilson-Turner correspondence in the Houghton Library, Harvard University.

10. According to one of his later students, Turner explored almost every leading interpretation and major field of research in national history (see Merle E. Curti, "Frederick Jackson Turner," *Instituto Panamericano de Geografía E. Historia, Comision De Historia*, no. 96 (Mexico, D.F., 1949). This perspective suggests a broadening of Turner's views, and Curti discusses Turner's ideas concerning the use of multiple hypotheses in American history. Some years ago, Homer C. Hockett informed me that Turner was talking in terms of multiple hypotheses at Wisconsin in 1904. See also Turner's essay, "Problems in American History," *Aegis* 7 (November 1892):48–52.

11. It will be recalled that Orin Grant Libby's dissertation was the first volume in the University of Wisconsin Economics, Political Science, and History series, *Geographical Distribution of the Vote of the Thirteen States on the Federal Constitution* (Madison, Wis., 1897).

12. For the relationship between Paxson and Turner, see Earl Pomeroy, "Frederick L. Paxson and His Approach to History," *Mississippi Valley Historical Review* 39:4 (March 1953):673–92. See also Richard W. Etulain, "After Turner: Western Historiography of Frederick Logan Paxson," in R. W. Etulain, ed., *Writing Western History: Essays on Major Western Historians* (Albuquerque, N. Mex., 1991), pp. 137-66.

13. Bolton mentions this point several times, but no major variance in Turner's interpretations has been found in comparing Turner's Wisconsin and Harvard periods (see also note 10).

14. Bolton is undoubtedly correct. No evidence has been found that Turner offered a course in "method in a pedagogical sense."

15. The supplements are in Bolton's hand, and in the left margin of "Supplement 1" is a note: "Over the weekend my assistants are not here, hence these hand written pages."

BIBLIOGRAPHICAL NOTE

The Turner Papers at the Huntington Library, designated as HEH TU, now include the most comprehensive collection of Turner's voluminous correspondence, his research collections and notes, and his unpublished essays, speeches, and abortive chapters for books (exemplified by the beginning chapters of a textbook). This collection is especially valuable because the library made an extraordinary effort to obtain copies of Turner materials found in other libraries. During the 1960s both Ray A. Billington and I assisted in obtaining letters from dozens of libraries that owned collections of papers belonging to individuals who had corresponded with Turner. Some of Turner's papers are still not in the collection. For example I have referred to a private family collection, the Turner-Edinger Papers, containing letters that passed between Turner and his brother Will. Jacobs, *The Historical World of Frederick Jackson Turner* (New Haven, Conn., 1968), pp. 256–59, offers a comprehensive and chronological identification of the various boxes, drawers, film reels, and manuscript volumes that contain such items as Turner's commonplace books.

The foundation of my perspectives on Turner is, of course, based upon the large Turner collection that contains both Turner's letters and those written to him. Additionally, I have consulted the Merle Curti and William Hesseltine collections at the State Historical Society of Wisconsin, which contain Billington's letters regarding a range of subjects relating to Billington's rise as a distinguished scholar and power broker in the former Mississippi Valley Historical Association (the Organization of American Historians). W. Eugene Hollon's long correspondence with Billington, preserved among his papers at the University of Toledo Library, reveals much about Billington's leadership techniques as a founder of the Western History Association. Billington's papers at the Huntington Library are closed, apparently for some twenty-five years at the request of his family, although Billington himself, according to his former student Martin Ridge, asked that the papers be opened five years after

329

his death. This book is also based upon dozens of interviews with western history scholars over a number of years; many of these interviews are cited in the notes. As might be expected, some of the individuals gave what I considered to be valuable but seemingly unrelated information. Paul Wallace Gates, for instance, in a long talk we had at a recent WHA meeting, declared that he never considered himself to be a Turnerian despite his training under Frederick Merk. Gates went so far as to say that he believed much of the Turnerian literature was inconsequential and amounted to "nonsense." Further, he was convinced that Ray Billington "wasted his time on that Turner stuff." Gates, in commenting on Billington's rivalry with Merk, said that Merk stated, "Billington had stolen my course" (interview with P. W. Gates, October 18, 1986, Billings, Montana). Interviews with Billington's former students and close friends show him to be a beloved figure. Ray Billington actually "changed my life," says William Brandon, who left fiction writing to become a historian. Lawrence W. Towner, a former pupil, said that Billington "especially loved" his students and was "loved in return."

I have discussed a number of books that have influenced my thinking on Turner and western history in the preceding pages. Although I have not cited them all, I am indebted to the enormous well of scholarship filled by eminent scholars, old and new, who have written on the West and on Turner. These Turnerians include Gerald D. Nash, Earl Pomeroy, David J. Weber, Walter Nugent, David Wrobel, Richard W. Etulain, Michael Malone, William Goetzmann, Martin Ridge, Allan Bogue, and Howard Lamar as well as new western historians Patricia Limerick, Richard White, Don Worster, William Cronon, and others. Their books, articles, and essays collectively form a massive bibliography on Turnerian–western history themes of the 1990s. Probably the most comprehensive immediate bibliographical reference is found in the notes and citations included in Allan Bogue's essay giving his overview of Turner and the legacy of western history in *Western Historical Quarterly* 34:1 (February 1993):45–68. For an excellent annotated compendium of Turnerian literature before 1985, consult Vernon E. Matteson and William E. Marion, eds., *Frederick Jackson Turner, A Reference Guide* (Boston, 1985).

No scholar of Turner and his work can overlook the superlative database of information found in *American History and Life*'s article abstracts and citations to reviews and dissertations covering the United States and Canada. All published volumes are indexed and have the most complete citations to material on Turner, the frontier, the West, and individual western states. The Clio Press has a computer reference database that can retrieve citations from printed volumes on the topics I have mentioned.

INDEX

331